Rāgas & Rāginīs

RAGINI DESA-VARATI

A Melody-Mode Grouped Under the Male Raga Hindola

JAIPUR SCHOOL

From a Private Collection

RĀGAS & RĀGINĪS

A Pictorial & Iconographic Study of Indian Musical Modes based on Original Sources

O.C. Gangoly

VOLUME I : TEXT

History of Ragas, Iconography, Ragmala Texts and Criticism.

Munshiram Manoharlal
Publishers Pvt. Ltd.

ISBN 81-215-0473-2
This edition 2004
First published in 1935

Printed in India.
Published by Munshiram Manoharlal Publishers Pvt. Ltd.,
Post Box 5715, 54 Rani Jhansi Road,
New Delhi 110 055.

TO

MR. V. N. BHATKHANDE, B.A., LL.B.,

OF BOMBAY

The Greatest Living Authority on Indian Music

THIS MONOGRAPH IS RESPECTFULLY

DEDICATED

1935

O. C. GANGOLY

PREFACE

In this volume, an humble, though a pioneer attempt has been made to trace the beginnings and the later evolution of the rāga-system of Indian Music—from authoritative sources, many of which are still buried in unpublished and rare manuscripts. Orthodox music practitioners, opposing any manner of new developments and innovations—on the belief that Indian Music is a stereotyped system hide-bound by strict rules and conventions prescribed by ancient musical Sages, to depart from which is to assail the individuality of Indian Musical thought—and, therefore, a musical crime, may find in this Volume much material which will contradict such a belief. Indeed, the history of the rāgas, of which a bare outline, is, here presented demonstrates that in all periods of its development—Indian Music has grown and progressed by assimilating new ideas from non-Aryan and aboriginal musical practices—and that the Classical Rāga-System is firmly based on and is heavily indebted to Primitive Folk-music, having never disdained from borrowing and assimilating new data from alien or foreign sources. Yet the Indian Rāga-System—has a structure of peculiar form—having fundamental rules and conventions of its own—which must be understood— in its essential character—before any innovation or a new development can be initiated. In the coming new order of things, Indian Music is destined to play a great part in vitalizing national culture. It is hoped that the free liberalizing rôle of music should not be restricted and subordinated by being harnessed to political propaganda. Both the necessity of saving Indian Music from such slavery and of extending its rôle—in a larger expansion of national life—in forms of new applications to newer needs—it is necessary for all kinds of votaries,—the Practioners, the Connoisseurs, the Innovators, the Reformers, and the Students—to have a thorough knowledge of the basics of Indian Music, its grammer and conventions, the secrets of its peculiar charm, and its power of intense emotional expressiveness—both in its thematic and abstract applications. It is believed that from this point of view—this monograph may offer valuable educational data. In many of the Indian Schools of Music—the syllabus includes not only a knowledge of the practice of the Rāgas—and their differentiations—but also of some rudiments of the theories on which they are based. But very often authoritative data is not readily available to the average teacher—who has no time to undertake independent researches to dig out the facts bearing on the history of Indian Music-theories. It is humbly claimed—the data put forward in this Volume may go in some way to provide this essential materials for the study of Indian Music. The Political Life—and the freedom to coin our new political destiny—may be imitated in the sphere of Music. As the history of Indian Music demonstrates—our musical authorities have never opposed innovations—but have welcomed fresh ideas—and have assimilated them according to the fundamental principles of Indian Music. In this conception, it is useful to recall the remark of Plato in his *Republic:* "The introduction of a new kind of music must be shunned as imperilling the whole State; since styles of music are never disturbed without affecting the most important political institutions."

This work has been respectfully dedicated to the great musical Savant the late Pandit V. N. Bhatkhande—whose services to Indian Music are invaluable. Unfortunately, the work could not be placed in his hands—until a short time before his death, when he was laid up with paralysis. It is reported that when the book was placed in his hands he sat up with great curiosity and enthusiasm and as he turned over the pages—in speechless silence—tears tracled down his cheeks—in affectionate appreciation of a tribute to the study of a subject of which he was a lifelong devotee, and an indefatigable exponent blessed with inexhaustible erudition.

Owing to circumstances beyond the control of the Author the work had to be published—in an extremely limited edition of only thirty-six copies which were subscribed for, two years before the actual date of publication,—so that the work was out of print and was un-available from the date of its birth, not only to the general reader but to an everwidening circle of friends of Indian Music and Specialists. This was a crime which has been crying for atonement ever since 1935—the original date of its publication. The Author is therefore grateful to Nalanda Publication for coming forward to rescue the work from practical oblivion.

It is to be regretted that it has not been possible to revise and improve the text, and it is sent out in its original form with all its imperfections and blemishes—for a wider circulation which was not possible to secure in its first edition. This is not, therefore, a new edition,—but a cheap re-issue. The only addition made—is the Supplementary Bibliography setting out a list of publications and articles which have appeared since the year 1935.

1st December, 1947. O. C. GANGOLY.

2, Ashutosh Mukherjee Road,
Elgin Road Post Office,
Calcutta, India.

CONTENTS

LIST OF ILLUSTRATIONS

Note:

The references to Illustrative Plates in Roman Numerals spread out throughout the Text of this Volume are Illustrations cited in Volume of *Ragas and Raginis* (Original Edition of 1935).

"रागाः षडेव रागिण्यः षट्-त्रिंशत् चारु-विग्रहाः ।
आगता ब्रह्म-सदसि ब्रह्माणम् समुपासते" ॥
नारदीय-पंचम-सार-संहितायाम् ।

"The six major melodies (Rāgas) and the thirty-six Minor Melodies (Rāginis)—with their beautiful bodies—emanated from the Abode of Brāmha—the Transcendental being—and sing hymns in honour of Brāmha Himself."

PANCHAM SARA SAMHITA—NARADA

INTRODUCTION

The conception of Rāgas is one of the basic principles of the system of Indian Music. A rāga (*Vulgo Rāg*) is generally mis-translated as a tune, air, or key. It is, in fact, a peculiar conception, having no exact parallel in any other system of music. Literally, rāga is something that colours, or tinges the mind with some definite feeling,—a wave of passion, or emotion.[1] In a special sense, a rāga is a sonal composition of musical notes (*svaras*) having a sequence, form, or structure of a peculiar significance. Some of its component notes stand in a significant relationship to one another to give a character to the rāga, *e.g.*, the starting, or initial note (*graha svara*), the predominant or expressive note (*amśa svara*), and the terminating, or the final note (*nyāsa svara*), has each a peculiar significance in the composition of a rāga.

The starting note (*graha*) and the terminating note (*nyāsa*) have now almost lost their significance. But the *aṃśa* (predominant note) is of great importance. It is also called the *vādī* (lit. the speaker, or announcer) *i.e.* the note which indicates, manifests, or expresses the peculiar character of the rāga, and receives the greatest emphasis in the structure of the rāga. It is also called the *jīva,* or the soul of the rāga. Just as the *vādī* note determines the general character of a rāga, the *vivādī,* or the dissonant note, distinguishes and differentiates it from other forms of rāgas, by avoidance of the *vivādī* note. For, this dissonant note destroys the character of the melody. The *vivādī* note gives the negative element, and, the other three, the positive determining elements of a rāga.[2] Every rāga has its special

(1) '*Rañjayati iti rāgaḥ*'='that which colours, is a rāga.'

(2) In the Sanskrit text-books on music (conveniently summarised by Sir S. M. Tagore in his *Saṅgītasaṅgraha,* p. 27), very

types of a serial of notes for ascent (*āroha*) and descent (*avaroha*) which determines its structure or *ṭhāṭ*. The degree of insistence or importance of particular notes lends flesh, blood, colour, and life to the scale and creates a Rāga.

Some definitions are given of the nature of rāga by ancient authorities. The earliest is that of Mataṅga (circa 5th century)—a fairly ancient authority, later than Bharata, but much earlier than Śārṅgadeva. His definition is repeated by all later authors. According to Mataṅga, 'A rāga is called by the learned, that kind of sound composition, which is adorned with musical notes, in some peculiarly stationary, or ascending, or descending, or moving values (*varṇa*), which have the effect of colouring the hearts of men'[1]. In this definition a technical word *varṇa* (value) is used. *Varṇas* (values) are of four kinds: 'values of duration'

picturesque definitions and descriptions are given of the characteristic composing notes of a rāga, *viz. vādī, saṃvādī, anuvādī,* and *vivādī* (sonant, consonant, assonant, dissonant) notes: "*sa vādī kathyate pracuro yaḥ prayogeṣu vakti rāgādiniścayam*"='That note is called a *vādī*, by the abundant use of which a rāga is clearly differentiated.'

"*Samaśrutiśca saṃvādī pañcamasya samaḥ kvasit*"='The *saṃvādī* note has similar quarter-tones (*śruti*) as the *vādī* note, or according to some, is equal to the fifth note.' '*Vivādī* is a note situated at a distance of two *Srutis* from the *vādī* note, *e.g. gāndhāra* (c) and *nikhāda.* (c). The other notes are *anuvādī.*

The following verses summarise the relationship:

"*Vādī rājā svarastasya saṃvādī syād amātyavat|*
Satrur vivādī tasy syād anuvādí ca bhṛtyavat|| [Ibid., p., 28]

'Of the notes, *vādī* is the king, *sāṃvādī* is the minister, *vivādī* is the enemy, *anuvādī* is in the position of a vassal.' The *vādī* note is translated by some as the 'regnal' note.

(1) "*Svara-varṇa-viśeṣeṇa dhvani-bhedena vā punaḥ|*
.Rajyate yena yaḥ kaścit sa rāgaḥ sammataḥ satām|| 290
Athavā: *Yo'sau dhvani-viśeṣastu svara-varṇavibhūṣitaḥ|*
*Rañjako jana-cittānāṃ sa rāga udāhṛtaḥ||*291
Ityevaṃ rāgā-śabdasya vyutpattir-abhidhīyate|
Rañjanājjāyate rāgo vyutpattiḥ smudāhṛtā|| 293
Mataṅga-muni : 'Bṛhaddeśī' (Trivandrum edition, p. 81)

(*sthāyī*); 'values of ascent' (*ārohaṇa*); 'values of descent' (*avarohana*); and 'values of movement' (*sañcārī*). This definition of rāga may be paraphrased as a note-composition having a peculiar musical significance, in their values of duration, ascent, descent, or movement, capable of affecting the human mind with peculiar feelings.

A secod definition ascribed to Bharata and quoted in the *Saṅgīta Nārāyaṇa* (circa 1750) is somewhat more subjective and vague.

" Those are called rāgas by Bharata and other sages by which the hearts of all the beings in the three worlds are coloured and pleased."[1]

A third version is also a paraphrase of the last two. 'By which all people are coloured, or elated as soon as they hear it, and by reason of giving pleasure to all, that is known as rāga.'[2] In all the three definitions, the word rāga is derived from the root *'rañja'*, "to colour," "to tinge."

Rāgas are usually said to have descended from a certain parent stock which is technically known as a *ṭhaṭ* (lit. an 'array', or a 'setting'). These *ṭhāṭs* represent modes, or types of some group of notes, from which distinct forms, or modes of somewhat similar texture can be derived. The difference between a *ṭhāṭ* and a rāga consists in the absence of any aesthetic value in the former which is only the ascent and the descent without the distinctive assonant, and consonant notes (*vādī, anuvādī,* or *saṃvādī*) and without the capacity of conveying any emotion. *Ṭhāṭ* is technically used in the instrumental music system of Northern India to denote the frets of string instruments (*Sitār, Vīṇā, Surbāhār*) for the purpose of playing a given pattern of modes, for, one setting will serve for several modes of the same type,—*e.g. Bhairavī ṭhāṭ, Kāfī ṭhāṭ.* Thus *ṭhāṭ* is used in a classifying sense, the corresponding Southern or the Karnatic word is *mela-kartā*—the 'union-maker,' that is to say, the group-maker which groups together several allied rāgas.

(1) *Yaistu cetāṃsi rajyante jagattritayavarttināṃ|*
Te rāgā iti kathyante munibhir Bharatādibhiḥ||

(2) *Yasya śravaṇa-mātreṇa rajyante sakalāḥ prājāḥ|*
Sarvānurañjanād dhetos tena rāga iti smṛtaḥ||

A rāga may, therefore, be, more correctly, rendered as a "melody-mould," a " melody-type," or a "musical pattern." "Except for the primary condition that certain notes are to come in a certain way, there is no other restriction imposed on the singing of a particular rāga" (R. Śrīnivāsa).

As Fox Strangways observes: "A Rāga gets its special flavour not so much from its being just what it is, as *from its not being something else, closely allied to it,* which is present all the time in the musician's consciousness."[1] [The italics are ours.] It is, however, the distinct individuality of the rāga which makes for the consciousness of the difference and not the difference which creates the individuality which seems to be suggested by the italicised expression. And it sometimes requires long education and trained connoisseurship to distinguish between two apparently identical, but subtly distinguished, rāgas, which the less trained ears of the uneducated frequently confuse.

S. G. Kanhere[2] observes: "In the language of music the arrangement of notes which colour or affect certain emotion of the mind is called rāga. The definition of rāga given in Sanskrit books is "that a particular combination or relation of several notes which is pleasing to the ear is called Rāga." Many conflicting explanations of rāga given by different scholars converge to the same centre, *i.e.*, "the pleasant effect of the arrangements of notes."

Clements in his excellent study of the fundamentals of type,—e.g. *Bhairavī thāt,*
Indian Music thus describes the rāga:[3] "The name of the Rāga connotes a scale bearing a fixed relationship to the drone, with its harmonic structure determined by a *Vādī* and *Saṃvādī*, a chief note ("aṃśa svara") occurring more frequently than others, a lower limit described in terms of the Mūrchanā, occasionally an upper limit also, certain characteristic turns of melody, recurring with frequency, certain rules regarding the employment of embellishments,

(1) Fox Strangways : *The Music of Hindostan*, p. 170.

(2) S. G. Kanhere : "*Some remarks on Indian Music*," Bulletin of the School of Oriental Studies, vol. IV, pp. 105-120.

(3) E. Clements : '*Introduction to the Sttudy of Indian Music*', London 1913, pp. 3-4.

RĀGINĪ KAKUBHĀ

and a stated time of the day for its performance. It is a common practice, after singing an air in a Rāga, to improvise a series of free fantasia passages each returning in due course to a characteristic snatch of the melody, only to wander off again in still more elaborate variations. The whole performance must be "within the Rāga," that is, without transgression of the elaborate rules governing its structure."

Philippe Stern ("La Musique Hindoue", *La Revue Musicale,* Mai 1923, p. 31, 55-6) thus defines a rāga:—"It is the deepening of the idea of mode .... that which gives not only the mode but also the choice of principal notes, the degrees to be avoided, the difference of the descending and ascending movements, the prescribed sequences, the movement, this ambient, this coloration, this peculiar physiognomy, this personality constitutes the rāga (lit. the taint). A rāga, when transcribed in notes, should include the rise, fall and often the prescribed sequences. It can be taken for a melody. Often however an actual melody is given as an example and we have there the appearance of a skeleton on account of the fact that the Indian notation does not generally indicate the ornaments. We are simply told that—it is that rāga. Indeed, but quite a different melody might also be that rāga and give that ambient. The Indian musician is in a situation which is analogous to that of the sculptor of the Middle Ages, who being a prisoner of the canons of religious iconography, tried there to specialise thoroughly in certain types, marked his personality with details so very striking for the initiated that these types remained enclosed within a limit, and he following the same rules created either a mediocre work, or a masterpiece."

In a recent article, the same author has made another attempt to translate the idea of a *rāga:* "What is a *rāga*? It is an atmosphere, a musical colouring. This colouring is associated with a mood of feeling, a sentiment. It is often, also, associated with the time of the day, and it is quite obvious that the musical colouring should differ for dawn or dusk, for heat or for middle of the night ...... How is this musical colouring attained? How is the rāga to be defined in musical terms? ...... The rāga belongs to the realm of modes and of different scales. In modes, Indian music is extremely rich, but the *rāga* is not *only* the scale. The various explanations of the *rāga* have often been misleading, because they stop short or go too far. It has been sometimes said that the rāga is a mode; but the *rāga* is far more precise and much richer than a mode. On the same mode there are several *rāgas*. The *rāga* is therefore in that direction, but goes further. The *rāga* has been also likened to a skeleton of melody which is to be clothed with varied ornaments. But this goes too far; the *rāga* is much less fixed and much richer than a musical outline given; several melodies, all different, can be composed on the same *rāga*; so that the definition as regards melody is beyond the truth. The *rāga* is more fixed than the mode, and less fixed than the melody, beyond the mode and short of the melody, and richer both than a given mode or a given melody. It is a mode with added multiple specialities."[1]

Mr. Fox Strangways defines *rāga* as "an arbitrary series of notes characterized, as far as possible as individuals, by proximity to or remoteness from the note which marks the *tessitura* (general level of the melody), by a special order in which they are usually taken, by the frequency or the reverse with which they occur, by grace or the absence of it, and by relation to a tonic usually reinforced by a drone." Mr. Popley paraphrases this definition in a simplified form: "*Rāgas* are different series of notes within the octave, which form the basis of all Indian melodies, and are differentiated from each other by the prominence of certain fixed notes and by the sequence of particular notes. We may perhaps find in the term 'melody-type' the best way to transcribe *rāga* in English."[2]

In rendering or interpreting a rāga, it is not necessary to reproduce, or repeat slavishly, or mechanically, its component notes in a given sequence. If one keeps to the main features, or outlines of the pattern, considerable latitude is allowed by way of improvizations. Indeed no rendering of the same rāga, even by the same interpreter need be, iden-

(1) Philippe Stern : "*The Music of India and the Theory of the Rāga*" (*Indian Art and Letters*, New series, vol. VII, no. 1 1933, p. 1-9).

(2) Herbert A. Popley : '*The Music of India,*' 1921, p. 39.

tically alike,—like 'copies' of a stereotype, or the repetitions of a gramophone. The actual form varies, according to the mood, or skill of the singer, or the response of the audience, though adhering to the main outline of the types, —so as not to call up the mental picture (*tasbīr*) of any other rāga, however, closely related. In order to keep to this identity of pattern, or mould, it is necessary to avoid notes, which will alter the individuality of the 'picture,' the peculiarity of the physiognomy, or in other words, will introduce dissonance, or a jarring feeling. This dissonant note to be avoided, is, as we know, the *vivādī* (the inimical note). *Saṃvādī* is, on the other hand, the consonant note. While the *anuvādī* (assonant, or subservient) note stands for all other notes which are not *vādī, saṃvādī,* or *vivādī*.[1]

According to the number of notes composing them rāgas are classified as *oḍava* (pentatonic) using five notes, *ṣāḍava* or *khāḍava* (hextatonic) using six notes, and *sampūraṇa* (heptatonic) using all the seven notes. With less than five notes, no rāga can be composed.[2]

According to Mataṅga, an ancient authority on Music, 'no classical melody (*mārga*) can be composed from four notes and less; melodies with notes of less than five are used by tribes such as Śavaras, Pulindas, Kāmbojas, Vaṅgas, Kirātas, Vālhīkas, Andhras, Draviḍas, and foresters.[3] An exception is made in the case of a class of stage songs known as *dhruvās,* which though regarded as classical melodies,

(1) It is sometimes believed that a *vivādī* note is to be avoided, and *is* absent in a rāga. This is not correct. A *vivādī* note is occasionally introduced to demonstrate its dissonant character in the scheme of a particular melody.

(2) According to some authorities, the Mālava-śrī rāgiṇi is a melody of less than five notes.

(3) "*Catuḥ-svarāt prabhṛti na mārgaḥ śavara-pulinda-kāmboja-vaṅga-kīrāta-vālhīkāndhra-dravida-vanādisu prayujyate|*
Tathācāha Bharatah:—'ṣat-svarasya prayogo'sti tathā pañcasvarasyaca|
catuḥ-svara-proyage'pi hyavakriṣṭa-dhruvāsvapi"||
Bṛhaddeśī by Mataṅga-Muni (Trivandram Sanskrit Series, 1928, no. VI, p. 59).

are found to be composed of four notes.

If the combinations, growing out of the component members or elements (*svaras*) of a rāga-composition, have any significant qualities, or functions, the *ensemble* of the rāga-form must spell and express some particular states of feelings and emotions. Indeed, they are believed to represent particular moods, association, or atmosphere of the human mind, or of nature,—and to be able to call up and invoke a distinctive kind of feeling answering to the state of the mind,—or its physical environment, for the time being. Rāgas have, therefore, the power of producing certain mental effects and each is supposed to have an emotional value, or signification which may be called the *ethos* of the rāga. Rāgas may be said to stand for the language of the soul, expressing itself variously, under the stress of sorrow, or the inspiration of joy, under the storm of passion, or the thrills of the expectation, under the throes of love-longing, the pangs of separation, or the joys of union.

HISTORY OF THE RAGAS

By legend and tradition Indian music is supposed to be derived from, and have its roots in, the Vedas.[1] Let us see if the music of the Vedic age offer any materials for the rāgas. The Sāman chants appear to be melodies of three notes (tetrachord?) known as *udātta* (raised), *anudātta* (not raised) and *svarita* (sounded, graced). This seems to be borne out by the sūtras of Pāṇini (5th century B.C.) who defines the *svarita* note as an adjustment or amalgamation of the two notes *udātta* and *anudātta*.[2] If the Vedic chants were music confined to three notes, they were not melodies or rāgas in our sense, for a *rāga* must at least have five notes (pentatonic). The *śikṣās* (branches of the Prātiśākhyas) seem to give a different interpretation to the three Vedic notes. According to this later definition, *udātta* stands for *niṣāda* and *gāndhāra*, *anudātta* for *ṛṣabha* and *dhaivata*, and *svarita* for *ṣaḍja*, *madhyama* and *pañcama*.[3] According to the tonic values of the notes, *ṣaḍja* and *madhyama* are made of 4 śrutis which is made to equate with the Vedic notes known as 'svarita.' The notes ṛṣabha and dhaivata are made of 3 śrutis and answer to *anudātta* notes, while *niṣāda* and *gāndhāra*, made of 2 śrutis, correspond to *udātta*. The seven notes therefore are implied in the three

(1) "*Jagrāha pāṭhyam ṛgvedād sāmabhya gītam eva ca.*|"
Nāṭyaśāstra, Ch. I, Verse 17.
"*Sāma-vedād daṃ gītaṃ saṃjagrāha pitāmahaḥ* |
Tadgītaṃ Nāradāyaiva tena lokeṣu varṇitaṃ ||"
Saṅgītamakaranda, I, 18.

(2) Pāṇini, IV. 2, 29, 30, 31 & 32:
"*Uccairudāttaḥ nīcairanudāttaḥ samāhāraḥ svaritah.* ||"

(3) "*Udāttau niṣāda-gāndhārau, anudāttau ṛsabha-dhaivatau* |
Svarita-prabhavāhy ete ṣaḍja-madhyama-pañcahāḥ ||"

2

notes of the Vedic melodies.

There is a long standing tradition, still surviving in current musical practices, that after Vālmīki had composed his *Rāmāyaṇa,* it was set to music by Bharata himself[1] and sung by Lava and Kuśa, who were fortunate in finding as their auditor Rāma himself. We have no means of knowing the character of the melodies to which the *Rāmāyaṇa* was sung.

Bharata.

It may be remarked that a greater part of what now passes under the name of classical music, at one time or other, belonged to the world of *deśi,* or folk music, and which being refined and affiliated to the rules and system of the traditional classic music have contributed to its growth and development. Materials are very scanty for tracing the processes by which rāgas evolved in their present forms, characters and classifications. It is certainly difficult to contend that the rāgas as understood to-day, had evolved and were recognized as such, at the time[2] when the *Nāṭyaśāstra* attributed to Bharata was compiled;[3] though there would be nothing improbable in the supposition that

(1) Rāmāyaṇa: *"Taṃ sa śuśrāva kākutsthaḥ pūrvācārya--vinirmmitaṃ"* which a commentator explains: *'gāthakānāṃ gāna?siddhaye pūrvvācāryyeṇa Bharatena nirmmitaṃ.'*

(2) According to Keith: "The date of that text *(Nāṭyaśāstra)* is uncertain, but we cannot with any certainty place it before the third century A.D." *(The Sanskrit Drama,* Oxford, 1924, p. 13.)

(3) The remarks of J. Grosset *(Contribution á l'étude La Musique Hindoue,* 1888, p. 88) are very pertinent in this connection: "We believe that the introduction of the theory of rāga is of relatively recent date, Bharata in his *Nāṭyaśāstra* no-where gives it a definition. He does not devote any *adhyāya* to the exposition of this musical element which had subsequently such an important development. Therefore in spite of the definition of rāga being attributed to our authority by W. Jones, Mohun Tagore etc., in spite of the quotations that they give as emanating from him (Bharata) and some commentators of dramas, we are of opinion that in the period of the composition of the *Nāṭyaśāstra,* the *rāgas* did not constitute one of the elements of the musical theory but that they were gradually substituted for the *jātis* which, however, they resembled, and, it seems, permitted a double use."

they may have evolved, though not known and recognized by definite names or associated with any cult, season, or particular areas of culture. In the musical data of the *Nāṭyāśāstra* (chapter 38) we have definite evidence of the theory of the consonance of notes (samavāditya) in the terminology used *viz.*, *vādī, saṃvādī, anuvādī, vivādī,*—words which are indeed as old as the second century A.D., for, they occur in the *Mahābhārata* (XIV, 14, 19), which is believed to have taken their present form some time between 400 B.C. and 200 A.D. In the *Nāṭyaśāstra* (ch. 38, śloka 23) we have not only a recognition of the relationship between the consonant, assonant, dissonant notes, but also an allusion to a theory of the relative values of initial and terminal notes *graha, nyāsa* and *apanyāsa* (ch. 28, ślokas 80, 81).

But these data appear to be forestalled by Dattila, a musical authority (Saṅgītācārya), who seems to be earlier than Bharata.[1]

According to the text attributed to Dattila,[2] *vādī, anuvādī* and *vivādī* notes are recognised and defined.

The text of Dattila also refers, in a summary way, to the 18 *jātis,* or species of melodies, of which seven take their names after the seven notes. The remaining eleven are also named and described according to their component parts. Of these, seven belong to the ṣaḍja scale (*grāma*) and the

(1) According to an old tradition, Dattila is supposed to be one of the five Bharatas (Nandi, Kohala, Dattila, Bharata and Mataṅga) who made the science of music and dramaturgy current in the world. Dattila is sometimes associated with Kohala, and they were supposed to have collaborated in a work known as *Dattila-Kohalyīam.* Kohala being undoubtedly an earlier authority than Bharata, who quotes Kohala, it follows that Dattila is earlier than Bharata. This view is supported by two scholars who have recently investigated into the relative positions of the early authorities on music: (i) V. V. Narasiṃhachary "The Early Writers on Music" (*The Journal of the Music Academy,* Madras, October, 1930, p. 259) and (ii) V. Raghavan: "Some names in early Saṅgīta Literature" (Ibid., Vol. III, 1932, No. 1 & 2, p. 12): "The present text (of Bharata) is later than Kohala and even Dattila".

(2) Published in the Trivandrum Sanskrit Series. No. CII.

rest to the madhyama scale.

We have also, a classification of melody-types according to the number of notes used, into three classes known as pentatonic (oḍava), sextatonic (khāḍava) and septatonic (sampūrṇā). Both Dattila and Bharata, therefore, give us all the ingredients or materials for the structure of a melody.

In fact Bharata, following Dattila, classifies the melodies under the name of *jātis* (species). These he classifies under two modes or scales (grāmas), the ṣaḍja-grāma and madhyama-grāma. Under these two modes (grāmas) Bharata enumerates the 18 *jātis* of melodies, the same as given by Dattila (See Anppendix 1 and 2).

According to Mataṅga (an authority who comes next after Bharata), the *jātis* generate the *grāma-rāgas* with the use of the tonic-initial the predominating or *aṃśa* note.[1] Mataṅga gives the following definition of *jāti*: "The *jātis* are born out of the initial notes and śrutis (microtones). Hence they are called *jātis,* from which is born (that is to say, from which begins) the consciousness of flavour *that* is *jāti.* In the alternative, by reason of the birth of all kinds of melodies, *jātis* are so-called."[2] The same author expounds the 18 jātis enumerated by Bharata, with somewhat greater elaboration.

In the next chapter (29), Bharata indicates the *rasa* (passion) and *bhāvas* (sentiments) of each of the *jātis* and what *jātis* should be employed to interpret a particular sentiment.

Bharata's *jātis,* therefore, for all practical purposes provide the *genus* out of which the rāgas have been derived although Bharata does not actually use the term rāga. In fact Mataṅga asserts that "he is including in his work informations on such subjects as "courses of rāgas" with their marks and characteristics,—matters which have not been dealt with by Bharata and other sages".[3]

Harivamsa.

That the rāgas, associated with the modes (grāma)

(1) *Bṛhaddeśī* (T. S. S. No. XCIV, p. 65).

(2) Ibid., p. 55-56.

(3) *"Rāgā-mārgasya yad rūpaṃ yan noktaṃ Bharatādibhiḥ |
Nirūpyate tadasmābhir lakṣaṇa-saṃyutam"* || *Bṛhaddeśī* (p. 81).

were in existence already before Bharata summarised them in his sections devoted to music, is proved by sifinificant allusions in the *Harivaṃśa*, (which is regarded as a supplement to the *Mahābharata*) and is ascribed to about 300 A.D.[1]

In more than one passages, *grāma-rāgas* are referred to and it is very likely, these *grāma-rāgas* were of the types indicated by Bharata. In the 89th chapter of the Viṣṇu-parva in connection with a water carnival, various musical and dramatic representations are described in the *Harivaṃśa*. The women of the descendants of Bhīma sang various songs.

"O king! the skill required to perform a fraction of the forms of the different varieties of the six *grāma-rāgas* (modal melodies), in their fine and subtle classifications (jātis), can only be attempted by human beings with great difficulty" [ch. 89, 82].

According to a different reading, the first passage in the quotation would refer to eleven varieties (*ekādaśa avayava*) of modal melodies answering to the eleven composite modes referred to in Dattila [Appendix 1].

* * *

(Chapter 93, verses 23, 24):

"Thereafter, the women of the Bhīma tribe sang *Chālikya* songs in the melody of Devagāndhāra,[2] sweet to the ear like nectar, and pleasant to the ear and a delight to the mind."

"Then they sang songs beautifully, having for their subject the *Descent* of *Gaṅgā* in the *grāma-rāgas* which

(1) The date 200 A.D. has been assigned to the *Harivaṃśa* on the ground of the occurrence of the word *dināra*. See Hopkins, *Great Epic of India*, p. 387; Winternitz, *A History of Indian Literature* (Cal. Ed. Vol. I, 1927, p. 464) remarks "We may assume that it did not come into existence very long before the 4th century A.D." R. G. Bhandarkar (*Vaiṣṇavism*, p. 36) assigns it to "about the third century of the Christian era."

(2) It is surprising to find, here, a reference to the well-known melody of Deva-Gāndhāra (Deo-Gāndhā). [See Notes on Plate LXLI]. It is a derivative of the archaic *grāma-rāga* known as Bhinna-ṣaḍja.

went up to Gāndhāra (grāma), with the grandeur of beautiful notes, pierced (*viddhaṃ*) and elaborated (*āsāritaṃ*)".

"The *grāma rāgas* referred to above, it may be assumed, were identical with the *grāma-rāgas* described in the *Nāṭya-śāstra.* Only the latter describes the *grāma-rāgas* appertaining to two grāmas viz. *ṣaḍja* and *madhyama,* while the passage of the *Harivaṃśa* alludes to *rāgas* belonging to the *gāndhāra-grāma.* As some ancient authorities have explained, the last named grāma (scale) was obsolete amongst men and were current in celestial practices. In fact, one text suggests that according to Nārada, the *ṣaḍja-grāma* has grown out of the terrestrial regions, the *madhyama-grāma* from the ethereal regions, and the *gāndhara-grāma* from the celestial regions, and not from anywhere else.

Anyhow, the *grāma-rāgas* of Bharata are referred to and described in the *Nāradīyā Śikṣā,*[1] under the names of "Niṣāda-Khāḍava", "Pañcama", "Madhyama-grāma", Ṣaḍja-grāma", "Sādhāritam", "Kaiśikam", and "Kaiśika-madhyama'. The two last named melodies are described as follows:

"After expressing the Kaiśika (V) in the presence of

(1) *Nāradīyā Śikṣā (Sāma-vedīya)* edited by Satyavrata Sāmaśramī, Calcutta, 1890. Popley *(The Music of India,* page 14) suggests that it was "probably composed between the tenth and twelfth century". Considering that its rāga system corresponds very nearly to that of the Kuḍumiyamālai inscription, the data, if not the text of the *Narādīya Śikṣā,* must be earlier than the 7th century and considering the fact that it only refers to seven melodies, while the *Pañcatantra* refers to thirty-six, the former must be earlier than the *Pañcatantra.*. Kielhorn suggests that some of the *Śikṣās* are not earlier than the date of Patañjalī (2nd century B. C.) "That the Śikṣās in verse were in existence when Patañjalī composed his great commentary on Kātyāyana's "Vārtikas" seems to me very probable. *The Indian Antiquary,* May 1876, p. 143., foot-note.

M. Rama Krishna Kavi ('Literature on Music,' *Journal, Andhra Historical Research Society,* Vol. III, 1928-29, pp. 20-29)) believes that the *Nāradīyā Śikṣā,* or, at least, the view of Nārada, the traditional author of the *Śikṣā,* is quoted by Bharata in Chapter 34. He is therefore inclined to place the musical data of the *Nāradīyā Śikṣā* earlier than Bharata.

all the notes, where (the melody) terminates in the *madhyama,* there arises "Kaiśika-madhyama" (VI) where the Kākalī (?sharp Nikhāda) is seen and the *pañcama* predominates. Kaśyapa calls it *"Kaiśika"*, born of the "Madhyama grāma" (VII), (11th śloka).

Kudumiya-mālai Inscription.

The next available evidence of the currency of the grāma-rāgas is furnished by the inscription of Kuḍumiya-mālai[1] in the Pudukkottai State (Southern India), written in characters of the seventh century. Though not designated as such, seven different varieties of melodies are given in the form of notations namely: (i) Madhyama-grāma (ii) Saḍja-grāma (iii) Sāḍava (iv) Sādhārita (v) Pañcama (vi) Kaiśika-madhyama (vii) Kaiśika, which seem to correspond to the grāma rāgas given in the *Nāradīyā Śikṣā* the text of which should, therefore, be considered as earlier than the seventh century.

In editing this inscription P. R. Bhandarkar[1] remarks: "It is clear that the seven rāgas of this inscription did not exist in the time of Bharatīya *Nāṭya-śāstra.* When they came into existence is not known, the present inscription being the earliest record." There is no doubt that these seven rāgas, even if they existed at the time, are not indicated in the *Nāṭya-śāstra.* But a glance at the seven melodies will show that they are identical with the seven melodies described in the *Nāradīyā Śikṣā,* quoted and translated above. In the last named text their compositional forms are verbally described, while in the inscription their "skeleton notes are given for the benefit of students" (*śiṣyahitārthāya kṛtaḥ svarāgamaḥ*). Excepting two *viz.* 'Pāñcama' and 'Kaiśika', none of the others in their names seem to suggest any of the rāgas known in later texts. There is no doubt that here we have the rāgas in their nascent stage, crudely described with reference to their salient notes, long before they came to be associatd with any season, region, or cult, and assumed proper names.

Pañcatantra.

It will be convenient to consider here, a curious reference to the so-called thirty-six rāgas in the *Pañcatantra* (dated about the fifth century, being anterior to A.D. 570).

(1) P. R. Bhandarkar: "Kuḍimiyamālai Inscription of Music", *Epigraphia Indica,* Vol. XII, 1914, p. 266.

In the tale of "Ass as Singer",[1] the ass inspired by the beauty of the night expresses a desire to sing, and, being exhorted by his friend the jackal not to sing, boasts of his knowledge of the musical science as will appear from the following extract:

"O! sister's daughter! Look here. It is a very clear beautiful night. I am, therefore, going to sing. Well then, in what melody (rāga) must I sing? * * * * What? Don't I know how to sing? Listen, I will tell you of the theory. It is thus. There are seven notes, three scales, twenty-one grace modes, forty-nine melodic improvisations, three units of time, three voice-registers, six ways of singing, nine emotions, thirty-six variations of the melody (*varṇa*); and forty minor melodies are known. Thus, the mode of singing will embrace all the 185 parts of song, pure as gold."

The word actually used in the last passage is *varṇa* which cannot be taken as equivalent to rāgas. On the other hand, in the first passage, the term rāga is actually used in the sense of a song being set to a particular melody. This would certainly suggest that more than one rāga, in the sense we understand to-day, had come into existence and were current in practice. Whether they were still in the stage of *grāmarāgas,* or had been recognized and labelled by proper names it is impossible to say from the data of this allusion to the science of music in the *Pañcatantra* (5th century). From the above reference it is difficult to say,—if the six rāgas and thirty-six rāgiṇīs, popular in North India, had been evolved by that time. The passage refers to thirty-six classes altogether.

Brhad-desi by Matanga-muni.

We now come to an important text, recently come to light, and known as *Bṛhad-deśī* by Mataṅga-muni,[2] which, though fragmentary, throws a flood of light on the history of the rāgas. As its name implies it is a comprehensive (*Bṛhat*) treatise on *deśī* or folk-music, current on the earth, as distinguished from the *mārga* or celestial music, cur-

(1) Book V, Tale, Vol. II, Harvard Edition, by J. Hertel, 1908 p. 271-72.

(2) Published in the Trivandrum Sanskrit Series (Vol. XCIV., 1928.)

rent in the heavens.

After devoting a chapter to the *Jātis,* Mataṅga devotes a special chapter to the rāgas. Indeed, it is in this chapter of the *Bṛhad-deśī* that we first come across the word "rāgas" as understood in all later literature on Indian music. In the history of the rāgas, *Bṛhad-deśī* is, therefore, a very important landmark. Chronologically, the work stands between the *Nāṭyaśāstra* of Bharata, and the *Saṅgita-makaranda* of Nārada, that is to say, some time between the 4th and the 7th century.[1]

Mataṅga regards rāgas as one of the seven classes of songs (*gītis*) current in his time. He cites Yāṣṭika, an earlier authority, according to whom the gītis were of five classes: śuddha, bhinna, vesara, gauḍa, and sādhārita. At the time of Mataṅga, the gītis were of seven varieties.[2] (1) śuddha (2) bhinnaka (3) gauḍika (4) rāga-gīti (5) sādhāraṇī (6) bhāṣā-gīti (7) vibhāṣā-gītis. The raga-gītis are fourth in Mataṅga's list (*rāga-gītis-caturthikā*). He defines the various classes of *gītis,* and describes rāga-gītis as follows: "Attractive note compositions, with beautiful and illuminating graces are known as rāga-gītis. Where the four *varṇas* (probably the four characters of values of duration, ascent, descent, and movement) are met with in

(1) According to V. Raghavan, Mataṅga cannot be earlier than the 9th century, while Ram Chandra Kavi seems to assign to him an earlier date, on the basis of an alleged reference by Mataṅga to Rudraṭa, who is not the great rhetorician of the 9th century. According to a quotation given by Kallinātha who cites Mataṅga as quoting Rudraṭa)*Saṅgīta-Ratnākara,* p. 82), V. Raghavan is of opinion that Mataṅga's *Brhaddeśī* cannot be earlier than the 9th century. Ram Chandra Kavi ("Literary Gleanings", *Journal, Andhra Historical Research Society,* Vol. III, 1929, nos. 2, 3, 4 at pages 200-206 takes Rudraṭa cited by Mataṅga, as Rudrācārya, the protégé of the kind Mahendra Vikrama, referred to in the Kuḍumiyamālai music inscription (7th century). (See the discussion of the date in V. Raghavan's paper "Some names in early Saṅgīta Literature", *Journal of the Music Academy,* Madras, Vol. II No. 1 & 2, 1932, p. 19, 25-26). Having regard to the archaic nature of the

(2) Published in the Trivandrum Sanskrit Series (Vol. XCIV., 1928).

data relating to rāgas cited in *Bṛhaddeśī*, it is difficult to assign it to a period as late as the 9th century.

a graceful combination that is known as rāga."

Of the seven classes of *gītis*, sub-divisions are enumerated. Thus 'śuddha' *(cokṣa)*, and 'bhinnaka' have each five varieties, 'gauḍas' three varieties; 'rāgas' are of eight varieties and 'sādhāraṇas,' of seven varieties; 'bhāṣās are of sixteen kinds and 'vibhāṣās, of twelve kinds. The eight varieties of rāgas went by the name of (1) Takka, or Taku (2) Sauvīra (3) Mālava-pañcama (4) Khāḍava (5) Voṭṭa-rāga (6) Hindolaka (7) Takka-Kaiśika.[1]

Here then we have the first enumeration of eight of the earliest rāgas known by name. Some of them may have been derived from the 18 jātis described by Bharata.

That the 'bhāṣā', 'vibhāṣā' and sādhāraṇa gītis,' were later related to and amalgamated with the rāga system appears to be suggested by the names given to these gītis.

Thus the 'sādhāraṇa gītis' bear six names (1) Śaka (2) Kakubha (3) Harmāṇa-pañcama (4) Rūpa-sādhārita (5) Gāndhāra-pañcama (6) Ṣaḍja-kaiśika. (Appendix 3).

Even from the time of Bharata, the melodies were used and they naturally developed in association with the different sections of the body of a drama. Thus, in a passage of Bharata quoted by Mataṅga *(Bṛhad-deśī*, p. 87), it is laid down that the madhyama-grāma melodies should be used in the *mukha* (opening of the drama), the ṣaḍja-grāma melodies in the *pratimukha* stages (progression), the sādhārita melodies in the *garbha* (development) stages, and the pañcama-jāti melodies for the *vimarśa* (pauses) and so on.[2]

It is from this point of view that the 18 jātis of melodies are assigned by Bharata (Ch. 29, 1-4 verses) their *rasa*

(1) *"Ṭaku-rāgaśca Souvīrastathā Mālava--pañcamaḥ|*
Khāḍavo Voṭṭa-rāgaśca tathā Hindolakaḥ paraḥ|| 314
Taka-kaiśika ityuktastathā Mālava-Kaiśikāḥ|
Ete rāgāḥ samākhyātā nāmato muni-puṅgavaiḥ"|| 315,
Bṛhad-deśī, p. 85.

(2) *Brihaddeśī*, p. 87.
This passage cannot be traced in the published text of the *Nāṭya-śāstra*.

values, that is to say, their appropriateness for particular passion, sentiment, or atmosphere of feeling, with reference to particular situations in the plot of a drama ("*tat pravṛtte rase kāyaṃ gānaṃgeye prayoktṛbhiḥ,*" Ch. 29, verse 11.) This is made clear by the more elaborate descriptions of jāti melodies or gītis given by Mataṅga who, while describing the component notes of each gīti, mentions the *rasa,* or the flavour of sentiment appropriate to each, and the place in the body of the drama where a gīti can be appropriately introduced. And it is very probable that the rāga-gītis, were first distinguished from other classes of gītis (*e.g.* Śuddha, Bhinna, Gaúḍī), on account of the *rasa*—quality, the power of evoking emphatic and clearly differentiated sentiments, or qualities of feeling.

The only other comment which the text of Mataṅga calls for is that it represents a very early stage in the development of the rāgas, when Kakubha, destined to be pushed to a subordinate position as a rāgiṇī, later on, figures as a major melody, to which several minor melodies (*bhāṣās*) are affiliated. At this stage, Bhairava, which was later derived from Bhinna-ṣaḍja,[1] an ancient jāti-rāga, had not yet come into existence. Unfortunately the successive developments are not supported by documents as there is a considerable gap between the text of Mataṅga and the next landmark.

Abhilāsārtha-cintāmani by Somesvara.

In the well-known encyclopædia known as *Mānasollāsa* or *Abhilāṣārtha-cintāmaṇi,*[2] by Someśvara which we owe to a royal author, there are two chapters devoted to music and music data. The work was composed in 1131 A.D. by king Someśvara, son of Vikramāditya of the Western Cālukya dynasty, who had their capital city at Kalyāṇī (Kalyān).

(1) *Saṅgīta-ratnākara,* Vol. 1, p. 191: *"Iti Bhinna-ṣaḍjaḥ| Bhairava-stat-samudbhavaḥ Dhāṃśo mānto ripa-tyvktaḥ prārthanāyāṃ samasvaraḥ"*|| 81.

(2) Portions of *Abhilāṣārtha Cintāmaṇi* have been printed and published in the Mysore Oriental Publication Series, 69, 1926, and in Gaekwad's Oriental Series No. 28, Vol. 1, 1925. But the published portions do not include the chapters on music. The informations here cited are borrowed from a Ms. in the collection of the Bhandarkar Research Institute, Poona.

As an authority on music, the Prince is mentioned by Śāraṅgadeva in his work.[1] He was also the author of a special treatise on music entitled *Saṅgīta-ratnāvalī* which is known only by references in other works.[2] The discussion of rāgas is confined only to the first 80 verses in the chapter in the encyclopædia devoted to music, but the chapter does not contain any reference to the system of rāga-classification, which is attributed to Someśvara in the *Rāga-darpana*, (Appendix 8) and other works; probably, the system was set out in the *Saṅgīta-ratnāvalī*.. The topic is introduced by tracing the rāgas indirectly from the Sāma-veda. 'From the jātis the *rāgas* were ascertained. From the rāgas came the *bhāṣās,* and then the *vibhāṣās,* and the *antara-bhāṣikās.*[3] According to the author, Deśī-rāgas derived from the names of regions, have been current in his time, in popular and beautiful forms.[4] "The rāga develops by hearing, and the mind is always pleased and elated by it, therefore they are called rāgas; I am proceeding to recite them by names."[5] Then, the author gives a catalogue of the different classes or types of rāgas, apparently current in his time. Thus, the five śuddha rāgas are stated to be: (1) Śuddha-ṣāḍava, (2) Śuddha-pañcama, (3) Śuddha-

(1) *"Rudraṭo Nānya-bhūpālo Bhoja-bhū-vallabhastathā||*
Paramārdi ca Someśo jagadeka-mahīpatiḥ"|| Saṅgīta-ratnākara.

(2) See discussion in the editor's Introduction to *Bhāva-prakāśana* (G.O.S., Vol. XLV, 1930, pp. 73-74). A work called *Saṅgīta-ratnāvalī* by Soma-rāja-pratihāra was announced for publication in the Gaekwad's Oriental Series, years ago.

(3) *"Sāma-vedāt svarā jātāḥ svarebhyo grāmosaṃbhavaḥ|*
Grāmebhyo jātayo jātā jātibhyo rāga-nirṇayaḥ||1||
Rāgebhyaśca tathābhāṣā vibhāsāśc āpi sañjātastathaivā antara-bhāṣikā||2||
Abhilāṣārtha-cintāmani

(4) *"Deśi-rāga***deśa-nāma-samudbhavāḥ|*
Pravartante vinodeṣu sāṃpratam sumanoharāḥ"||3|| Ibid.

(5) *Rāgaḥ pravardhate śrutyā rajyate mānasaṃ sadā|*
Tena rāgāḥ samākhyātā nāmatastān vravīmyaham||4|| Ibid.

sādhārita, (4) Śuddha-kaiśika-madhyama, (5) Śuddha-kaiśika. The names of the five Bhinna-rāgas are: (1) Bhinna-ṣaḍja (2) Bhinna-tāna(?) (3) Bhinna-kaiśika-madhyama (4) Bhinna-pañcama (5) Bhinna-kaiśika. The three Gauḍas are: (1) Gauḍa-pañcama, (2) Gauḍa-kaiśika-madhyama, (3) Gauḍa-kaiśika. The rāgas proper are said to be eight in number: (1) Ṣāḍava, (2) Voḍda-rāga, (3) Mālava-pañcama (4) Takka-kaiśika, (5) Sauvīra, (6) Mālava-kaiśika, (7) Hindola, (8) Taka.[1] Of Sādhāraṇa melodies, seven names are given: (1) Narta, (2) Śaka, (3) Kakubha, (4) Harmāṇa-pañcama, (5) Rūpa-sādhārita, (6) Gāndhāra-pañcama, (7) Ṣaḍja-kauśika.

The author then gives a series of verses describing the structure of the following melodies: Śrī-rāga, Soma-rāga, Mālava-kauśika, Harṣa-purī(?) Hindola, Deśi-Hindola, Bhairivī, Mahlāra, Sāverī, Valiti (? Vahuli), Vaṅgāla, Karṇāṭa-Vaṅgāla, Gurjarī, Saurāṣṭrī, Pun-nāṭa, Kaiśiki, Śuddha-varāṭī, Karṇāṭa-varāṭī, Drāviḍa-varāṭī, Śuddha-naṭī, Megha-rāga, Āhirī, Chāyānaṭī, Toḍi, (?), Dullī-Toḍī, Vahlānā, Vahuri, Velā-ullī, Chāyā-velā-ullī, Cundyī, Haṃsa, Khambhārī, Kāmoda, Siṃhalī-Kāmoda, Deśānaka (? Deśākhya), Danthibhi(?), Kolāhala, Saindhavī, Dāṃva-kṛti, Rāmakṛti, and Nuṇḍa-(? Tuṇḍa)-kṛti. This is an interesting list and helps us to realise that many of the melodies had come into existence of a century before Śāraṅgadeva wrote his treatise. The different varieties of Toḍīs are of interest. The original form of the name Velā-ullī, apparently an aboriginal melody, later sanskritized into Velāvalī, also deserves notice.

Unfortunately, the successive developments are not supported by documents, as there is a considerable gap between the text of Mataṅga and the next landmark.

The text of *Saṅgīta-makaranda,* the next available record of the history of the rāgas, though bearing testimony to the considerable development that has taken place bet- **Sangita-makaranda by Nārada.**

(1) *Sāḍavo Voḍa-rāgaca tathā mālava-pañcamaḥ|*
Taka-kauśika-sauvīra Tathā mālava-kauśika||9||
Hindola-ṭaka-rāgasca ityaṣtau rāgā-bhavantyasu
(? ami)||10||. If we compare this list with the 8 rāgās catalogued by Mataṅga (ślokas 314-315, at pp. 84-85), we find that they are identical.

ween the fifth and the eleventh century,[1] is very poor in actual musical data. Beyond giving some important lists of names of rāgas the text does not offer any descriptions of the melodies mentioned. Nārada, the author of this work, (not the mythical sage associated with the early legends of Hindu music), for the first time, perhaps, gives us an elaborate enumeration and classification of rāgas as known to the Northern system at the time of its composition. The author in fact gives two stages in the development of the classification. (Appendix 4).

But the most important data, furnished by this text, is the origin of the distinction between rāgas and rāgiṇīs. Here, we have for the first time a classification of the melodies into masculine and feminine groups, thus initiating the differentiation between rāgas and rāgiṇīs. In fact, Nārada gives three classifications, *viz.*, Masculine melodies (*puṃ-liṅga-rāgāḥ)*, Feminine melodies (*strī-rāgāḥ)* and Neuter melodies (*napuṃsaka-rāgāh*). The principle of classification is according to the character of the feeling *(rasa)*

(1) On the basis of a reference to Mātṛgupta, a contemporary of Śilāditya partāpśīla of Mālava (A. D. 550-600), Mr. M. R. Telang the Editor of *Saṅgīta-Makaranda* by Nārada (Gaekwad's Oriental Series, No. XVI), ascribes this text to a period between seventh and the eleventh centuries. Mr. Telaṅg in discussing the date omits to consider the bearing of the word Turuṣka, as the melody Turuṣka-tunḍī (=Turuṣka-Toḍī?) is twice mentioned (p. 16, 18), suggesting a contact with Mussulman music which is believed to have taken place about the time of Āmir Khusru, the court-poet of Sultan Alau-d-din Khiliji (1290-1360). The connotation of the word Turṣka as such would not necessarily imply the Moslem invaders of the eleventh century. For, Kalhaṇa (11th century) in his *Rāja-taraṅgiṇī* uses the word to refer to the Kuṣāna Kings who came from Central Asia (Turkestan=*Turuṣka-deśa*). It is doubtful if the word could have been applied to the Hunas, the nomad hordes, from Central Asia which poured into India in 455 A. D. 'The land of the Turuṣkas' is actually referred to in seventh century. (Bāna's *Harṣa-carita,* Cowell & Thomas' Translation, London, 1897, p. 290). So that the name Turuṣka-Toḍī, would not, necessarily, imply a contact with the Mussulmans, and may stand for a Kuṣāna melody like the Śaka-rāga.

evoked by the melodies. Thus it is laid down that in interpreting feelings or sentiments of *passion, admiration* or *heroism,* the masculine melodies should be employed. In interpreting feelings of *love, humour*, and *sorrow,* the feminine melodies should be employed. In interpreting feelings of *terror, abhorrence,* and *peace,* the neuter melodies should be employed.[1] Mataṅga, as we have seen, indicated the emotive values of the major melodies described by him. Unfortunately, none of these figures in the list given in the *Saṅgīta-makaranda,* and we have no materials to compare the *rasa* values of melodies prevailing during the respective periods represented by Mataṅga and Nārada. The latter prefaces his list of the three sets of rāgas, with the remark that the names given by him represent the principal melodies whose numbers are incalculable and vary in different regions.[2] So that we cannot take his enumerations as exhaustive. He gives a list of 20 masculine rāgas, 24 feminine rāgas, and 13 neuter rāgas.

Whatever may have been the basis of the subsequent development, the six rāgas enumerated in the *Saṅgīta-makaranda* formed the earliest group and was made the foundation of the earliest mythology of the melodies. The earliest legends ascribe to Śiva, or Naṭarāja, the origin of the science of music and dramaturgy. Śiva the cosmic dancer, is known as the arch-dramatist, and the whole of the *Nāṭya-śāstra* (embracing singing, dancing, and dramatic representations) is derived by ancient legend from this great-god (Mahā-deva). According to this legend, the rāgas are said to have been derived from the union of Śiva and Śakti (female energy),—Pārvatī, or Giri-jāyā. From the five faces of Śiva at the beginning of his dance *(narttārambhe)* came out the five rāgas:—Śrī-rāga, Vasanta, Bhairava, Pañcama, and Megha, while the sixth rāga, Naṭa-

(1) *'Raudre' dbhute tathā vīre puṃ-rāgaiḥ parigīyate|*
Śṛingāra-hāsya-karuṇa strī-rāgaiśca pragīyate||62||
Bhayānake ca vībhatse śānte gāyannapuṃsake| *Saṅgīta-makaranda*, p. 19.

(2) *Evaṃ pradhāna-rāgāḥ syur lakṣaṇoktaṃ yathā-kramaṃ||50||*
Anantāḥ santi sandarbhāḥ nānā-deśyāḥ prakīrtitāḥ|
Ibid. p. 18.

nārāyaṇa came out of the mouth of Pārvatī (Giri-jāyā), the daughter of the Himālaya when she performed the elegant *lāsya* dance.[1]

Pañcama sāra-saṃhitā:

One is inclined, not without some diffidence, to place the text of the *Pañcama-sāra-saṃhitā*,[2] attributed to Nārada, after the *Saṅgīta-makarànda.* It has some archaic features, particularly in the peculiar absence of the Bhairava rāga.[3] On the other hand, the allusions to names of some rāgas which distinctly bear the impress of later times (*e.g.* Koḍā, Kānoḍā, Sindhuḍā, Āsāvarī, Māhārāṭi etc.) tend to pull the date of the text towards a period, centuries later than the *Saṅgīta-makaranda.* This apparent contradiction may, perhaps, be explained by the fact that the melodies mentioned in this text were current, as suggested by the author, in an area embracing some parts of Rajputana, Guzerat, Cutch and the regions near the sea,[4] that is to say, surviving in a small area, long after other developments had overtaken other musical centres of Northern India. The text evidently relates to musical theories prevalent in the North, at the time, and belongs to a period, when out of the large mass of floating melodies, six had been selected as major melodies

(1) *Śiva-śakti-samāyogād rāgāṇāṃ sambhavo bhavet*|
Pañcāsyāt pañca rāgāḥ syuḥ ṣaṣṭhastu Girijāmukhāt||9||
Sadyo vaktrāttu Śrīrāgo vāmadevād vasantakḥ| 10
Aghorād bhairavo 'bhūt tatpuruṣāt pañcamo' 'bhavat||10||
Īśānākhyād megha-rāgo nāṭyārambhe Śivādahūt|
Girijāyā-mukāllāsye naṭṭa-nārāyaṇo' bhavat||11||
Saṅgīta-darpaṇa, Calcutta Edition, p. 72.

(2) There are several Mss. of this work. The quotations here given are based on a Bengali Ms. (No. 716), in the collection of the Bangīya Sāhitya Parisad, Calcutta. The copy of this text, made by one Vaiṣṇava Vairāgī, is dated 1700 Śakāvda=1778 A. D.

(3) This state of the melodies, namely Bhairava omitted, while Bhairavî is included, also occurs in the rāga data furnished by the *Nāṭya-locana.*

(4) "*Meroruttarataḥ pūrvve paścime dakṣiṇe tathā*|
Samudra-kacchape deśās tatrāmīṣām pracāraṇā||
Bhārate yaśca-bhū-bhāgaḥ pāramparyyopadeśataḥ|
Rāgāḥ ṣaḍ atha rāgiṇyaḥ ṣaṭ-triṃśat khyātimāgatāḥ|
Pañcama-sāra-saṃhitā, Ch. III, *Rāga-nirṇaya.*

RĀGINĪ SĀRANGĪ

to each of which five or six minor melodies are related and assigned. According to this text, the major melodies, or rāgas proper, come in the following order: "First comes Mālava, the king of the rāgas, then comes Mallāra, and after it comes Śrī-rāga and then Vasanta, Hindola and Karṇāṭa coming next,—these are the rāgas known by fame, and they are dressed as males."[1] We have, here, for the first time, the minor, or the derivative melodies designated as the 'wives of the rāgas' (*rāga-yoṣita*) and the word 'rāgiṇī' is used in the text, for the first time. They are assigned to their appropriate rāgas in a scheme given in Appendix 13.

Nātya-locana: This would be a convenient and appropriate place to notice the rāga data offered by the unpublished manuscript of the *Nāṭya-locana,* a compendium of dramaturgy of somewhat uncertain date, not earlier than the ninth century and not later than the thirteenth.[2] The rāgas enumerated in this text, offer some peculiar features, which suggest an early stage. They belong to a time, when the distinction between 'male' or 'female' rāgas had not come into existence. It purports to cite 44 rāgas, of which eight are stated to be *śuddha rāgas,* sixteen of the *sālaṃka* class *(chāyā* ***laga*****),** and twenty-two are said to be *sandhi rāgas.*[3] In the muti-

(1) *Ādau Mālava rāgendrastato mallāra-saṃjñakaḥ|*
Śrī-rāgastasya paścāttu vasantastadanantaraṃ.||
Hindolaścāthakarṇāṭa ete rāgāḥ prakīrttitāḥ|
Puruṣa vastra-bhūṣāḍhyā rāgāḥ ṣaṭ Mālavādayaḥ.|| Ibid.

(2) The work seems to survive in a single Ms. in the collection of the Asiatic Society of Bengal No. III, E. 158. As it quotes *Anargha-rāghava* (c. 850) the upper limit of the date cannot be earlier than the ninth century. Its lower limit can only be inferred from the list of rāgas which it enumerates and which include some very archaic names, *e.g.* pañcama-mālava, śuddha-nāṭa, sālaṃka, mādhavāri, sāverī, vicitrā and himakīrika. It does not mention Bhairava the absence of which suggests an early date.

(3) It is not clear what class *sandhī rāgas* represent. It may mean *miśra* or *saṅkīrṇa* (mixed type). Perhaps it corresponds to the *jāti-sādhārana* of Bharata who calls it 'sandhi' or 'twilight of the rāgas'. (See Fox-Strangways' *Music of Hindosthan,* p. 138-139). Alternately, *sandhī-rāgas* may mean rāgas suitable for singing at

lated text available, some of the names cannot be read and accurately deciphered. The first group of eight consists of:—Pañcama-mālava, Mādhavāri, Hindola, Mālasikā, Velāvali, Toḍi, Gāndhāra, and Naṭa. The second group consists of: Lalitā, Bhairavī, Bhāṣa, Vasanta, Gurjjarī, Koḍā-Deśākh, Deśa-Varāṭī, Vicitrā, Gaunḍa-kirī, Varāḍī, Mānavati, Vāṅgāla, Karṇāṭa, Rāma-Kirī, Sālaṃka, Navanāṭa, Deśākh, Nṛpa-mālava. The third group consists of:—Mallāra, Patha-mañjarī, Dhanāsikā, Karṇāṭī, Hemakirīkā, Savarī, Divāḍī, Khaṃvāvati, Takka, Kāmoda, Devakirī, Laungirātī (?), Moṭaki, Bhallāta, Vāheḍī, Guṇakirī, Kokīrikā, Madhukarī, Gauḍī and Anunī(?) (Appendix 6).

The list undoubtedly includes many archaic and obsolete melodies which did not survive in later times. The absence of Bhairava provides an additional archaic feature, while the presence of Bhairavī in the list suggests that the Bhairava came into existence later and was related to Bhairavī, already in existence.

Old Bengali Buddhist Songs

We have a very interesting corroboration of the existence of some of these melodies at last some time prior to the tenth century in the archaic Bengali songs of the Buddhist mystic of the Sahajiyā sect, by name Siddhācārya Luipā, whom Haraprasad Sastri, associating with Dīpaṃkara Śri-jnāna, places in the tenth century,[1] while Benoytosh Bhattacharya believes Luipā lived about 669 A.D.[2] Each of these songs collected under the name of *Caryācarya-viniścaya,* bears on the heading of each song, the name of the melody in which it is required to be sung. The following names of rāgas are indicated: Paṭamañjarī, Gauḍā, Gavaḍā (Gauḍa), Aru, Guñjarī (? Gujjarī), Deva-krī, Deśākh, Bhairavi, Kāmod, Dhanasī, Varāḍī, Valāddī, Mallārī, Mālaśī, Mālasī-Gavuḍā (Mālava-Gauḍa), Kahnu-Guñjari, Vaṅgāla, Śīvarī Śavarī (Sāverī). Nearly all of

the five *sandhis,* 'intervals' of the five portions of a drama, cp. "*Viniyukto garbha-sandhau śuddha-sādhāritobudhaiḥ*". (*Saṅgīta-ratnākara,* part i, p. 157).

(1) Hara Prasad Sastri: *Bauddha Gān O Dohā,* Calcutta, 1323, Introduction, p. 15-16.

(2) Benoytosh Bhattacharya: *An Introduction to Buddhist Esoterism,* 1932, p. 69.

these melodies are cited in the *Saṅgīta-makaranda*.

A very interesting reference to the uses of melodies in connection with rituals is furnished by the rules as to the consecration of the *Nava-patrikā* ('a new plantain shoot', symbolizing the great goddess) laid down in the *Kālikā-purāṇa* in connection with the initiatory ceremonies of the Durgā-cult, the great autumnal festival *(śāradīyā-pūjā)* still current in Bengal. The rules and the formulas for the consecration are not set out in the printed edition of the *Purāṇa*, and have been borrowed, here, from a manuscript in the possession of a professional priest. The ritual consists of bathing and consecrating the 'new shoot' by waters from eight different sources collected in eight different jars. As each jar of water is poured over the shoot, it has to be accompanied by singing a particular rāga, with specified manner of drum accompaniment, together with the recitation of *mantraṃ* invoking the auspicious influences of eight different gods and celestial beings: Kālikā-purāna

"The Lustration of the New Shoot: It should be placed in the court-yard of the house and then consecrated by bathing with waters from the eight jars.

"After singing the Mālava-rāga, with drum accompaniment of 'victory', pouring from the jar filled with water from the (river) Ganges, (the following words to be recited): 'Oṃ! Let the Gods Brahmā, Viṣṇu, and Maheśvara sprinkle Thee with this first jar filled with water from the celestial Ganges'||1||

"After singing the Lalita-rāga, with accompaniment of the drum *dundubhī*, pouring from the jar filled with rain-water, (the following words to be recited): 'Oṃ! Let the devoted celestial Winds *(Marutah)* sprinkle Thee, O! Thou goddess of the Gods! with this second jar, filled with water from the Clouds'||2||

"After singing the Vibhāṣa-rāga, with accompaniment of the drum *dundhubī*, pouring from the jar filled with water from the river Sarasvatī, (the following words to be recited): 'Oṃ! Let the Vidyādharas sprinkle Thee, O! Thou the Best of the gods! with this third jar, filled with water from the Sarasvatī'||3||

"After singing the Bhairava-rāga, with drum accompaniment in the 'Bhima-measure,' pouring from the jar filled with water from the Sea, (the following words to be recited): 'Oṃ! Let Śukra and the other Lokapālas descend and sprinkle Thee with this fourth jar, filled with water from the sea'||4||

"After singing the Kedāra-rāga, with drum accompaniment proper for the lustration of Indra, pouring from the jar filled with water mingled with pollens of lotuses, (the following words to be recited): 'Oṃ! Let the Nāgas (the snake-gods) sprinkle Thee with this fifth jar, filled with water fragrant with pollens from lotuses'||5||

"After singing the Varāḍī-rāga, with accompaniment of the blowing of the conch-shell pouring from the jar filled with waters from the water-falls, (the following words to be recited): 'Let the Himavat (Himālaya), the Hemakūṭa and other Mountains sprinkle Thee with this sixth jar filled with water from the Cascades'||6||

" After singing the Vasanta-rāga, with accompaniment of the 'Five Sounds,'[1] pouring from the jars filled with waters from all the sacred pools, (the following words to be recited): 'Oṃ! Let the Seven Sages (*Ṛṣis*) sprinkle Thee O! Thou Goddess of the Gods, with this seventh jar filled with waters from all the sacred pools of the Holy places'||7||

"After singing the Dhanāsī (Dhanā-śrī)-rāga, with drum accompaniment of 'victory,' pouring water from the jars filled with pure consecrated water, (the following words to be recited): 'Oṃ! Let the Vasus sprinkle Thee with water from this eighth jar. I adore Thee! Goddess Durgā, with accessions of eight sacred and auspicious influences!"||8||

[Ritual for the Worship of Durgā, as enjoined in the Kalikā-Purāṇa].

(1) 'The Five Sounds' (*pañca śabda*) is probably the same as the 'Five Great Sounds' (*Pañcamahā-śabda*) which an Imperial Sovereign is entitled to use as the Royal insignia of his office. According to a text cited in the *Prabandha cintāmaṇi* (Tawney's translation, p. 214), they represent five kinds of music emanating from metal, throat, drum, vīnā, and bugle. The matter is discussed by Grouse (*Indian Antiquary,* Vol. V, p. 534), Pathak (*Ibid,* Vol. XII, p. 96) and recently in the *Journal of the Bombay Royal Asiatic Society* 1933.

The reading of the text suggests that words are to be preceded by singing of the rāgas. Very probably, what is intended is that the priest should sing the words of the eight invocations in the melodies prescribed for each, with the specified accompaniment in each case. The *Kālikā-purāṇa,* one of the minor *purāṇas,* is of uncertain date, but must belong to a period prior to the currency of the Durgā-pūjā as an established cult in Bengal about the tenth, or eleventh century, to which date this text may be approximately assigned.

Sarasvatī-Hrdayālamkāra by Nānyadeva.

The next important text is that attributed to king Nānyadeva who is supposed to be a prince of a later branch of the Rāṣṭra-kūta (Karṇāṭa) dynasty and who, according to Jaysawal[1], reigned in Mithilā between 1097 and 1133 A.D. His capital was at Simarampur (modern Simraon) now lying within the border of Nepal. Professedly written as a commentary (*bhāṣya*) on Bharata's *Nāṭya-śāstra,* his work Sarasvatī-hṛdayālaṃkāra[2] is in a way an independent

(1) *Journal of the Bihar and Orissa Research Society,* Vol. IX, pp. 200-310; Vol. X, pp. 31-46. Mr. R. C. Mazumdar in his article 'Nānya Deva of Mithila,' (*Indian Historial Quarterly,* Vol. VII, 1931, p. 679), discusses his date. Following Sylvain Lévi, Mazumdar accepts 1037 A. D. as the date of his accession, and suggests that Nānya Deva must have died before 1154 A. D. Manmohan Chakravartty in his 'History of Mithila during the Pre-Mughal Period (*Journal, Asiatic Society of Bengal,* Vol. XI, 1915, pp. 407-433) discusses the position of general culture during the period. The other outstanding musical composition of the time is Jagaddhara's *Saṅgīta-Sarvasva* and the chapters dealing with music in Jyotirīśvara's Maithil Encyclopædia, *Varṇa-ratnākara.*

(2) The work survives in a unique Ms. of 221 folios in the Collection of the Bhandarkar Oriental Institute, Poona, No. 111, 1869-70, catalogued under the title *Bharatabhāṣya.* It is an incomplete Ms. with the 16th and 17th chapters missing. Each chapter ends with a Colophon. The terminating Colophon runs as follows: "*Iti mahā sāmantādhipati dharmāvalauka Śrī-man-Nānyapati-viracite Sarasvatī-Hṛdayālaṃkāra Bharata-vārtike vācikāṃśo ṣaṣtho kadhyāya samāptaḥ.*" We are indebted to Ramchandra Kavi who discovered the work and drew our attention to it. By the courtesy of the

treatise as he has introduced much new matters not touched by earlier authorities, the grāma and jāti rāgas being very fully treated. The treatise stands between the *Bṛhad-deśī* and *Saṅgīta-ratnākara,* the date of which are anticipated in this work. Nānyadeva derives most of his materials from Nārada, Yāṣṭika, Kaśyapa,[1] and Mataṅga, the last two of whom are profusely quoted as important authorities. He remarks: "How could people of lesser intelligence succeed in swimming across the ocean of melodies which such early exponents of rāgas as Mataṅga and others failed to cross,"[2] meaning thereby that it is impossible to describe the melodies exhaustively. Yet he devotes two long chapters (sixth and seventh) in describing the *lakṣaṇa* (structure), the *ālāpaka* (improvisation), and the *rūpaka* (notation) of numerous melodies current during his time. In each case, the definitions of Kaśyapa and Mataṅga are given followed by the notation for each melody. Following Mataṅga, he gives the various classifications of melodies (Appendix 6). He divides gītis under five instead of under the seven groups given by Mataṅga (Appendix 3). He uses the word root-rāgas (*mūla-rāga*) for the major melodies (*mukhyā*) which are so called "because of their extremely soothing qualities."[3] He uses a new term called 'Svarākhya rāgas', *i.e.,* melodies which take their names according to the notes (svara) *e.g.* the grāma rāgas such as Ṣaḍjī, Ārṣabhī, Dhaivatī, etc. A similar term used in Deśākhya rāgas, *i.e.,* melodies which borrow their names from the country, province, or region of their origins.[4] They are five in number, and, are classed as Upa-rāgas: Dākṣiṇātyā, Saurāṣṭrī, Gūrj-

Bhandarkar Institute the original Ms. was lent to the writer for the purpose of study.

(1) He quotes from two musical authorities of the same name of Kaśyapa, one of whom he describes as Bṛhat-Kaśyapa the Senior" (in describing the melody 'Gandharvamodana' at folio 111).

(2) *"Yo na tīrṇo Mataṅgādyaiḥ rāgā-dvaiḥ rāga-sāgaraḥ|*
Svalpa-buddhyā pūrveṇeha sanataritum śakyate katham||

(3) *"Rañjanādatiśayatvena tāstu mukhyāḥ prakīrttitāḥ"|*

(4) *"Deśākhyā Dākṣiṇātyāca Saurāṣṭrī Gūrjarītathā|*
Vaṅgālī Saindhavī cobhe (?) *pañcaitu tettupagrāgajāḥ"||*

jarī, Vaṅgālī, and Saindavī.[1] Of various melodies described by their note structures and notations we come across some new names such as 'Stambha-patrikā' and 'Tumburu-priya'.[2] An interesting information is cited by the author as to the authorship of the well-known rāga known as 'Reva-gupta.' It is said that a person called Saṃgrāma Gupta was the creator of this melody.[3] It is tempting to believe that he may have been a music expert associated with the Gupta dynasty. Nānyadeva devotes a small section of his work in indicating the presiding deity of the principal melodies. Some indications are also given as to the appropriate hours and seasons for the melodies.

Sāranga-deva's Sangīta-Ratnākara:

The most elaborate and authoritative exposition of Indian musical theories and practices is furnished by the *magnum opus,* known as *Saṅgīta-Ratnākara,* which we owe to Śāraṅgadeva, who is justly regarded as the greatest authority of the mediæval period. He lived in the first half of the 13th century (A.D. 1210-1247) and was associated with the Court of the Yādava dynasty of the Deccan which had its capital at Devagiri (Daulatabad) which was a centre of intellectual activity having contact with both the north-

(1) *Ṣaḍjāṃśa-dhṛta-ṣaḍjā sampūrṇo nysta-dhaivata*
Dhvani-kāriti-pā-khyākā gamaka-yutā Kakubhokto
Staṃbha-patrikā-bhihitā: Tathā ca Brahaddeśyāṃ|
Ṣaḍjāṃśā dhaivatānyāsa saṃpurṇo saptabhiḥ svaraiḥ|
Kavibhiḥ Kakubho-tthā(?) ca kathyate Staṃbha-patrikā||

(2) *"Gāndharāṃśo madhyamā nyāso ni-dhi-na su sapaaṃ-dhanikaḥ|*
Dhaivata-ṣaḍjo peta-rāgaḥ syāt Tumvuru-priyaḥ||
Tathāca-Kaśyaspaḥ: Gāndharāṃśo niṣādānto madhyama nyāsa saṃyutaḥ|
Ṣaḍja dhaivata ni-mukto vijneyas Tumvaru-priyaḥ||

(3) *Vīra-roudrādhbhūta-rase tāna jīvana saṃjnake*
Abhi ṣaḍja tāyāṃ mūrccha-grayaṃ (?) madhyama śruto
Ārṣadhyāṃ ṛṣabha aṃśa nyāsayoḥ||
Ṣaḍja-varjita-jita-saṃgrāma-gupten Reva-gupta prakīrttitaḥ|
Tathāca Kaśyapaḥ:
Ārṣbhī-jāti sambhūto ṛṣabhāṃta staḍḍāṃtakah||
Sampūrṇo Reva-gupta stu vidvadbhiḥ ṣaḍja-ṣāḍvah||
Folio 68.

ern and southern streams of art and culture. Śāraṅgadeva's work undoubtedly bears signs of this contact with the music of the Northern and as well as the Southern School. "It is possible," as Popely has suggested, "that he (Śāraṅgadeva) is endeavouring to give the common theory which underlies both systems." After considering the texts of Bharata, Dattila, Mataṅga, and Nārada, one can have no doubt that Śāraṅgadeva, gives an elaborate résumé of the general system of Indian music in theory and practice as had been developed in the centuries previous to the thirteenth. He gives detailed exposition of th *jātis*, and the *grāma-rāgas*, accompanied by actual notations. He devotes a large section of his chapter on melodies (*rāga-vivekādhyāya*) to the deśī melodies famous in ancient times (*prāk-prasiddha-deśī-rāgāḥ*). He gives an historical survey of rāgas according to Yāṣṭīka and Mataṅga. He then gives a preliminary list of 8 *uparāgas* : Tilaka, Śaka, Takka-saindhava, Kokila, Pañcama, Revagupta, and Pañcama-ṣāḍava. Next he gives a general list of 20 rāgas namely: Bhāvanā-pañcama, Nāga-gāndhāra, Nāga-pañcama, Śrī-rāga, Naṭṭa, Vaṅgāla, Bhāsa, Madhyama-ṣāḍava, Raktahaṃsa, Kollahāsa, Prasava, Bhairava-dhvani, Megha-rāga, Somarāga, Kāmoda, Ābhra-pañcama, Kandarpa-deśākhya, Kakuba, Kaiśika, Naṭṭa-nārāyaṇa (Appendix 9).

We notice here several melodies of the *bhāṣā* class accepted as major rāgas. He then enumerates, on the authority of Yāṣṭika, fifteen melodies—which are asserted as generic rāgas from which the minor melodies *bhāṣās* (*rāgiṇīs*) are derived.[1] These are: Sauvīra, Kakubha, Ṭakka, Pañcama, Bhinna-pañcama, Ṭakka-Kaiśika, Hindolaka, Vhoṭṭa, Mālava-kaiśika, Gāndhāra-pañcama, Bhinna-ṣaḍja, Vesara-ṣāḍava, Mālava-pañcama,[2] Tāna, Pañcama-ṣaḍava.

The list of so-called major or generic rāgas improves on the list of the eight generic rāgas given by Mataṅga, by incorporating some melodies of the Bhinnaka and Sādhārita

(1) "*Bhāṣāṇāṃ Janakāḥ pañca-daśaite Yāṣṭikoditaḥ*," *Saṅgīta-ratnākara*, p. 152.

(2) "*Mālava pañcamāntaḥ*," probably stands for 'Mālava-pañcama'.

types. Then he proceeds to enumerate the different *bhāṣās* or derivative melodies affiliated to these rāgas. In the next section he describes the further subdivisions of the melodies into *rāgāṅgas, bhāṣāṅgas* and *kriyāṅgas* on the authority of Kaśyapa, son of Sodhala[1] and enumerates 34 melodies. "These 34 rāgas are said to have been famous in early times."[2] "Now," says Śāraṅgadeva, "I am proceeding to enumerate those which are famous in modern times."[3] These are famous in modern times" "The aggregate numbers of these rāgas amount to 264," so says Śāraṅgadeva.[4] Kallinātha, commenting on this list, explains Deśavāl as equivalent to Kedāragauḍa, and Tauruṣka as equivalent to Mālavagauḍa.

But the most valuable information that this text conveys to us is as to the ancestry of several of the rāgas, whose names occur for the first time in the *Saṅgīta-makaranda* and which rāgas must have acquired those names some time before the last named text, say about the eighth century. The text of Śāraṅgadeva affords the only evidences as to the sources from which these well-known rāgas derive their character and existence.

Very instructive examples are offered as to the melody-bases from which some of the rāgas famous in later times, derive their character, though no clue is available as to their proper names. Thus, we are informed by Śāraṅgadeva for the first time, that the rāga Bhairava is derived from the archaic melody, Bhinna-ṣaḍja. "It has 'dha' for its tonic note, 'ma' for its finale, and it avoids the notes 'ṛi' and 'pa'; it is a melody of equivalent values for prayers."

(1) *Rañjanādrāgatā bhāsā rāgāngāderapiṣyate|*
Deśī-rāgatayā proktaṃ rāgāṅgādi catuṣṭayaṃ.|| 2
Prasiddhā-grāma-rāgādyā keciddeśi tyapiritāḥ|
Tatra pūrva-prasiddhānāmuddesaḥ kriyate' dhunā.|| 3 ||
Ibid, p. 155.

(2) *Catus-triṃśadime rāgāh prāk-prasiddhāḥ prakīrtitāḥ.* 8.
Ibid, p. 155.

(3) *Athādhunā prasiddhānāmuddeśaḥ pratipādyate.||* 9

(4) *Ete'dhunā prasiddhāḥ syur dvāpañcaśanmanoramāḥ|* 18
Saravesāmiti rāgāṇāṃ militānāṃ śata-dvayaṃ|
Catuḥ-ṣaṣṭya-dhikam vrūte śāraṅgi śrī-karṇāgraṇī.|| 19 ||

5

Sangīta-Samayasāra by Pārsva-deva:

After Śāraṅgadeva, the musical authority that claims our attention is Pārśvadeva. Born of Brahmin parents he was a convert to Jainism. He wrote a work entitled *Śaṅgīta-Samayasāra,*[1] devoted to music and dancing. Very probably he was a contemporary of *Śāraṅgadeva,* or lived shortly after him,[2] say, about the middle of the thirteenth century. Most probably he belonged to the group of musical authorities of Northern India, as he quotes Mātṛgupta king of Kashmir, king Bhoja Pāramāra of Malva, king Someśvara of the Cālukya dynasty of Anhilwara (Gujerat), and king Pramārdi of the Candela dynasty. Pārśvadeva, who calls himself as a 'Mine of music' (*Saṅgitākara*), devotes a short chapter of 75 verses to the rāgas. He does not state what are the major rāgas, and he principally deals with the minor melodies under the various sub-divisions of *rāgāṅgas, bhāṣāṅgas, upāṅgas* and *kriyāṅgas* which he defines as follows: '*Rāgāṅgas* are so-called by the learned as they imitate the appearances (shadows) of rāgas. Similarly *bhāṣāṅgas* are imitators of the visages (shadows') of *bhāṣāṣ*. The *upāṅgas* are so-called by the learned by reason of imitating the visages of *aṅgas*.[3]

The author then proceeds to enumerate the *rāgāṅgas, bhāsāṅgas, upāṅgas* and *kriyāṅga-rāgas* under the three

(1) Edited by T. Ganapati Sastri from a single Ms. and published in the Trivandrum Sanskrit Series, No. LXXXVII, 1925.

A second Ms. of this work is in the Madras Oriental Library, No. 13028.

(2) He is not mentioned by Śāraṅgadeva. He quotes King Bhoja, (1010-1055 A.D.), King Someśvara (C. 1330 A.D.) and King Paramārdi (C. 1165-1203 A.D.). He is quoted by Singha Bhūpāla (C. 1330 A.D.), he must therefore have lived some time between 1200 and 1300 A.D. V. Raghavan, who discusses his date ('Some names in early Saṅgīta Literature,' *Journal Music Academy of Madras,* Vol. III, Nos. 1 and 2, 1932, at p. 30), suggests that his date falls between 1165 and 1330 A.D.

(3) *Rāga-cchāyānukāritvād rāgāṅgāni vidurabudhāḥ|*
Bhāṣāṅgāni tathaiva syuḥr-bhāṣā-chāyānukārataḥ|| 1 ||
Aṅga-chāyānukāritvādupāṅgaṃ kathyate budhaiḥ.|
Tānānāṃ karanam tantryāḥ kriyābhedena kathayate.|| 2 ||
Kriyāyād bhavedaṅgaṃ kriyāṅgaṃ tadudāhṛtam."|
Saṅgīta-samaya-sāra (T.S.S. Vol. 87, 1925, p. 15).

groups of sampūrna, ṣāḍava, and oḍava.

It is curious that Pārśvadeva does not mention which of the 101 melodies cited by him he considers as rāgas *proper*, or major melodies, except that the early major rāgas (*e.g.* Takka, Mālava, Pañcama etc.) are mentioned incidentally as the sources of the derivative melodies described by him. Out of his list, he gives the characteristics of 43 rāgas which he says are popular in practice.[1] (Appendix 10).

A typical example of his descriptions may be cited in the description of Varāṭi, "Varāṭikā is the vibhāṣā (*i.e.* rāgiṇī) of Pañcama, the king of the melodies. It has 'dha' as its tonic note, 'sa' for its initial and final notes, 'dha' in the high scale and the madhyama in the soft tone. It is a fully toned melody applicable to sentiments of passion, according to Yāṣṭika".[2] It appears that at the time of Pārśvadeva, Pañcama occupied the place of honour among the melodies.

After the *Saṅgīta-samaya-sāra*, one is inclined to place the work *Rāgārṇava* which we owe to an unknown author. The exact date of the upper limit cannot be definitely fixed, but the lower limit is furnished by *Sāraṅgadhara-paddhati*, an encyclopædia in Sanskrit, compiled in 1363 A.D. As the latter work derives all its musical materials from *Rāgārṇava*, it may be reasonably accepted that the last named work must have been composed at least about half a century before. The fact that Śāraṅgadhara borrows some of his materials from *Rāgārṇava*, seems to place this work in the position of the leading authority on music about the end of the thirteenth century, in Northern India. Rāgārnava

Its rāga-system deserves notice, and, compared with an analogous system referred to in the *Saṅgīta-makaranda*, indicates changes in the 'system' of the major-melodies. Confin-

(1) *Ityekottara-śata-saṃkhyā-pariganita-rāga-madhye,*
loka-vyavāhāra-siddhānāṃ keṣāncid
rāgāṇāṃ lakṣaṇam vakṣye."|
Saṅgīta-samaya-sāra, p. 16.

(2) *"Vibhāṣā rāga-rājasya pañcamasya varāṭikā.*|| 23 ||
Dhāṃśā ṣaḍja-graha-nyāsā dha-tārā
mandra-madhyamā|
Sama-śleṣa-svarā-pūrṇā śṛṅgāre yāṣṭikoditā.|| 24 ||
Ibid, p. 18.

ing itself to the system of thirty-six melodies, *Rāgārṇava*, accepts the following six as the generic melodies : Bhairava, Pañcama, Naṭa, Mallāra, Gauḍa-Mālava, and Deśākha. The list is somewhat nearer to the one given in *Saṅgīta-makaranda*,[1] with the peculiar difference that Megha, Śrī-rāga and Vasanta are replaced by Mallāra, Gauḍa-Mālava, and Deśākha as major melodies. The derivative rāgas ascribed to the major rāgas are, however, quite different from those given in the *Saṅgīta-makaranda* as will appear from the scheme set out in Appendix 4. It should be noted that these derivative melodies are designated as *rāgas* and not yet as *rāgiṇīs*. The new names of derivative melodies offered are Sālaga (? Sālaṅka), Triguṇā, Dhānī, Haripāla, and Dhoraṇi.

Subhamkara: Samgāna-sāgara

To the beginning of the fourteenth century, belongs a very curious text called *Saṃgāna-Sāgara* which we owe to Śubhaṃkara, who lived in Nepal, during the reign of Mahārājā Bhūmalla Deva. The work survives in a very much mutilated palm-leaf Ms. written in Newāri character with Colophon which gives the date 428 Newāri saṃvat equivalent to 1308 A.D.[2] The author enumerates the eighteen *jātis*, and mentions and describes 34 rāgas. He seems to give the same system which we find elaborated in the *Saṅgīta-ratnākara*. He mentions such rāgas as *Madhyamādi* and *Śaṅkarābharaṇa*.[3] He also quotes the opinion of Someśvara. Owing to the mutilated condition of the Ms., it is not possible to obtain detailed information as to the state of the melodies prevalent at the time of the author.

Joytirīsvara: Varna-ratnākara.

Belonging to the first quarter of the fourteenth century, there is an interesting document hailing from Mithilā which was, for several centuries, a seat of Hindu culture, particularly, of music and poetry. This work which is an encyclopædia in old Maithilī language, known as "Varṇa-

(1) *Saṅgīta-makaranda* (G. O. S. m XVI), page 20, verse 74.

(2) Colophon: "*Śroyastu sāṃvāt 428 Phālgun Kriṣā Kṛitipadyāyāṃtithou śanivāsare likhitamiti Mahārājādhi rāja-śri-mat-Bhūmalladevasya vijaya-rājye Iti gitādhyāya samāptaḥ. Śubhaṃkara viracita saṃgāna-sāgara.*" Ms. Asiatic Society of Bengal, Calcutta.

(3) "*Śṛṅgāre prastute nityaṃ madhyamādi-rihocyate*"...... "*Chāyāntarina kṛyate śankarābharaṇsthā.*" Ibid.

Ratnākara"[1] we owe to a learned scholar and connoisseur of music named Joytirīśvara. He was a high official attached to the court of king Harisiṃha Deva of the Karṇāṭa dynasty, who ruled in Mithilā some time between 1300 and 1324 A.D., having his capital at Simraon. In the seventh section of this encyclopædia entitled *Bhaṭṭādi-varṇana* (folio 60b. ff.) there are references to poetry, music, and dancing. In this connection the qualification of a *Vidyāvanta* that is to say, a professional singer and music-master, a person now commonly known as *Kalāvanta* or *Kalāwāt* is described. This leads to an enumeration of the śrutis (semi-tones) and the rāgas. Unfortunately, the list is a mere string of names without any order and without any indication of the system of the rāgas, or principles of classification known at the time:

"Madhyamādi, Mālava-Kaiśaka, Mallāra Megha, Mālasī, Muddhaki, Malāri, Desākhī, Dīpaka, Desī, Devakiri (Devakriyā, Devagiri), Vasanta, Vangāla, Vegha-ravani, Valāra (? Bhallāra, Bhallārī) Varāṭi, Vicitra, Karkka, Toki-Kauha (? Takka-Kaiśika), Kāmoda, Karṇāṭa, Kambhuda (? Kaṃbhātī),[2] Bhairava, Bhairavī, Paṭamañjarī, Trāna, Ganugara, Gunagari (Gunakriyā=Gunakali), Gāndhāra, Guñjari (? Gujjarī), Gaula (? Gauḍa), Larita (? Lalita), Pañcama, Hindola, Vati, Rāmakari (Rāmakelī), Andhāri, Dhanacchi (Dhannāsī), Naṭa, Cokhasara (? Cokṣa), Khambhāvatī, Śrī-Rāga, Sakabja (Sakañja), Savari (Sāverī), Saṃkarābharina ādi aneka rāgaka gāyan."

As the last four words "and various other melodies are sung" indicate, the list is not exhaustive and merely enu-

(1) The work survives in a single palm-leaf Ms. in the Government Collection of the Asiatic Society of Bengal No. 48134, with a Colophon dated 388 of Lakṣmaṇsaṃvat corresponding to 1507 A.D. The Ms. is analysed and described by Prof. Suniti Kumar Chatterjee in the Proceedings and Transactions of the *Fourth Oriental Conference*, Vo. II, Allahabad, 1928, pp. 553-621, in an article entitled "The Varṇa-Ratnākara of Joytiriśvara Kaviśekharacārya." The general dynastic history and culture of Mithilā of this period is very ably described by Manmohan Chakravarti in an article published in the *Journal of the Asiatic Society of Bengal*, 1915, at pp. 407-433.

(2) Kambhātī, or Kambhātikā is described in "*Saṅgīta-samaya-sāra*" (T.S.S. No. LXXXVII, 1925) p. 21, verse 58.

Amir Khusru

merates the principal popular melodies current at the time.

The beginning of the fourteenth century marks the most significant stage in the development of Indian music. The differentiation in the classification of the rāgas had already marked a cleavage between the Northern and the Southern systems, two centuries before. But the new contact with Persian melodies in the fourteenth century further accentuated the differences, so that while the Southern system remained immune from the contact of Persian music, the Northern system received the new-comers with open arms, and absorbed and assimilated many new melodies imported from Persia, and incorporated them in the indigenous rāga-system, giving them their places in the classified lists, according to their structural affinities. Indeed, this was not the first time, that Western Asiatic melodies were adopted by Indian musicians. As we have seen, the Śaka rāga and the Turuṣka-Toḍī indicate that in earlier times, melodies from Chinese Turkestan had already established contacts with Indian music. The comparative era of peace established by the Khiliji dynasty afforded opportunities for cultural developments. And the new contacts with Persian music was an interesting phase of this cultural revival. The great pioneer of this contact was Hazarat 'Āmīr Khusrau, the great Persian poet, musician, and administrator who was associated with the reign of Sultan Alauddin Khiliji (1296-1315 A.D.). To 'Āmīr Khusrau, a liberal-minded connoisseur, we owe the first pioneer effort of foreigners to approach Indian culture and to understand and appreciate the principles of Indian music. The later royal patronage of the art under Akbar seems to be anticipated by this cultured poet and administrator. The part that 'Āmīr Khusrau took in developing the growth of the Indian melodies is indeed valuable. By a judicious combination of Persian airs (*muqqams*) and Indian *rāgas,* 'Āmīr Khusrau introduced many derivative melodies, hitherto unknown to the Indian rāga-system. Having acquired sufficient proficiency in Indian musical science, 'Āmīr Khusrau made very interesting innovations by producing a number of mixed melodies (*saṅkīrṇa rāgas*), in which Indian rāgas were crossed with Persian airs.

In the life of 'Āmīr Khusrau by *Shibli,* known as *Shir-u'l-'Ajam* (Lit. 'verses from Persia'), a chapter is devoted to Music, from which we have a list of the hybrid melodies invented by the Persian exponent under the Indian rāga-system. We quote below a free English translation of the chapter:[1] "Music: 'Āmīr's versatile genius turned to this delicate and fine art too, and raised it to such a degree of excellence that he has remained unrivalled during the long period of six hundred years. Naik Gopal who was acknowledged as a master all over India was the famous world-renowned *ustād* (master) of his time. He had twelve hundred disciples who used to carry his Siṃhāsan that is, throne, upon their shoulders, like palanquin-bearers. The fame of his perfection and consummate skill (in music) reached the ears of Sultan (Alauddin Khiliji, who called him to his *durbār* (court). 'Āmīr Khusrau made the submission (to His Majesty) that he would conceal himself under the throne, and that Naik Gopal be commanded to sing. Naik displayed his perfect skill in six different assemblies. On the seventh occasion 'Āmīr, too, came to the *durbār,* along with his disciples. Gopal too had heard of his fame, and asked him to sing. Āmīr said 'I am a Moghul. I have just a smattering knowledge of Hindustāni songs. You please let us hear something first, and then I, too shall sing a little.' Gopal commenced to sing. 'Āmīr said, 'I set this *rāga* (melody) long ago, and then he rendered it himself. Gopal commenced another *rāga,* Āmīr rendered that too, and said that he had rendered it long ago. In short, 'Āmīr continued to prove every *rāg rāginī,* and *sur,* (tune, scale) rendered by Gopal to be his own invention. In the end he (Khusrau) said: 'These were all hackneyed, vulgar (*am bazāri*) rāgas. Now I shall let you hear my own special inventions.' Then he started singing and Gopal became mute with astonishment."

As Āmīr Khusrau was conversant with Persian *rāgas* along with Hindu ones, he compounded the two music, and created a new world, or chapter of musical practice. Thus the rāgas invented by him are as follows:

(1) We are indebted for this translation to Mr. A. Alim, one of the translators of High Court, Calcutta.

MAJIR	.. ..	Ghar and one Persian rāg.
SAZAGARI	.. ..	Pūrvi, Gorā, Kāṅglī and one Persian rāg.
IMAN	.. ..	Hindol and Nairez.
USHA-SHAQ	..	Sārang, and Basant and Nawa.
MUWAFIQ	.. ..	Tori, and Mālvi, and Dogah and Hosainī.
GHANAM	.. ..	A slight modification of Pūrvi.
ZILF	.. .. ..	Shāhnāz mixed with Khat rāg.
FARGHANA	..	Ferghana mixed with Kāngli and Gorā.
SARPARDĀ	.. ..	Sārang, Patawal and Rast compounded together.
BAKHARĀR	..	One Persian rāg mixed with Deskār.
PHIRDOST	.. ..	Kānrhā, Gauḍi, Pūrvi, and one Persian rāg.
MANAM	.. ..	One Persian rāg added to Kalyān.

"It is mentioned in the *Rāga-Darpaṇa* that out of these rāgas, he has shown the perfection of music in Sazgari, Bakharār Ushashaq, and Muwafiq. In the remaining rāgas he has made some alterations and given them new names: Qawl, Tarana, Khyal, Naqsh, Nigar, Baseat, Talana, Suhla—all these, as well, are 'Āmīr Khusrau's inventions. Some of these are specially his own inventions. The names of some others existed previously in Hindu music. 'Āmīr made some modifications in them and changed their names." (*Shir-u'l-'Ajam*, by Shibli, p. 135).

The invention or adoption of new melodies and affiliation thereof to Indian rāga-system was no new innovation in the 14th century. As we have seen, the process has been going on throughout the long career of the development of music.

Śaka and Pulinda rāgas were apparently non-aryan melodies accepted by the Hindu musicians in early times. Turuṣka-Toḍī a new version of Toḍī was apparently composed in contact with some airs from Turkestan. The power of receiving new-comers and assimilating them in the forms of rāgas, bespeaks the strong vitality and living quality of the growth and development of Indian music. This interesting contact of Indian rāgas with Persian melodies at the time

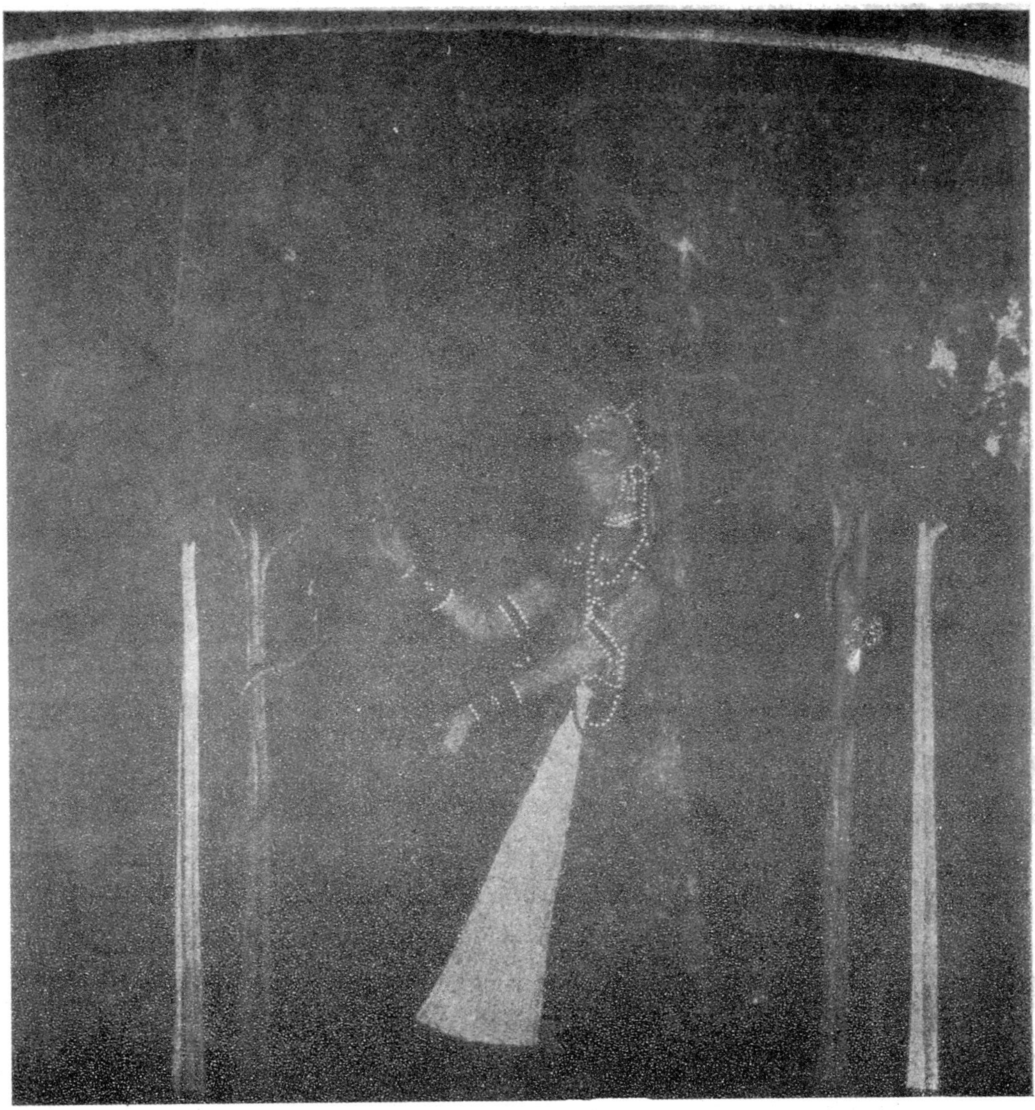

RĀGINĪ SHĀVIRĪ

of 'Āmīr Khusrau has been somewhat misinterpreted as a record of the dominating influence of Persian music on Indian music. Indeed, Indian music quite held its own against the tide of Persian culture, and by adopting new rāgas tinged with Persian airs, did not sacrifice one iota of the principles of its rāga-composition, or the basic foundations of Indian musical science. The sympathetic interest and patronage that was extended to Indian music under the influence of such an able connosseur, lent an impetus to the indigenous art which had no parallel, before the age of the Moghuls.

Sāranga-dhara-paddhati:

The rāgas current in the North about the middle of the fourteenth century, can be gleaned from the well-known Sanskrit anthology, already referred to, *Śāraṅgadhara-paddhati.* It was composed in the year 1363 A.D. In chapter 81, under the heading 'gāndharva śāstraṃ' (verses 1942-2081), the author summarises the current musical data[1]: He gives a list of 36 generic (*pravarataka*) rāgas, on the basis of the *Rāgārṇava.*[1] We have already cited these rāgas, (*ante* p. 19). After reciting the 36 rāgas, the author states that there are various melodies prevailing in particular localities or areas such as Mārū etc. which are regarded as local melodies. So that the enumeration of Śāraṅgadhara is not at all exhaustive. In fact he says that 'there is no end of 'rāgas' or 'tālas', they are to be sung by the learned for the pleasure of Śiva.'[2]

Locana Kavi's Rāgata-ranginī:

It would be convenient to notice here the text of *Rāga-taraṅgiṇī* by Locana Kavi, of uncertain date.[3] The author

(1) *Atha ṣaṭ-triṃśat-pravartaka-rāgā ucyante:*
2052: *"Bhairavaḥ, pañcamo nāṭo mallāro gauḍa-mālavaḥ|*
Deśākhaśceti ṣaḍrāgāḥ procyante loka-viśrutaḥ"|| 111

(1) 2054: *"Matā rāgārṇave rāgāḥ pañcaite pañcamāśrayāḥ"||* 113

(2) 2059: *"Anye ca bahavo rāgā jātā deśa-viśeṣataḥ|*
Mārū prabhṛitayo loke te ca taddeśikāḥ smṛtāḥ|| 118
2060: *"Na rāgāṇaṃ na tālānām antaḥ kutrāpi vidyate|*
Saṃtoṣāya śivasyaite geyā vudha-janaiḥ sadā|| 119

(3) Edition of D. K. Joshi, printed at Arya Bhusana Press, Poona City, 1918.

According to the date given in the colophon, Locana Paṇḍita's *Rāgataraṅgiṇī* comes in order of chronological sequence before the

asserts that the ancient masters of the melodies sang twelve melodies on which all the other melodies are based.[1] He enumerates the following twelve melodies as the basic rāgas:—Bhairavī, Ṭoḍī, Gaurī, Karṇāṭa, Kedāra, Iman, Sāraṅga, Megha-rāga, Dhanāśrī, Pūravī, Mukhārī and Dīpaka. The author describes these 12 melodies with their characteristics.

On the authority of this text it may be asserted that by this time, the Pañcama melody had been dethroned, and that at this time the Megharāga was now on the throne, occupying the place of honour amongst the melodies. Curiously, the Dīpaka rāga is not described and it is euphemistically suggested that the structure of this melody should be settled by an assembly of musicians which suggests that Dīpaka had lost its place in current practice.[2] The author gives a list of derivative melodies (*janya rāgas*) which are said to be

Saṅgīta-Ratnākara, but the reference to the new Indo-Persian melody of the name of Phirodast which is supposed to have been invented by Āmîr Khusrau, makes it incumbent on students to push the date of *Rāga-taraṅgiṇī* to a period after Āmir Khusrau (c. 1375-1400). The colophon runs as follows:

Bhuja-vasu-daśamita-śāke śrimad-vallāla-sena-rājyādau
Varṣaika-ṣaṣṭī-bhoge munayastvāsan viśākhāyāṃ.

This chronogram yields the date of 1082 *śeka* (*i.e.* 1160 A.D.). But if the poet Vidyāpati referred to in the work is the great Maithili poet (1395-1440 A.D.) of the same name, patronized by Śiva-Siṃha, then *Rāga-taraṅgiṇī* cannot be earlier than the fifteenth century.

The melody Phirodast is referred to in the following passage:—

Dhanāśrīḥ Kānarāyogāt
vāgīśvaryākhya-rāgiṇī|
Phirodastastu pūravi-gaurī śyāmābhireva ca||
Varāḍī-vaṅga-pālābhyāṃ vibhāsa-milanā api|
Aḍānā-rāgiṇī proktā, phirodastāt dhanena ca||
Rāga-taraṅgiṇī, p. 9.

(1) *Tāstu saṃsthitayaḥ prācyo rāgāṇāṃ dvādaśa smṛtāḥ|*
Yābhi-rāgāḥ pragīyante prācīnā rāga-pāragaiḥ||
Eteṣām eva saṃsthāne ṣarve rāgā vyavasthitāḥ||
Rāga-taraṅgiṇī, p. 3.

(2) *Dīpakaḥ sarvair militvā dīpako'pi lekhyaḥ.||*
Rāga-taraṅgiṇī, p. 6.

founded on each of the twelve major melodies cited by him. The list set out in Appendix 16 indeed is very curious and does not give any clue to the principle of the system. In this list, we come across, for the first time, many new rāgiṇīs, which became very common in the Northern system *e.g.* Khamāicī. Probably, Khamāicī is the well-known melody familiar to us under the name of Kammāj (Khamvāj), and which is distinguished from 'Khamvāvatī' which is ascribed to the group of Karṇāṭa.

Pañcama-sāra-samhitā by Nārada:

A short but important treatise, bearing on the iconography of rāgas, *Pañcama-sārasaṃhitā* (sometimes called *Pañcama-Saṃhitā*) *composed* by an author called Nārada deserves notice. It survives in two Mss., one[1] in the collection of the Baṅgīya Sāhitya Pariṣad (the copy bearing a date 1700 Śaka=1778 A.D.). The second Ms. belongs to the Asiatic Society of Bengal[2] with a Colophon dated 1440 A.D. (1362 Śaka). It is the most important document for the history of the Northern rāga-system. It must have existed in earlier recensions, and appears to have undergone changes and modifications by later hands. In its chapter on Rāgas, it suggests that the melodies treated by the author have been current in the region to the north of the Vindhyā mountains and its immediate vicinities, including the region of Cutch

(1) Ms. No. 716 in the collection of Sanskrit Mss. in the Vaṅgīya Sāhitya Pariṣad, Calcutta entitled: '*Nārada-kṛta Pañcama-sāra-saṃhitā:*

"*Meroruttarataḥ pūrvve paścime dakṣiṇe tathā*|
Samudra-Kacchape ye deśāḥ tatrāmīṣāṃ pracāraṇā|
Bhārate yaśca bhū-bhāgaḥ pāraṃ-paryopadeśataḥ|
Rāgāḥ ṣaṭ atha rāgiṇyaḥ tṛṃśaṭ khyātimāgatā||
Colophon: "*Iti śrī-Nārada-kṛta Pañcama-sāra-saṃhitāyāṃ caturtho' dhyāyaḥ*|
Likhitaṃ śrī Vaiṣṇava Vairāgī| *Śakābda* 1700."

(2) Ms. No. 5040, in the collection of the Asiatic Society of Bengal. The colophon runs as follows: "*Iti Nārada-kṛta Pañcama saṃhitāyāṃ rāga-nirṇayo nāma tṛtīyo 'dhyāyaḥ*|| *Yuga-tṛṣaṭ-candramite śāke notha* (?) *prayatnataḥ saṅgīta-mālā bahubhī rātrau vārau raver api*|| *Śrī Hariḥ*|| *Śrī Curave namaḥ*"|| This chronogram yields two alternative dates: 1632 or 1932.

bordering on the sea. Its rāga-system consits of the six rāgas : Mālava, Mallāra, Śrī-rāga, Vasanta, Hindola and Karṇāṭa. This seems to point to an early time, as in this list, Mālava rāga is described as the 'King of the Melodies'[1] and Bhairava which came to occupy the throne, later, has no place in this group, the rāgiṇī Bhairavī being assigned to Mālava-rāga. The six rāgiṇīs attributed to each of the rāgas, according to this system is set out in Appendix 13. The names of some of the rāgiṇīs are curious, and seem to indicate later interpolations. The list includes Pūravī, Koḍā, Gaḍā, and Mārhāṭī. The late form of the last-named rāgiṇī militates against the suggestion of an early date for this work. At the same time, the inclusion of some early rāgiṇīs e.g. Māyurī, and Dīpikā suggests an early date. It is quite possible that the system was confined to a particular region, and its earlier system had undergone modifications, from time to time, by the affiliation of later melodies. But the most important feature of the work is the citation of contemplative verses for the *dhyāna* formula of the melodies giving the iconographic pictures of the six rāgas and thirty-six rāgiṇīs belonging to the system. The citations of these prayer-formulas are preceded by a significant assertion that 'the beautiful images of the six rāgas and the thirty-six rāgiṇīs have emanated from the 'Abode of Brahmhā,' the Supreme Being, and they love to offer their prayer to the same Supreme Deity'.[2] The descriptive verses visualizing the melodies, cited in this work, have been frequently quoted by later text-writers from this work, and the work and its author are referred to by names.

Krsna-kirtana by Candīdās:

It is well-known that the advent of Chaitanya, the great Vaiṣṇavaite preacher (1486-1533 A.D.), flooded Bengal with torrents of devotional songs and music. But it is seldom recognized that the age preceding this new religious wave was rich in mystic Vaiṣṇavaite lyrics and songs, of which the central figure was the great poet Caṇḍīdās (c. 1400 A.D.),

(1) "*Ādau Mālava-rāgendra-stato Mallāra saṃjñakaḥ*"|

(2) We owe the discovery of this work to V. Raghavan. The work
Āgatā Brahma-sadasi Brahmāṇaṃ samupāsate"||
Asiatic Society of Bengal Ms., Folio 2.

the Chaucer of Bengali literature. His early poems "Kṛṣṇa Kīrtana" ('songs of Kṛṣṇa'), of which more than one early Mss. have now come to light, is a collection of songs, which were set to music and musical accompaniments. In two old Mss. (one of them dated 1237 sāl=1830 A.D.) recently discovered in the collection of the University of Calcutta.[1] Scholars have agreed to date this work in the second half of the fifteen century.[2] In these lyrical composition by Caṇḍīdās, each song is set to a rāga (melody) and tāla (time-measure) and the name of the melody and of the time-measure[3] in which each song is to be sung are indicated at the top of each. The names of these rāgas are very interesting, as they introduce to us many new names not previously known Vāgaśrī, Rāgiṇī Maṅgala, Rāgiṇī Diṃpanāśrī, Rāgiṇī Pāhiḍā, Rāga Vasanta, Rāga Vāḍārī, Rāg Ṣui (? Yui), Rāgiṇī Dhānaśī, Rāgiṇī Rāmagirī (? Rām-Kirī=Rāmakelī). The most surprising name in the list is the melody named 'Ṣui' and 'Dhiṃpanāśī', which has not, so far, been cited in any of the texts. It is quite possible that they were local Bengali melodies adopted in the pantheon of the rāgas.[4]

To about the middle of the fifteenth century belongs an important musical text by a royal author, recently brought to

Sangītarāja by Rānā-

(1) These Mss. are described by Manindra Mohan Basu in the *Sāhitya Pariṣad Patrikā* (Bengali) Vol. 39, No. 3, 1339, pp. 176-194, in an article: "Śrī Kṛṣṇa Kīrtaner Navāviṣkṛta Puthi."

(2) On philological data, Prof. Radha Govinda Basak and Prof. Suniti Kumar Chatterjee have assigned *"Śrī-Kṛṣṇa-Kīrtan"* to the second half of the fifteenth century, *vide* "Comments on the Ms." by Prof. S. K. Chatterjee, *Ibid,* p. 198.

(3) The authority for the tālas used is borrowed from 18 tālas described in the text of Nārada from which a quotation is cited in the manuscript. Unfortunately, the authority for the rāgas indicated is not cited.

(4) Harekrisna Mookerjee in a paper published in the *Sāhitya Pariṣad Patrikā,* vol. 38, 2nd part, has conjectured that the songs of the *Kṛṣṇa Kīrtana* were originally sung in popular folk-melodies known as "jhumur" which never attained the dignity of classical music, or were used for devotional songs.

Kumbha-karna Mahimendra:

light. It is the *Saṅgīta-rāga*[1] composed by Rāṇā Kuṃbha-karṇa of Mewar (c. 1419-1460 A.D.). It is an important contribution to Indian music. The author extends a graceful invitation to those interested in music to listen to him, *i.e.* to study his work. 'If you have curiosity in songs, if you have skill in music, then listen, oh! connoisseurs and learned men! to Kuṃbha-karṇa' ("*Yadi kautikino gāne saṅgīte cāturī yadi rasika Kuṃbha-karṇasya śṛṇvantu budha-sattamaḥ*" quoted in *Rasika-priyā*). In the preliminary sections, he gives the mythical history of music and then proceeds to provide definitions of the various technical terms. The author does not cite any other ancient authorities save and except Yāṣṭika, 'according to whom the bhāṣā gītis are thirty in number.'[2] His definition of rāga is a revised paraphrase of those of older authorities : 'A pleasant composition of notes, (initiative notes and others), distinguished by descents, ascents, and movements, and also by decorative graces, is called a rāga'.[3] A distinction between 'gīta' and 'rāga' appears to be indicated. All gītas (songs) are not rāgas, but only those which have the ten characteristics

(1) We owe the discovery of this work to V. Raghavan. The work is extensively quoted by the author himself in his commentary on '*Gīto-Govinda,* called *Rasika-priyā,* published by the Nirnaysagar Press, Bombay, 1913, under the editorship of Telang and Pansikar. The work survives in a single Ms. in the collection of the Bhandarkar Oriental Research Institute, Poona, No. 365, 1879-80. Unfortunately, the Ms. is a fragment and contains the introductory portions and definitions, but the portions bearing on the rāgas are missing in the Ms. The data on rāgas have, therefore, been cited, here, from the fragmentary extracts quoted by the author in his *Rasika-priyā.* In the Poona Ms. the work is also described as *Pādya-ratna-kośa.* Each section has a colophon which runs as follows: "*Iti śrī rājādhirāja śri Kuṃbha-karṇa viracite saṅgīta-rāje pādya-ratna-kośe parīkṣaṇaṃ nāma dvitīyaṃ samāptaṃ.*"

(2) "*Bhāṣādhya gītaya-stiśro Yāṣṭiken-orarī-kṛtāḥ*|
Tatra bhāṣā samākhyātā
mukhyān anyopajīvinī|| 38 | *Saṅgīta-rāja*

(3) "*Vicitra-varṇālaṃkāro viśeṣo yo dhvanir iha* (?)|
Grahādi svara-sandarbho rañjako rāga ucyate"|| 34 || Ibid.

(*Nāṭya-śāstra* ch. 26, verse 16-46).[7]

In the available fragments of the work, no principle of classification of the rāgas is indicated. The author, however, cites two different lists, or catalogues of important rāgas, eighteen, according to one view, and, seventeen, according to another. The lists are as follows:

A. (1) Madhyamādi, (2) Lalita, (3) Vasanta, (4) Gurjarī, (5) Dhanāśī, (6) Bhairava, (7) Gauṇḍa-Kṛti, (8) Deśākṣikā, (9) Mālava-śrī, (10) Kedāra, (11) Mālavī, (12) Ādi-Gauṇḍaka (?) (Ādi-Gauḍa), (13) Sthāna-Gauṇḍa (Gauḍa), (14) Śrī-rāga, (15) Mahlāra, (16) Varāṭikā, (17) Megha-rāga, (18) Dhoraṇa.

B. (1) Naṭṭa, (2) Kedāra, (3) Śrī-rāga, (4) Sthāna-Gauḍaka, (5) Dhoraṇi, (6) Mālavī, (7) Varāṭī, (8) Megha-rāga, (9) Mālava-śrī, (10) Deva-śākha, (11) Gauṇḍa-kṛt (12) Bhairavī, (13) Dhannāsikā, (14) Vasanta, (15) Gurjarī, (16) Mahlāra, (17) Lalita.

Of the citations of rāgas, given in short sections (*prabandhas*), two typical examples are quoted below.[2] The

(1) "*Prabandho rūpakaṃ vastu nibanddhaṃ gītam-ucyate*|
Nibaddhāvayava dhātur-dharādhīśasya sammataḥ"|| 57 ||
Ibid.

"*Rāgo 'bhidhīyate gīta daśa-lakṣaṇa lakṣitaḥ*"|
Lakṣaṇāni ca tatrāṃśa-nyāsau ṣāḍava mau puna (?)" || **55** ||
Ibid.

(2) "*Tathā ca saṅgīta-rāje*| *Mālavīyaāḥ smṛto gauḍo rāgastālo'ḍḍa-tālakaḥ*|
Śṛṅgāro vipralambhākhyo raso devādi-varnamaṃ|
Pada santatitas-tenāḥ pāṭhāḥ svara-samuccayah||
Tataḥ padyāni yatra syur-laya-madhya-mānataḥ||
Sa prabandha-varo jñeyo dhanya-vaikuṇṭha-kuṅkumaḥ||
Iti dhanya-vaikuṇṭha-kuṅkuma-nāma- dvādaśaḥ prabandhaḥ||" *Sangīta-rāja.*

According to this authority, Mālava-gauḍa rāga is appropriate in anecdotes of 'love in separation,' and for descriptions of gods.

"*Tathā ca saṅgīta-rāje*| *Rāgaḥ syāt Sthāna-gauḍākhyas-tālo varṇayati rasaḥ*|
Śṛṅgāro vipralambhākhyaḥ pramadā madanākulā||
Pakṣanāmāvaleḥ pāṭhā-gumphitā yatra gītake|
Snigdha Madhu-Sūdano'yaṃ rāsa-valaya-nāmakaḥ||

author does not describe their structures, but indicate their *rasa*-values, or emotional flavours, that is to say, their significance in arousing particular flavours of emotion. As will appear from the examples of the sections quoted, that very picturesque names are given to each section.

But the most important contribution of Rāṇā-Kuṃbha—is the view which appears to be propounded in this work, namely, that each rāga has its appropriate time-measure (*tāla*) which brings out the genius of the rāga in its characteristic qualities.[1] As the author seems to suggest that it is the time-measure which gives the true interpretation of a rāga ("*tālo varṇayati rāsaḥ*"), it is the time-measure which reveals its real flavour ("*tālo varṇayati rasaḥ*"). It does not follow that a rāga can only be interpreted in a fixed time-measure, but what is intended to be suggested is that particular rāgas receive the happiest interpretation and expression in particular time-measures.

A very interesting text called *Rāga-mālā*,[2] available in

Prabandhaḥ pṛthivī-bhartā prabaddha prītaye Hareḥ||
Iti snigdha-Madhu-sūdana-rāsa-valaya-nāmā pravandhas-trayodaśaḥ"|| *Sangīta-rāja.*

According to this authority, songs which are set to the 'Sthānagauḍa' rāga make the lady-lovers in separation, stricken with the shafts of Cupid.

(1) "*Yatra syāt-Gurjarī-rāgas-tālo jhampeti bhāgaśaḥ*"|
"*Śrī rāgo yatra-rāgaḥ syāt tālastu druta-manṭhakaḥ*"|
Sangīta-rāja.

(2) Asiatic Society of Bengal, Ms. No. 1195 (211) Govt. Collection. The colophon which gives the date of the copy of the Ms., not of its composition, is as follows: "*Iti śrī-rāga-mālā samāptā*|| *Saṃvat* 1833|| *Subhaṃ bhūyāt*|| *Grantha saṅkhyā śloka* 275|| The first few ślokas seem to contain a reference to the king in whose reign it was composed:

"*Manuja-danuja-devairvanditaṃ mama-devaṃ dhṛta-śaśi-dhara-mauliḥ kṣemakarṇaṃ praṇamy*|
Apahata muru-daityaṃ sundaraṃ rāga-mālāṃ racayati sukha sidhyai Jaṭivā bhūpateśaḥ"||

It is difficult to identify the king referred to under the name of "Jaṭivā bhupateṣaḥ."

Three verses about the end of the manuscript furnish (folio 13)

two manuscripts, one with a colophon dated Saṃvat 1431 (1509 A.D.), deserves to be noted here. It comes from Rewa and is the work of Kṣema Karṇa (Meṣa Karṇa) son of Maheś Pāṭhak, the family priest of a chief named Jāṭalendra, reigning in the Fort of Rewa. This work follows a scheme of classification on the basis of six major rāgas,[1] *viz.* Bhairava,

Ksema karna's Rāga-mālā:

further informations relating to the author of the work and the prince who patronized him.

The verses seem to describe the fort of Rewa at the foot of which the city lay washed by a river. There ruled a line of chiefs of whom three names are given in succession viz. Surava, Virajit, and Jāṭalendra (=Jaṭivā), the last of whom was the patron of the author who was, in fact, the priest of the royal patron. The author's name, twice stated as Meṣa-Karṇa, probably the dignified form of the vulgarised Khem Karan, a name very common in the North and Rajputana.

A Ms. copy of this work (No. 1125-15165) with a similar colophon is in the India Office (Eggeling: *Catalogue,* p.). The name of the author is given as Kṣemakarṇa Pāṭhaka.

The Colophon runs as follows: "*Iti Maheśa-Pāṭhakātmaja-śrī-Kṣema - karṇa - Pāthaka - Jātiava - bhūpatisukhārtha-viracitā Raga-mālā samāptā śubhaṃastu Śrī-mad-Akbara-rājye saṃvat 1867 jaiṣṭha vadi 8 vāra Bhṛgu-vāsare li(khitam) śiva-vālaka Brahmanamidam pustakam samāptaṃ*||

As pointed out by Eggeling, 'The copyist's allusion to Akbar (1556-1605 A.D.) seems to have come either from the author's own Ms. or from an early copy'. As a matter of fact that Asiatic Society Ms. proves that the work is earlier than Akbar.

The name of the work is called Rāgamālā, but the author also seems to suggest that it is not an original work, and that probably its materials are derived from an earlier work called Saṅgīta-ratnākara (*Iti Saṅgīta-ratnākara-sāroddhāraḥ,* folio 13, line 9). This must be a treatise quite different from the famous work of Śāraṅgadeva.

A work called *Rāgamālā,* attributed to Kshem Karana and said to be dated 1570 A.D. is referred to by Fox Strangways (*The Music of Hindustan,* p. 105).

(1) "*Rāgādau bhairavākhyastadanu nigadito mālakauśir-dvitīyo*||
Hindolo dīpaka śrīriha vivudha-janair-aṃudākhyaḥ kramenạ|

Mālava-Kauśika, Hindola, Dīpaka, Śrī and Megha (Aṃvuda), each having five wives and eight sons, set out in Appendix 15. The list offers many new names of rāgiṇīs, and melodies with similar names are differentiated and separately described. Thus Velāvalī and Velāval are treated as two different melodies, which are justified by different descriptive verses and also by distinct pictorial conceptions. Similarly Vaṅgāl, and Vaṅgālī are sought to be distinguished as two different melodies. Illustrative pictures corresponding to them may be taken to be represented by Plates VIII, IX & X.

Mān-kutūhala: The next stage in the development of the rāgas is represented by the contributions made by Rājā Mān Siṃha Tomar of Gwalior (not to be confused with Rājā Mānsingh of Amber). Rājā Mān, who succeeded Kalyāṇa Malla in 1486, died in 1517 A.D. According to Cunningham,[1] Rājā Mān was a "proficient composer, as well as a munificent patron, and many of his compositions still survive to justify the esteem in which they are held by his contemporaries. He was specially fond of the *saṅkīrṇa rāgas,* or mixed modes of which no less than four specimens are named after his favourite Gujarṇi (Guzerati) queen, *Mṛga-nenā (Mṛga-nayanā),* or the "fawn-eyed." These are *Gujari, Bahul-Gujari, Māl-Gujari,* and *Maṅgal Gujari.*" Gunningham thinks that the lady had a hand in their composition. Rājā Mān's love of mixed rāgas is particularly noteworthy. Rājā Mān's valuable contribution to Indian music is represented by a Hindi treatise known as "Mān-Kutūhala ' (Curiosities of Mān).[2] It is said to contain the records of the proceedings of a great conference of musical experts assembled under the order of the Rājā. This seems to be corroborated by Abdul Fazl (Gladwin, *Āīn-i-Akbarī,* p. 730) who states that three

Ekaikasyāṣṭa-putrāḥ sulalita-nayanāḥ pañca-bhāryyāḥ prasiddhāḥ|
Sve sve kāle ṣaḍete nijakula-sahitāḥ sampadaṃ vodiṣanantu"|| 3 || *Rāgamālā* (A. S. B. Ms.)

(1) Archaeological Survey of India Reports, Vol. II, 1862, pages 387-388.

(2) A Ms. of this work is in the possession of H. H. the Nawab Saheb of Rampur.

of Rājā Mān's musicians, Naik, Mukshoo, and Bhanau formed a collection of songs suited to the tastes of every class of people." According to Sir W. Ouseley (*Anecdotes of Indian Music*)[1] Rājā Mān Siṃha's work was translated into Persian by Fakur Ullah. Three of these masters patronized by Rājā Mān, viz. Bikshoo, Dhondee and Charjoo, contributed a new type of Mallāra, to the stock of Indian melodies, called after them, "Mukshoo-ki-mallār," "Dhondia Mallār," and "Charjoo-ki-mallār." Bukshoo's name is also associated with a new variety of Velāval, and the melody 'Bāhādurī-Ṭoḍī.' These artists subsequently passed into the service of Sultan Bāhādur of Gujerat.

Rāmāmātya's Svaramela-kalānidhi:

Before we proceed to consider the development of the rāgas during the sixteenth century in the North, it is necessary to notice the changes and development in the old Indian system as preserved in Southern practices and theories. After Śāraṅga-deva (c. 1210-1247), the great landmark in the South is provided by a short but an eminently scientific treatise entitled *Svara-mela-kalānidhī,*[2] the composition of which we owe to Rāmāmātya (1550), said to be a minister (amātya) of the Vijayanagara prince, Rāma-rāja, and a descendent of the famous commentator Kallinātha.

The most important contribution of Rāmāmātya was in the formulation of a scientific principle of classification of the rāgas, on the basis of the common elements of their characteristic note structures. This was certainly a great improvement on the system of classification recorded in *Saṅgīta-ratnākara,* which Mr. Aiyar characterises as nothing more than a mere catalogue. Śāraṅgadeva's classification, though not exactly an enumeration of a catalogue, was more an historical presentation of the older and current systems of classification, rather than an attempt to classify the melodies on a new system on any empirical basis. Following the

(1) Reprinted in Captain N. A. Williard's *A Treatise on the Music of Hindustan,* 1882, p. 167.

(2) This text is available in two editions, one published with *a commentary in Maharatti by Bharadvāja Sarma (Pandit V. N.* Bhat-khande) san 1910, and the other published by the Annamalai University (1932) and edited with an excellent critical introduction and translation by M. S. Ramaswami Aiyar.

precedent of Yāṣṭika, whom he cites, he merely enumerates the fifteen major melodies, but he also indicates that these fifteen melodies are the father *(janaka)*, that is to say, the genus of the minor melodies (*bhāṣās*).[1] This old *janya-janaka* system (corresponding to the *rāga-rāgiṇī-putra* system of the North) is replaced by Rāmāmātya by an independent analysis of the melodies and by a scientific classification based on a study of the common elements of the note compositions of the different varieties of melodies, unified *(mela)* by a recognition of their basic structural unity of the groups tabulated under a common *genus*. As Mr. Aiyar concedes, "doubtless the germ of the idea of the *genus-species* system may be found long before Rāmāmātya." But "he was the first to introduce a chapter on *mela* called Mela-prakaraṇa." In this chapter, he enumerates, the *melakas* (unifiers) and then explains their characteristics. As Pandit Bhatkhande has pointed out, the *mela* corresponds to what is called in the North, the *ṭhāṭ,* (the array or moulds of particular types under which a group of minor melodies can be classified on the basis of their unity). Following an older precedent, Rāmāmātya takes the Mukhārī mela, as the *śuddha* scale and gives it the place of precedence.[2] "Of all the melas Mukhārī is the first. Other melas are as follows: Mālava-gaula, Śrī-rāga, Śāraṅga-nāṭa, Hindola, Śuddha-rāma-kriyā, Deśākṣī, Kannaḍa-gaula, Śuddha-nāṭa, Ahīrī, Nāda-rāma-kriyā, Śuddha-varālī, Rīti-gaula, Vasanta-Bhairavī Kedāra-Gauḍa, Hejujjī, Sāma-varālī, Reva-gupta, Sāmanta, Kāmbhojī. Thus there are twenty melas." (Appendix 17).

Tān Sen

With the advent of Akbar (1542-1605), the most enthusiastic patron of Indian culture in all its branches, North Indian music approaches the most glorious period of its his-

(1) "*Bhāṣāṇāṃ janakāḥ pañca-daśaite Yāṣṭikoditāḥ*"| 20 | *Saṅgīta-ratnākara,* Vol. I, p. 152.

(2) Although he accepts Mukhārî, as the Śuddha scale, following the older practice, he was inclined to take Mālava-gaula as his model for the Śuddha scale: "*Rāgo Mālava-gaulaśca**rāgāṇāmuttamottamaḥ*|| (*Svara-mela-kalānidhi,* p. xxxi). As Mr. Aiyar remarks: "Evidently he did not come to deduce his twenty *melas* form any kind of principles but perhaps recorded such of the *melas* as were in vogue during his time."

tory. At the head of the new development under Akbar was the famous singer Mīyān Tān Sen, who was a close associate of Sūr Dās, the great poet-saint, and who received his musical education at Gwalior under the discipleship of a great musician Rām Dās Svāmī. It is generally believed in conservative musical circles, that Tān Sen was principally responsible for abjuring many old traditions and for introducing innovations and questionable novelties which lead to the deterioration of the old Hindu system. "He is said to have falsified the *rāgas* and it is stated that two, Hindola and Megha, of the original six have disappeared since his time."[1] There is no doubt that Tān Sen introduced new rāgas and new versions, or unconventional variations of old forms. It is well-known that Tān Sen was the first to introduce the E-Flat *(Komala gāndhāra)* and both varieties of Niṣāda (B flat and sharp) into the *rāga mallār* which came to be known as "Mīyān-ki-mallār." Similarly, he is the inventor of a new type of *Ṭoḍī* known as *Mīyān-ki-Ṭoḍī.* The modified forms of Kānarā known as Darbārī Kānarā are attributed to him. Nevertheless, our innovator was not tardy in paying his respects to the rāgas of hoary antiquity. In a Hindi treatise on music, called Rāg-mālā,[2] he accepts the six rāgas (*ṣaṭ-rāg*) enumerated by the school of Hanumān and analyses them into their component parts. He claims to have examined the schools (*mats*) of Śiva, Bharata, and Hanumāna and describes his own views, set forth in the work as the School of Tān Sen' (*Tānseni mat*),[3] based on the authorities of Mataṅgamuni and Bharata. The author claims to analyse the six principal rāgas and to give their component

(1) *Rāg-mālā, prasiddha Miyān Tān Sen racita,* Lahiri Press, *Kasi (Benares), 1907.. Pandit Bhatkhande believes that this is a* spurious work compiled by some later authors and fathered on Tān Sen to lend a halo of authority to the work. The fact that the name of Tān Sen is introduced somewhat aggressively in almost every alternate line throws ample doubts on the authenticity of the attribution.

(2) *Dekhyou Śiva-mat Bharat-mat, Hanumān-mat joyi|*
Kahai saṅgīt vicāri kai, Tānseni mat soyi.|| 2 || *Rāg-mālā.*

(3) Francis Gladwin: *Ayeen Akbery,* 1800, London, Vol. II, pp. 456-464.

elements, an analysis of which would apparently suggest that these rāgas are mixed melodies (*saṅkīrṇa*) compounded of other independent melodies. What is really meant is that the so-called component melodies, are affiliated to and, hence, can be derived from these major rāgas considered as *genus*.

Like Āmīr Khusrau, Akbar himself is credited with the introduction of many Persian melodies to the India rāgas of his time. According to the *Akbarnāmā* (Beveridge, Vol. I, p. 50), His Imperial Majesty had "composed over 200 of the old Khwarizmite tunes, especially the tunes of Jalasahi, Mahamir, Karat, and Nauroj, which were the delight of the young and the old." We have no records of their musical characters, but the melody Nauroj, later sanskritized as "*Navarocikā*" still survives in current practice. The author of the *Āīn-i-Akbarī* devotes a chapter under heading *Sungeet*[1] where he cites certain data collected from some contemporary treatises. He mentions six rāgas or 'musical modes': *Sree Rāg, Bussunt, Behrowng, Punchem, Megh,* and *Nutnārain.* Under each rāga, he cites rāgiṇīs, which he describes not as *rāgīnis,* but as "Variations" of the *rāgas.* He refers to the two classes of songs *marug* (*mārga*) and *deysee* (*deśī*). And under the former he cites seven out of the melodies then current in the Deccan: *sūrya-prakāś, pañca-taleśvara, sarvato-bhadra, candra-prakāśa,* and *rāga-kadamba.*

Pundarīk Viththal: Sadrāga-candrodaya:

But the most important contribution to the developments of the Akbar period we owe to a great scholar, named Puṇḍarīk Vittal, who came from some part of the Deccan.[2] He was the author of four remarkable treatises in Sanskrit[2] in which the theories and the musical practices of his time are systematised. Although he cites the Southern Mukhārī or Kanakāṅgi scale, the music that he treats of is without doubt Northern music. Our author wrote his works under the aus-

(1) As indicated in the concluding portion of the "*Sadrāga-candrodaya*", he came from a village called Sātanūrvā (?) near Śiva-gaṅgā in Karṇāṭa (Kanarese District).

(2) Three of his treatises have been published by Prof. V. N. Bhatkhande and the data available has been very lucidly discussed by him in his article in *Saṅgeeta* (Vol. I, No. 4) under the title: *A comparative study of some of the leading music systems of the 15th, 16th, and 18th centuries.*

pices of three successive royal patrons. The first one *Sadrāga-candrodaya* was written some time between 1562 and 1599 under the service of the Faroqi Prince Burhan Khan of Khandesh which was incorporated in the Moghal empire after the seige of Asirgarh in 1599.[1] In this work he deals with both the Southern and Northern systems of rāgas and classifies them under nineteen ṭhāṭs or parent-scale, *viz.*: Mukhārī, Mālava-gauḍa, Śrī, Śuddha-naṭṭa, Deśākṣī, Karṇāṭā-gauḍa, Kedāra, Hijeja, Hamir, Kamode, Toḍī, Ābhīrī, Śuddha-varāṭī, Śuddha-rāmakrī, Devakrī, Śāraṅga, Kalyāṇa, Hindola and Nāda-Rāmakri. Out of these nineteen original (*mela*) rāgas, he attributes to five of them their respective derivative forms (*janya-rāga*). (See Appendix 18). As Prof. Bhatkhande remarks, "the Hindusthāni musician will find this classification very interesting. He will find many of his own rāgas in the list. Some of these latter seem to have retained their original *svaras* (notes) to this day." The work, is, therefore, of great significance for the data provided for the history of the rāgas. It is noteworthy, that when the author composed his works, the recognized melodies in the north far exceeded the limits of an exhaustive enumeration as is evident from the author's remark: "Owing to the rāgas being innumerable it is impossible to describe each individual ones, I am reciting, here, some of them, following a particular school."[2]

Rāga-mālā: In his next treatise *Rāgamālā*, written probably under the patronage of the Jaipur princes, Mādho Singh and Mān Singh Kacchwas,[3] Puṇḍarīk Viṭṭhal classifies the melodies

(1) "*Tajjaḥ śrī-burahāna-khāna-caturaḥ kāmānukārī varaḥ*
Saṅgītādi-kalā-prapūrṇa-vimalaḥ sāhitya-tejomayaḥ|| 5
Sadrāga-candrodayaḥ, p. 7.

(2) *Anantatvāttu rāgāṇām pratyekaṃ vaktumakṣmaḥ*|
Keṣāñcin-matam-āśritya kati rāgān vadāmyahaṃ||
Rāga-mālā, p. 12.

(3) The colophon to a Ms. of *Rāga-mālā* in the Collection of the Bhandarkar Oriental Research Institute (Ms. No. 1026 of 1884-87) runs as follows: "*Śāke vasvambaka-vedābja ka parigaṇite dhātṛ-saṃvatsare'smin*| *Āṣāḍhe kṛṣṇa- pakṣe-śaśa-dhara-sudine pañcamī revatibhe*| *Nāgāmvā dharma-sūnur-dvijavara-tilako Viṭṭhalo'sti?*

under six male rāgas, and attributes to each, five 'spouses' (*bhāryyās*) and five 'sons' which may be conveniently set forth in a table in Appendix 18.

In this list of 66 melodies, we miss some of the rāgas cited in the first treatise, given above. The 66 rāgas tabulated in the list probably represented the current melodies as Puṇḍarīk Viṭṭhal found them in Northern India when he sat down to compose his work. But the *Rāgamālā,* from our point of view, is the most important document, as it is in this work that we come across *for the first time* descriptive verses, actually giving the visual pictures, along with the component notes of the melodies, and also an indication of the time allocated to the singing of the rāgas.

Rāga-mañjari: The third treatise, *Rāgamañjarī,* was probably composed by the author under the patronage of Rājā Mānsingh Ka'chwa and after he was introduced to the Imperial Court at Delhi. In this work, he cites twenty melodies as parents of the derivatives. They are as follows: Mukhārī, Soma-rāga, Ṭoḍī, Gauḍī, Varāṭī, Kedāra, Śuddha-nāṭa, Deśākśī, Deśī-kāra, Sāraṅga, Āherī, Kalyāṇa, Kāmoda, Hijeja, Rāma-krī, Hindola, Karṇāṭa, Hamīra, Mālava-kaiśika, and Śri-rāga.

But the most important feature of this work is the recognition of the place of as many as sixteen Persian melodies and relating them to the Indian melodies by their nearest equivalents. Most probably these imported melodies had already obtained a place in current Indian music of the North and the author only confirmed the practice by including them in his work and by indicating their characters by assigning them to their places in relation to the Indian models. As Professor Bhatkhande remarks that the use of the locative case termination of the Indian rāgas named "is intended to show that the Persian melody is not exactly the same as the Indian but that the two are founded on the same scale." He accepts them as part of the Hindusthāni system though he

vidvān| Teneyaṃ rāga-mālā rasika-jana-gale bhūṣaṇārthaṃ kṛtā hi"||

This chronogram yields the date śaka 498 i.e. 1576 A.D. See discussion in 'Notes on Indian Chronology XI. Date of Rāga-mālā of Puṇḍarīk Viṭṭhal, *Annals of the Bhandarkar Research Institute,* Vol. XIII, 1931-32, pp. 337-346.

characterized them as "Persian" and recognized that they are "the gift from others" (*parada*). They are sixteen in number and are known as: Rahāyī, Niśāvar, Māhura, Jaṅgula, Māhaṅg(?), Vārā, Sunhath, Irāya, Husenī, Yaman, Sarpharadā, Vākhreja, Hijejaka, and Muśak.

It is significant that Turuṣka Ṭoḍi, which must have received an earlier affiliation is not mentioned in this list. On the other hand, Sarpardā, which is ascribed by tradition to Āmīr Khusrau, is here enumerated as a new-comer.[1]

By this time, the melodies had too far exceeded in number to be confined within the limits of the six rāgas and their wives. In this connection, two texts of uncertain date (and perhaps dateable about the second quarter of the 16th century), deserve to be noticed here.

Cattvārimsacchata-rāga-nirūpanam:

The first text bears the name *Cattvāriṃśacchata-rāga-nirūpaṇaṃ*, attributed to Nārada.[2] Whoever may be this author, who wrote under the cover of a name revered in musical history, he must have belonged to the sixteenth century when the melodies could not be conveniently grouped under the two categories of male and female rāgas, and a third category was a severe necessity. And the device of classifying the new-comers as 'sons' (kumāra) of the known rāgas and rāgiṇīs was resorted to. More than one author adopted this device.[3] But this author appears to be the ear-

(1) "*Anye'pi Pārasīkeyā rāgāḥ parada-nāmakāḥ*|
Sampūrṇāḥ sarva-gamakāḥ kākalyan taritāḥ sadā||
Rahāyi Devagāndhāre (1) *Kānare ca niśāvaraḥ* 2|
Sāraṅge māhuro nāma (3) *Jamgūlo' tha vaṅgālake* (4)||
Deśyā-māhaṅgako nāma (5) *vārā malhāra-rāgake* (6)|
Kedāre'pi ca sūhnātha (7) *Dhanāsyām ca irāyakā* (8)||
Jijāvantyāṃ ca hausenī (9) *Mālave musalīkakaḥ* (10)|
Kalyāṇe yamano gāyet (11) *Sarpardo' tha vilāvale* (12)||
Deśikāre vākharejaḥ (13) *Āsāvaryyāṃ Hijejakaḥ* (14)
Devāgaryyāṃ muśakākhyaḥ (15) *evamanye'pi yojaye*"||
Rāga-manjarī, p. 19.

(2) It survives in various Mss., one of which is in the Tanjore Palace Library (No. 6651). It has been published by M. S. Sukthankar (Arya Bhusan Press, Bombay, 1914).

(3) It is generally asserted that this fanciful system of classification of dividing the melodies into groups of 'families', consisting

liest to adopt this mode of classification. For, he builds his rāga-system on the earlier phase of ten major melodies, described as ten masculine rāgas: Śrī-rāga, Vasanta,, Pañcama, Bhairava, Kauśika, Megha-rāga, Naṭa-Nārāyaṇa, Hindola, Dīpaka, and Haṃsaka. This classification he attributes to Nārada.[1] The author proceeds to give the contemplative verses (*dhyāna*) the verbal image of each masculine rāga, and then enumerates five wives for each, and four sons for each couple. (See Appendix 19).

Somanatha: Rāga-vivodha:

To the early part of the reign of Jahāṅgir (1605-1627 A.D.) belongs an important music text, specially treating of the melodies. It is the *Rāga-vivodha* by Somanāth, son of Mudgala, composed in 1609 A.D. (1531 śaka) as indicated in the colophon.[2] The author has added to the text a commentary of his own which is of great assistance in interpreting the text. It is difficult to say if the author wrote his

of 'husbands,' 'wives' and 'sons' is an essentially Northern and unscientific method, is not authorized by the ancient texts, and has not been followed in the Southern School. This is generally true. But the germ of the idea is certainly derived from *Saṅgīta-ratnākara.* At page 152, (part 1) Śāraṅgadeva describes 15 major rāgas as "*janakas*" (fathers) of the minor melodies (*bhāṣās*). Then he describes (p. 238) a few rāgas, which he could not group under any class and assign to any family, as melodies of unknown parentage (*anukta-janakā*).

(1) This must mean the author himself, and not the author of *Saṅgīta-makaranda,* (p. 18) who enumerates the masculine rāgas as twenty in number. The author of *Cattvāriṃśacchata-rāga-nirūpaṇaṃ,* represents a time, when in Northern India, the major melodies (*puruṣa-rāga*) were growing less and less in number, and approaching towards the stage of being limited to six rāgas. It is quite possible that our author, though living in a later epoch, was adhering to the older and conservative school.

(2) "*Kudahana-tithi-gaṇita śake saumyāvdasyeṣa-māsi śuci-pakṣe.*"||

The work is available in the edition of Puruṣottama Gharpure printed at Poona, 1895, and also in a recent edition by M. S. Aiyar, with an elaborate Introduction and Translation, Triplicane, Madras, 1933.

PUHUPA RĀGINĪ

work in the North, or in the South.[1] He classifies the melodies by selecting 23 melodies as major melodies (*pravartaka-rāga*) and Mela-kartās ('unifiers', or genuses), taking the Mukhārī as the Śuddha scale,[2] and derives the other melodies, by classifying them under one, or other of these 23 types or classes. He does not, however, give any exhaustive enumeration of all the melodies which he remarks are innumerable according to the various ancient schools (*mata*)", and incidentally cites Mataṅga, Niśaḥnka, and *Rāgārṇava*, in his commentary (Ch. IV, pp. 1-3). He also cites the classification into six major rāgas, with five rāginīs each, making up a system of 36 rāgas, and also cites the classification of six rāgas, with five wives, and five sons each, making up a total of 66 melodies.[3] He however follows the Carnatic system by devising a scheme of generic rāgas (*melas*), giving a system of 23 Mela-rāgas from which he derives the other melodies. (See Appendix 20).

This scheme differs from that of the 20 melas of Rāmāmātya's *Svarakalānidhi* not only in the additional five melas, Bhairava, Mallāra, Kalyāna, Śuddha-vasanta and Hammira, but we also miss in Somanāth's list—the rāgas Hindola, and Hejujji. Bhairava is sometimes accepted in place of Mālava-gauḍa.[4]

Dāmodara Misra's Saṅgīta-darpana:

To the reign of Shāh Jahān belongs, the short but popular treatise known as the "*Saṅgītadarpaṇa*" (the Mirror of Music) written by Dāmodara Miśra about 1625 A.D.[5] It is more a compilation than an original work, and the author freely quotes from various authorities. His definition of 'Saṅgīta' (song and music) evidently borrowed from some

(1) Pandit Bhatkhande takes him to be an authority of the Northern School.

(2) "*Santi mukhāri-mele śuddhāḥ ṣaḍjādayaḥ svarāḥ sapta*"||
Rāga-vivodha, Chapter 3, 32.

(3) "*Rāgāḥ ṣaṭ-puruṣāsteṣāṃ pañca pañca tu yoṣitaḥ*|
Sūnavaḥ pañca pañcaiva ṣaṭ-ṣaṣṭiriti te'khilāḥ"||
Rāga-vivodha, Ch. 4, 2, commentary.

(4) See Aiyar's Edition of *Svarakalānidhi*, Intro. XLVI.

(5) It is available in the edition of Raja Sir S. M. Tagore who published it with his own commentary and notes (Stanhope Press, Calcutta, 1881).

earlier text-writer is worth quoting: "The quality of pleasing is the common factor underlying the art of singing songs, accompaniments, and dance. Therefore that which fails to give pleasure cannot deserve the name of music (Saṅgīta).[1]

In his chapter on rāgas, he gives a list of twenty major rāgas :—Śrī-rāga, Naṭṭa, Vaṅgāla, Bhāṣa, Madhyama, Ṣāḍava, Rakta-haṃsa, Kohlāsa, Prabhava, Bhairava, Dhvani, Megha-rāga, Soma-rāga, Kāmoda, Āmra-pañcama, Kandarpa, Deśākhya, Kakubha, Kaiśīka, Naṭṭa-nārāyaṇa.

This list is quite distinct from the system of six rāgas and thirty-six rāgiṇīs. The author cites two different systems of 'six-rāgas', one according to the school of Hanumān, and the other according to the view of *Rāgārṇava.* He also cites the view of Someśvara on the time-theory of the melodies. The chapter ends with a series of descriptions of the six rāgas, and thirty rāgiṇīs, according to the school of Hanumān, together with prayer-formulas (*dhyānas*) for each of the melodies described. The prayer-formulas of some of the uparāginīs,not given elsewhere, are cited by the author.

Govinda Dīksit's Sangīta-sudhā:

The next available text belongs to the South and the Karnatic system. *Saṅgīta-sūdhā,* composed by Govinda Dīkṣit, the minister at the Court of Prince Raghunath Naik (1614-1640 A.D.) of Tanjore, was ascribed by the author to his royal patron.[2] It is an elaborate treatise, and treats of the melodies very fully. The descriptions of the jāti-rāgas, including the composite *jāti*-melodies, are illustrated with actual songs, with notations. The author gives to the *Śuddha-jātis* a picturesque name, *viz., Kapālānī* (skulls), associating their origin with Śiva, as he went about in his begging role (*vikṣāṭaṇa veśa*) with the skull as his begging bowl.[3] Improving on Mataṅga (Appendix 3) the author classifies melodies under ten divisions: (1) Grāma-rāga, (2)

(1) *Gita-vāditra-nṛtyānāṃ raktīḥ sādhārāṇo guṇaḥ|*
Ato-rakti-vihīnaṃ yanna tat saṅgītamucyate|| 6 || *Saṅgīta-darpaṇaṃ.*

(2) The text together with a free translation is being published in a series of articles, in the *Journal of the Music Academy,* Madras, Vol. 1, Nos. 1-2, p. 57, 1930, 1932, 1933, by P. S. Sundaram Ayyar, and Subramanya Sastri.

(3) *Journal Music Academy,* Vol. II, No. 3, p. 166.

Uparāga, (3) Śuddha-rāga, (4) Bhāṣā, (5) Vibhāṣā, (6) Antara-bhāṣā, (7) Rāgāṅga, (8) Bhāṣāṅga, (9) Kriyāṅga, (10) Upāṅga. He cites and describes 30 Grāma-rāgas, 8 Upa-rāgas, 20 Śuddha-rāgas (nearly the same as given in *Saṅgīta-darpaṇa, ante* p. 32) and the 'derivative melodies' (*janya-bhāṣā-rāga*).

While *Svara-kalā-nidhi* cites 20 melas, (generic melodies which unify the derivatives under a genus-species system), *Rāga-vivodha* cites 23 mela-kartā rāgas; by the time of Govinda Dīkṣit, 72 melas had been evolved. Though the system of Melakartās had been in existence before, Dīkṣit gives it an emphatic status, and appears to have codified it, and given it a proper name, calling it, after the name of his patron, as 'Raghunātha-mela'. The author is said to have introduced some new rāgas, e.g., Jayanta-sena and others.[1]

Hrdaya Nārāyana Deva's Hrdayakautaka and Hrdaya-prakāsa:

The two following texts, *Hṛdaya-kautuka* and *Hṛdaya-prakāśa,* come from the North.[2] The author of both is Hṛdaya Nārāyaṇa Deva who ruled in Gadā deśa about 1724 Saṃvat (=1646 or 1660 A.D.) In the first work, the author borrows his 12 parent scales (*saṃsthānas* or *ṭhāṭs*) from *Rāga-taraṅginī.* He, however, invents a new melody called Hṛdaya-rāma, in which two peculiar notes are used, e.g., tri-śruti 'ma' and tri-śruti 'ni', and on the basis thereof lays down an additional thirteenth *ṭhāṭ.* His derivative rāgas are very fully described with their complete note-compositions. In his *Hṛdaya-prakāśa,* the author confines himself to 12 types of *melas* or *ṭhāṭs,* commenting that 'there are innumerable *melas* in the ocean of music, but only 12 of these are useful here.' He defines *mela* as 'a collection of notes capable of producing rāgas.' He emphasises on an important point. 'The use of two, three, or four notes may produce pleasing improvisations (*tānas*) but not rāgas.' The Śuddha scale of *Hṛdaya-prakāśa* seems to correspond to *the Kāfī*

(1) "You have codified the new Melā, Raghunath Melā by name" (65).

"You have sung the new Rāgas Jayantasena and others" (64). Ibid. Vol. I, No. 2, 1930, p. 120.

(2) Both these texts have been edited by D. K. Joshi and published by B. S. Sukthankar, Arya Bhusan Press, Poona, San 1918.

ṭhāṭ of the modern Hindustani musicians.

Venkatamakhi's Caturdandi-prakāsikā:

Passing over Harivallabha's Hindī treatise (1653 A.D.) interesting only for its iconographic data, we come to the most important text of the South, the *Caturdaṇḍi prakāśikā* by Veṅkaṭamakh[1] the son of Govinda Dīkṣit. The work was composed about 1660 A.D., and offers a very pungent criticism of the *Svaramelakalānidhi.* Thę author develops the *melas* into as many as 72 different types.[2] These 72 melas, the author considered as final, and exhaustive. He had asserted that 'even Śiva could not add to the 72 melas'.[3] This challenge has however been taken up by a later theorist the nameless author of *Melādhikāra-lakṣaṇa.* Many musicians hold that 72 melas are not possible. Veṅkaṭamakhi's system is based on the following 12 svara sthānas: (1) Ṣaḍja, (2) Śuddha-ṛṣabha, (3) Catu-śruti ṛṣabha=Śuddha-gāndhāra, (4) Ṣaṭ-śruti-ṛṣabha=Sādhāraṇa gāndhāra, (5) Antara-gāndhāra, (6) Śuddha-madhyama, (7) Pratimadhyama, (8) Pañcama, (9) Śuddha-dhaivata, (10) Catusruti-dhaivata= Śuddha-niṣada, (11) Śaṭ-śruti-dhaivata=Kaiśika-niṣāda, (12) Kākalī-niṣāda. "The point to be noticed about this scheme is that with these twelve *sthānas* alloting two for Ri, Ga, Ma, Dha, and Ni, we can have only 32 *melas* in all, and in fact that position has been taken by some of the musicians of the present day. But Veṅkaṭamakhi intended to provide for both the Ris, or Gas, or Dhas, or Nis, occurring in the same *mela,* and so he classified the same *sthāna* both as Ri, Ga, Ga; and as Dha, or Ni. Thus we get Śuddha-gāndhāra, Ṣaṭ-śruti-ṛṣabha, Śuddha-nisāda, Catuḥ-śruti-dhaivata. Thus the seventy-two *melas* are made up". (T. L. Venkatarama Iyer, in *Journal Music Academy,* Madras, Vol. I, No. 1, p. 42). He sets out a table of 19 *melas* (Appendix 24) which were current when he came into the field.[4]

(1) Available in two editions: (1) published by Joshi and Sukthankar, Arya Bhusan Press, Poona, 1918 San, (2) published by the Music Academy, Madras.

(2) "*Dvi-saptati melakānāṃ nirmātā veṅkateśvara.*"

(3) "*Nahi tat-kalpane bhāla-locano'pi pragalbhate.*"

(4) "*Itthaṃ pradarśitā melā lakṣya-lakṣaṇa-saṅgatāḥ|*
Ekona-viśadasmābhiḥ samprati pracaranti ye||" Ch. IV. 174||
Catur-daṇḍi-prakāśikā.

Veṅkaṭamakhi classifies the rāgas into six kinds of Mārga-rāgas and four kinds of Deśi-rāgas.

Ahovala's Saṅgīta-Pārijāta:

A text datable about 1665 A.D., and which became very popular in the North is the *Saṅgīta-Pārijāta* by Ahovala Pandita[1] having been translated into Persian by Pandit Dīnanāth in 1724 A.D. The translation bearing the seal of the librarian of Emperor Mohamed Shah (1719-1724) is still in the collection of the Rampur State Library. The most important feature of this work is the fixing of the exact places of the *śuddha* and *vikṛta* notes in terms of the lengths of the sounding string of the *vīṇā*, in the same manner as that of *Hṛdaya-kautuka*. Ahovala does not appeal to give any classification of the rāgas under any types of parent-scale (*ṭhāṭ*) or otherwise, although he claims to describe the rāgas according to the characteristics laid down by Hanumān.[2] But occasional references to *ṭhāṭas* seem to indicate, that in his time, classification of rāgas under *ṭhāṭas* had become current in the North. He gives a list of 122 rāgas, which he describes with accurate notations.[3] He groups them according to the time and watches (*prahara*) assigned to their appropriate periods for singing, dividing them into three groups, for the first, second or third watches, while a string of 19 rāgas are grouped together as suitable for all hours ("*sarvadā ca. sukha-pradā*").

Bhavahatta's Anūpa-saṅgīta-vilāsa, Anūpa-saṅgīta-ratnākara, Anūpasaṅgītāṅkusa:

Passing over the short Hindī treatise of Deo-kavi (c. 1673 A.D.), mostly of iconographic interest, we come to a very interesting group of texts: *Anūpa-saṅgīta-vilāsa*, *Anūpa-saṅgīta-ratnākara* and *Anūpa-saṅgītāṅkuśa*, all composed by Bhavabhaṭṭa under the patronage of Raja Anūp Singh (1674-1701 A.D.) of Bikanir. This group of texts[4] is of great interest

(1) It was edited and published by Jîvānanda Vidyāsāgara, Sarasvati Press, Calcutta, 1884.

(2) "*Lakṣaṇāni vruve teṣāṃ sammatyā ca Hanūmataḥ*"|| 333 ||
Saṅgīta-Pārijāta.

(3) "*Dvāviṃśatyā śataṃ te ca proktā loka-sukhāya ca*"|| 488 ||
Ibid.

(4) The three texts have been printed and published by Joshi and Sukthankar, Arya Bhusan Press, Poona, San 1921, in one volume.

for the history of the rāgas. By adopting the data offered by nearly all the earlier texts, the author gives an historical view of the rāgas, and their various classifications as gleaned from the preceding theorists, beginning from Yāṣṭika. In the first text, the author gives various prayer-formulas from earlier authors whose original texts are not otherwise available. In the second text, the author cites variegated forms of 18 different melodies, e.g., 16 forms of Naṭa; 14 forms of Karṇāṭa; 16 forms of Velāvalī; nine forms of Ṭoḍī; and so on; He catalogues 37 varieties of grāma-rāgas with their respective derivatives (*vibhāṣās* &c.). He gives a very interesting history how the first group of six major-rāgas came to be recognized at first. 'The ancient authorities had given the status of major rāgas to the following (four): (i) Naṭṭa-nārāyaṇa, (ii) Megha, (iii) Bhairava, (iv) Śrī-rāga. To this, the grāma-rāga called 'Pañcama' was added, and also the rāgāṅga 'Vasanta' (thus making a group of six).'[1] Then the author cites four other different groups of six-rāgas, including that of the *Rāgārṇava,* with their respective rāgiṇīs for each of the five systems. Next, he gives the name of 20 *melas*: Ṭoḍī, Gauḍī, Varāṭi, Kedāra, Śuddha-nāṭa, Mālava-kaiśika, Śrī-rāga, Hammira, Ahirī, Kalyāna, Deśākṣī, Deśikār, Sāraṅga, Karnāṭa, Hijeja, Nādarāmkriyā, Hindola, Mukhārī, and Soma. This is followed by full descriptions of numerous important melodies, mostly accompanied by prayer-formulas. In the third text *Anūpa-saṅgītāṅkuśa,* the author confines himself to the system of Hanumāna, with slight variations, viz., Sāveri, substituted for Āśāvarī (See Appendix 33). Descriptions of the note-structures of the melodies are borrowed from various earlier authorities. It is obvious that Bhava-bhaṭṭa does not record any new developments, but follows current and prevailing practices. Similarly, the *Saṅgīta-dāmodara* by Śubhaṅkara (*c.* 1690) is mostly based on *Saṅgīta-darpaṇa* and does not offer any new materials or data for the history of rāgas.

Sangīta-nārāyana by Purusottama Misra:

During the eighteenth century the available texts have

(1) ***Naṭṭa-nārāyaṇasyāpi Meghasya Bhairavasya ca|***
Śrī-rāgasya ca samproktaṃ rāgatvaṃ pūrva-sūribhiḥ|| 142 ||
Pañcamo grāma-rāgaḥ syādrāgaṅgaṃ ca Vasantakaḥ"|
Anūpa-saṅgīta-ratnākara, p. 28.

very little to record by way of new developments. Thus the treatise called *Saṅgīta-nārāyaṇa*[1] composed by Puruṣottama Miśra under the patronage of Nārāyaṇa Deva of Parlakimedi of the Southern Gajapati dynasty about the years 1730-1750 freely uses the earlier texts.[2] The most interesting of the citations in this work are the verses from Nārada's *Pañcama-sāra-saṃhitā,* and Mammaṭā-carya's *Saṅgīta-ratnamālā,* the original text of the latter being not yet traceable. The principal feature of the work is contributed by the descriptive prayer-formulas from various earlier authors. The author follows the six-rāga system with the following major rāgas: Bhairava, Vasanta, Mālava-kauśika, Śri-rāga, Megha-rāga, and Naṭṭa-nārāyaṇa.

Sangīta Sārāmrtod-dhāra by Tulāji:

To the closing years of the eighteenth century belongs a short but interesting text, *Saṅgīta-sārāmṛtoddhāra*[3] attributed to a royal author, King Tulāji of Tanjore (1763-1787) A.D.). Though a late work, it has some interesting features. He refers to a musician (gāyaka) named Sautika[4] and cites pithy definitions of the classification of rāgas into rāgāṅga, bhāṣāṅga etc. He cites Mataṅga, Viṭṭhala, and the *Caturdaṇḍi-prakāśikā.* He cites the melodies as current in his time (*"samprati pracaranti ye,"* verse 14). He attributes to Someśvaradeva,

(1) The text is available in an unpublished Ms. in Bengali, in the collection of the Asiatic Society of Bengal No. 2513-69-E4. The colophon runs as follows: *"Iti śrī-man-nikhilānvayottuṅga-garva-śāva-stasyākhila-guṇa-sadma-padma-nābha-bhūmi-pati-tanū-janmano -mahārājasya-sāhitya-saṅgītārṇava-karṇadhāra(kara)kamalergajapati -vīra-śrī-Nārāyaṇa-devasya-kṛtau Saṅgīta-Nārāyaṇe śuddha-prabandho-dhāraṇaṃ nāma caturthaḥ paricchedaḥ * * * Śrī-Kaviratna Puruṣottama-Miśra-Kṛta Saṅgīta-Nārāyaṇonāma granthaḥ."*

(2) A chief called Nārāyaṇa Deva of Parlakimedi, is referred to in R. D. Banerjee's *History of Orissa,* Vol. II, p. 120ff. See also Ramachandra Kavi : "Literary Gleanings," *Journal Andhra Historical Research Society,* Vol. III, 2, 3, 4, p. 206.

(3) The work is represented by two imperfect Mss. in the Collection of the Tanjore Palace State Library, Nos. 6629, and 6632 (Burnell's *Catalogue,* p. 60). It has been published in an edition now out of print, printed in Bombay by Bhāla Chandra Sarmā.

(4) *"Bhāṣāngastena Kathyante gāyakaiḥ Soutikādibhiḥ,"* Verse 12.

the well-known verses describing the origin of the six major rāgas from the mouth of Śiva and Pārvati, already cited here (*ante* p. 13, foot-note 1). As a characteristic Southern text, it classifies the melodies under the system of *melas*. As compared with the *Caturdaṇḍi-prakāśikā,* the text offers several peculiarities. If we compare the *mela* and *janya-rāgas*—as given in the Appendices 24 and 2 and we find that the Mukhārī mela, popular in the earlier period, has given up its position of honour to Śrī-rāga.[1] Śuddha-rāma-kriyā, and Sindhu-rāma-kriyā are cited as two independent major rāgas, and a new major rāga (*melaka*) is cited under the name of Vega-vāhinī. The Saindhavī rāga, an evening melody, is described as giving victory in times of war.[2] The melody Madhyamādi is said to be very moving and stimulating when played on a flute.[3] The melody Kannaḍa-gauḍa, an *Upāṅga-rāga,* is said to be very popular in Orissa ("*Utkalā-nāmatipriyaḥ*"). Among the list of derivative melodies the following new names are cited: Mādhava-manoharī, Śrī-rañjanī, Jayanta-sena, Mani-raṅga, Udaya-ravi-candrikā, Ārdra-deśi, Meca-vauli, Pūrṇa-pañcama, Nārāyaṇī, Pūrṇa-candrikā, Sura-sindhu, Chhāyā-taraṅginī, Julāvu (Sanskrit form of Jilaf?), and Manoha. Some interesting varieties of older and familiar melodies are cited, *e.g.*, Yadu-kula-kāmboji, Nārāyaṇī-deśāksī, Naṭa-kurañjī, Mohana-kalyāṇī, Indu-ghanṭā-rava. The new names appear to prove that music was still a living science, growing by the development of new melodies.

Saṅgīta-sāra by Mahārāja Pratāpa Simha:

The Hindi text *Saṅgīta-sāra*[4] compiled by Mahārāja Sawai Pratāpa Siṃha Deo of Jaipur (1779-1804 A.D.) offers

(1) "*Atra sarvveṣu rāgeṣu Śrī-rāgaścottamottamaḥ*"|| 74||
"*Śrī-rāga rāga-rājo' yaṃ sarvva-sampat-pradāyakaḥ|*
Itucyate tatra lakṣmya Tulājendrena dhīmatā|| 85 ||
Saṅgīta-sārāmṛtoddhāra.

(2) "*Śrī-rāga-mela-sambhūtaḥ Saindhavī-rāga īritaḥ|*
Saṃgrāma-karmmaṇi jaya-pradaḥ sāyaṃ pragīyate
Sampūrṇa-svara-saṃyuktaḥ ṣaḍja-nyāsa-grahāṃśakaḥ"||
Ibid.

(3) "*Raktiretasya rāgasya muralyāṃ dṛśyate'dhikā*"|| *Ibid.*

(4) Published by Poona Gayan Samaj, Printed at Arya Bhusan Press, 7 parts, 1910-12.

no data bearing of the history of the rāgas. He however describes several new rāgas e.g. Laṅkā-dahana, Līlāvati. The work is of more interest for the materials offered for musical iconography. The work is the result of a conference of experts and musical practitioners called at Jaipur for the purpose of compiling a standard work on Hindusthani music. In the work the standard of Śuddha scale accepted is that of Vilāval.

The eighteenth century has very little to record in the history of the development of Indian music, in theory, or science—though eminent practical exponents continued to carry on the brilliant traditions of the Moghul periods as late as the reign of Muhammad Shah (1719-1748 A.D.).

Nagamat-e-Asaphi by Muhammad Rezza Khan:

During the early part of the nineteenth century an important Persian text offers a new development in the classification of rāgas. This is a Persian text compiled in 1813 A.D. by Muhammad Rezza, a Prince of Patna. It is known as *Nagmat-e-Asaphi* and appears to survive in manuscripts. This eminent connoisseur of music had the courage to call into question the classification of the northern system, based on a picturesque divisions of the melodies into 'wives' and 'sons' of rāgas. He devised a new system based on a study of the structural similarities of the rāgas. He based his classification by accepting the Vilāval scale as the standard of Śuddha scale. He built up his system after consulting the best practising artists of his time. z

Sangīta-rāga- kalpadruma by Krishnananda Vyāsa:

A pretentious treatise compiled during the early part of the 19th century, and printed in 1842 we owe to a musical expert Kṛishṇānanda Vyāsa, a Gauḍa Brahmin from a village in Udaipur. It is an encyclopædia in Sanskrit of songs collected from different parts of India and published under the title *Saṅgīta-rāga-kalpadruma.*[1] It also deals with dancing and drumming and rhythm. It is hardly an original contribution to music and merely summarises the works of previous text-writers. In the section on rāgas the author follows

(1) The work has been printed twice, the first edition during 1842-49, and the second edition in two volumes in 1916 by the Baṅgīya Sāhitya Pariṣad, Calcutta, *vide* O. C. Gangoly's note on 'Date of the *Saṃgīta-rāga-kalpa-drumḥ*' in the *Annals of the Bhandarkar Oriental Research Institute,* Vol. XV, Parts 1-11, 1934, p. 117.

the *Saṅgīta-darpaṇa* basing his classification on the School of Hanumān. He describes the 36 melodies and quotes the prayer-formulas as cited in the *Saṅgīta-darpaṇa.* As an anthology of old songs, both in Hindi and Persian, which are collected under different melodies, the work is of great value, the materials having been collected during a period of 32 years, from a wide field of researches.

Sangītasāra-Samgraha by Sir S. M. Tagore:

The compilation of Raja Sir Sourindra Mohun Tagore, (one of the greatest connoisseurs and patrons of Indian Music) under the title of *Saṅgīta-sāra-saṃgraha*[1] and published in Saṃvat 1932 (1875 A.D.) offers the latest study on the old Sanskrit musical texts. His chief sources are the text of *Saṅgīta-ratnākara, Saṅgīta-dāmodara,* and *Saṅgīta-darpaṇa.* His work is of great interest for the collection of prayer formulas *(dhyānas)* of rāgas according to the three schools.

Sri-mal-Laksa-Sangītam and Abhinaya-rāga mañjarī by Pandit Bhat-Khande:

A more original contribution to the science of the rāgas is furnished by *Śrī-mal-lakṣa-saṅgītaṃ and Abhinava-rāga-mañjarī*[2] two short Sanskrit treatises composed in 1921 by Pandit Bhat-Khande (under the pseudonym of Viṣṇu Śarmā) an eminent scholar and one of the foremost living connoisseurs of Indian music to whom this volume is dedicated. The author adopts the system of unifiers *(melakas)* and derivatives *(janya).* Accepting the Velāvala as the fundamental scale,[3] he divides the rāgas into 10 groups (*melakas*=group-makers): Kalyāṇa, Kammāj, Bhairava, Pauravī, Māravā, Kāphī, Āśāvarī, Bhairavī and Toḍikā. The derivative rāgiṇīs coming under each group are set out in the table given in Appendix 35).

Dr. Rabindranath Tagore:

This hasty, summary, and bird's eye-view of the development of the rāgas will be imperfect, without reference to the recent innovations introduced by Dr. Rabindra Nath Tagore. His experiments are chiefly interesting for their harmonious combinations of apparently inconsistent, or

(1) Printed by I. C. Bose & Co., Stanhope Press, Calcutta, 1875.

(2) Printed at the Arya Bhusan Press, Poona, and published by Bhalchandra S. Sukthankar, 1921 (Saka 1843), Bombay.

(3) "*Ādīmaḥ sarva-melānaṃ velāvalī-su-melakaḥ*", verse 89, *Abhinava-rāga-mañjarī,* p. 9.

temperamentally divergent, or structurally incompatible rāgas—into happy and melodious compositions. As we have seen (*ante* p. 27-28), numerous old masters of Indian music had changed the current forms of rāgas in new and attractive versions, and novel forms of interpretations. "Knowing the old rāgas perfectly well, he (Tagore) too had the right to use and change them as his own inspiration told him to do."[1]

(1) A. A. Bake : 'Rabindranath Tagore's music', *The Golden Book of Tagore*. 1931, pp. 273-276.

RAGAS AND RAGINIS

The differentiation of rāgiṇīs from rāgas is a topic of some complication. The evolution of the rāgiṇīs as a class of melodies to be distinguished from rāgas properly so-called is a matter of later history. The word rāgiṇī does not occur in the works of Dattila, Bharata, or in the *Bṛhaddeśī*. Rāgiṇīs are believed to be graceful, minor, diminutive, or abbreviated forms of rāgas. At an earlier stage, such as we find in the *Bṛhaddeśī,* they were looked upon as the derivatives of the root-rāgas, and as reflecting the character of the rāgas' (*Chāyā-mātrānuga*). They are then designated as *bhāṣās,* and *vibhāṣās,* and *antara-bhāṣās.* And each of the several earliest grāma-rāgas, or rāga-gītis (see Appendix 3) had particular *bhāṣā-gītis* assigned to them. According to the definition of Mataṅga, 'the *bhāṣās* were derived from the grāma-rāgas, the *vibhāṣās* spring from the *bhāṣās,* and the *antara-bhāṣās* were born of the *vibhāṣās*'.[1] In the nomenclature of this definition, and in the feminine endings given to these early derivatives of the root-rāgas, we have the seeds for the later classifications of rāgas and rāgiṇīs, picturesquely called as the wives of the rāgas, and the classification of rāgas and their derivatives picturesquely called as the sons (*putras*) of the rāgas. The three types of derivative rāgas, mentioned by Mataṅga, have names with feminine endings (*strī-pratyaya*).

According to an ingenious suggestion by a modern scholar of music,[2] it is the placing of the emphasis on the cadential notes (*nyāsa, vinyāsa, apanyāsa, sannyāsa*) on the stronger or the weaker pulses of the rhythm of a melody that determines its sex. And that when the musical phrases or

(1) "*Grāma-rāgodbhavā bhāṣā bhāṣbhyāśca vibhāṣikāḥ|*
Vibhāṣābhyāśca sañjātā tathā cāntara-bhāṣikāḥ||"
Mataṅga, *Bṛhad-deśī,* p. 105.

(2) Paṇḍit Kṛṣṇa Chandra Ghose Vedānta-Cintāmaṇi.

structure of a melody have an upward or ascending tendency (*ārohaṇa*) with the cadential notes resting on the stronger pulses—then it is called a rāga (a masculine melody). And when the phrases and structure have a downward or descending tendency (*avarohaṇa*) with the cadential notes resting on the weaker impulses,—it is characterized as a rāgiṇī (a feminine melody).

The conception of rāgiṇī, as a graceful, or a diminutive phase of a rāga, and designated with a feminine ending appears to be a peculiarity of the Northern system. Śāraṅgadeva does not recognize rāgiṇīs, but only *bhāṣās, vibhāṣā* and *antarabhāṣās.* The differentiation of female melodies is first come across in the *Saṅgīta-makaranda* of Nārada, who gives three classes of melodies under the headings of (i) male rāgas (*puṃliṅga-rāga*), (ii) female rāgas (*strī-rāgas*), and (ii) neuter rāgas (*napuṃsaka-rāgas*). This classification is ascribed to Brahmā, and the three groups are allocated to three different types of emotive values. The male melodies are assigned to the sentiments of Wonder, Courage, or Anger, the female melodies are assigned to the sentiments of Love, Laughter, and Sorrow, while the neuter melodies are assigned to the sentiments of Terror, Fear, Disgust, and Peace.[1]

It should be noted that Nārada does not actually use the word rāgiṇī, but uses the term *strī,* or '*yoṣit*' (wife) of a rāga. If Mammaṭa (8th century) is the author of *Saṅgīta-ratnamālā,* then the earliest reference to rāgiṇīs is to be found in this text; it has been freely utilized by the author of *Saṅgīta-nārāyaṇa* and various later authors. But this is somewhat problematic, as Nānyadeva, (12th century) an authority of the Northern School does not mention *rāgiṇīs,* so the term does not appear to have been used very much before the date of the *Rāgārṇava* (c. 14th century), though the recognition of a female rāga must be fairly old in the Northern system.

Gurjarī, Saindhavī, Gāndhārī, Ābhirī, are some of the earliest feminine melodies designated by Mataṅga under the

(1) "*Raudre'dbhūte tathā vīre puṃ-rāgaiḥ parigīyate|*
Śṛṅgāra-hāsya-karuṇām (?) *strī-rāgaiśca pragīyate*|| 65 ||
Bhayānake ca vibhatse śānte gāyannapuṃsake||
Saṅgīta-makaranda, (G. O. S. Vol. XVI, p. 19).

name of *bhāṣā*. According to the terminology of the mythology of the *tantras*, the minor melodies have been born of the union of the male and the female phases of the melodies.

Nomenclature of Rāgas:

As Nārada has remarked, 'curious, indeed, are the names of Rāgas'.[1] If we study their names we find three distinct phases. At the first stage, about the time of the *Nāṭya-Śāstra* the melodies took their names from the dominant or significant note prevailing in their compositions. Thus, one of the *grāma-rāgas* is called Ṣaḍjī, from the note Ṣaḍja; Ārṣabhī, from the note Ṛṣabha, *Gāndhārī,* from the note Gāndhāra, and so on. The last-named melody still survives in current practice. The name 'Madyamādi' (now regarded as a rāgiṇī of Bhairava) is so-called as it begins with the note 'Madhyama' (F). Vibhāṣā, originally a generic name for a class of derivative melodies (a sub-division of bhāṣās) now survives as a proper name for a rāgiṇī. In the second stage, the melodies derived their names from the ancient tribes inhabiting various parts of India. Thus the Śakas, the Pulindas, the Ābhīras, the Savars, and the Bhaīravas[2] appear to have lent their names to the following rāgas: Śaka-rāga (with variants called Śaka-tilaka, Śaka-miśrita), Pulindi-rāga, Ābhīrī, Sāverikā (Sāvirī) and Bhairava-rāga. Three of the earliest rāgas, (a) Mālava (with its derivatives Mālavikā, Mālavaśrī, Mālava-pañcama, Mālava-vesara, Mālava-kaiśika,[3] vulgarized into Mālkausa), (b) Āndhrī, and (c) Gūrjarī, may have come from the ancient tribes known as the Mālavas, the Andhras, and the Gurjaras respectively. As is well-known, the Mālavas

(1) "*Nāradena vicitreṇa santi nāmāni vakṣyate*"| *Saṅgīta-makaranda,* p. 18, 56.

(2) The Bhīravas were an aboriginal sect mentioned along with the Śakāras, Ābhīras, Chandālas, Pulindas and Savaras in Sāradātanaya's *Bhāva-prakāśana* (Gaekwad's O. S. Vol. XLV, 1930. Introduction, p. 61).

(3) According to Mataṅga (*Bṛhaddeśī,* T. S. S. p. 98) Mālava-Kaiśika is so called because it is derived from the Kaiśikī-jāti melody' ("*Kaiśikī-jāti-sambhūtiḥ rāgo Mālava-kaiśikaḥ*"|| (346). The term 'Kaiśikī' (literally—'hair breadth') is derived from the theory of Śrutis (microtones). Thus, 'Kaiśikī nī' is nikhāda (B) less by one Śruti.

TODĪ RĀGINĪ

were ancient martial tribes (*āyudhaj-jivī-saṃghas*), mentioned by Patañjalī, and who were formerly settled in the Punjab where they offered resistance to Alexander, and latterly settled in the North-west part of Central India, to which they gave the name the Mālwā.[1] The Andhras, a Dravidian sect, played a more important part in the political and cultural history of India, and founded ruling dynasties occupying various parts of Central, Eastern, and Southern India at different periods.[2] Similarly the Gurjara clans, probably foreign immigrants associated with the White Huns, formerly settled near Mount Abu, and, later, occupying the peninsula known as Guzerat,—played important parts in developing Indian culture and religious history. They are also associated with an important ruling dynasty known as the Gurjjara-pratihāra dynasty.[3] The aboriginal races of India appear to have contributed many shining and colourful threads to the rich and variegated texture of Indian musical tapestry.

Other names of rāgas are derived from geographical place names and regions. The most typical example is Vaṅgāla, 'the celestial form of which', Mataṅga points out, 'is derived from the Vaṅgāla country'.[4] Cognate examples are (a) Saindhavī, from Sindhūdeśa, modern Sind, (b) Sauvīra (with its derivative, Sauvīraka, Sauvīrī) from the ancient region in the South-west,[5] (c) Takka (sometimes called

(1) "The Mālavas" by Adrish Ch. Banerji, *Annals of the Bhandarkar Oriental Institute*, Vol. XIII, 1931-32, pp. 218-229.

(2) "Andhra History & Coinage" by Vincent Smith (*Z. D. M. G.*, 1902, 1903).

(3) D. R. Bhandarkar : 'Foreign Elements in the Hindu Population' (*Indian Antiquary*, Vol. XL, 1931, pp. 7-37.

C. V. Vaidya: '*History of Mediæval Hindu India*, Vol. I, p. 84.

J. C. Ghosh: 'Paḍihār's (*Indian Antiquary*, Vol. LX, 1931, pp. 239-246).

(4) "*Vaṅgāla-deśa-sambhūta vaṅgālī divya-rūpiṇī*," *Bṛhad-deśī*, p. 127.

(5) 'The Mārkaṇḍeya Purāṇa assigns Sindhu-Sauvīra to the South-west' (Cunningham's '*Ancient Geography of India*, S. Majumdar's Edition, 1924, p. 7).

'Taku', later vulgarized as 'Taṅka'), from Takka-deśā[1] (d) Saurāṣṭrī (vulgarized in forms, such as, Saurаṭhī, Surat, Suraṭ-mallār) from the Saurāṣṭra-deśa and (e) Karṇāṭa (Karṇāṭī), from regions of same names. Similarly, the rāgiṇī Kāmbhojī (still surviving in the South in the popular variety known as Hari-Kāmbhojī) is derived from Kāmbhoja-deśa, and the rāgiṇī Vairāṭī may have come from Berar, or Virāṭa kingdom, figuring in the epic anecdotes of *Mahābhārata.* Bhoṭṭa, a very early melody, may have come from the region of Thibet (Bhoṭṭa), just as Gauḍa (Eastern Bengal), to be distinguished from Vaṅgāla, and Gauḍī must have been melodies imported from the Eastern part of Bengal. Likewise, the melody Pauravikā (Pūravī, Pūrvī), literally meaning 'eastern', may have come from that region. It is quite possible that the melody known as Kakubhā derives its name from an ancient village, famous in Gupta history, as a culture-centre, 'a very jewel amongst villages, sanctified by the habitations of sages'.[2] The village *Kakubhā* still survives under the name of *Kahāyuñ,* five miles to the west of the chief town of Salampur-Majhauli in the district of Gorakhpur. The rāgiṇī Khaṃvāvatī, an ancient melody, probably derives its name from the city of the name of Cambay; the site of the ancient city is three miles away from the modern city. The Venetian traveller, Marco Polo, in the thirteenth century, calls it "Cambat.[3] According to Col. Todd, the proper Hindu name of the city, was Khambavatī, 'the city of the pillars.' 'The inhabitants write it Kambayat. It is spoken of as a flourishing city by Mas'udi who visited it in 915 A.D.' Ibn Batuta (14th century) speaks of it as a very fine city, remarkable for the elegance and solidarity of the mosques and houses built by wealthy foreign merchants.

(1) The melody may have come from an ancient aboriginal tribe known as the Takkas (Tāks, or Tauks of later times) who occupied portions of the Panjab in early times and who are believed to have given the name to the ancient city of Takṣa-śilā (Taxila) and of Attak (Attoc). See "*Early Turanians: Takkas*" (Cunningham, A. S. Reports, Vol. II, 1862-65, Simla, 1871, pp. 6-11).

(2) "*Khyāte'smin grāma-ratne kakubha iti janaiḥ sādhu-saṃsarga-pūte*" (Fleet's *Gupta Inscriptions,* No. 15, p. 67).

(3) Marco Polo, Yule's edition, 1875, Vol. II, p. 389.

The melody does not appear to find its place in the *Saṅgīta-makaranda,* nor in the *Saṅgīta-ratnakara,* nor even in the *Saṅgīta-samaya-sāra,* and is mentioned for the first time in Locana Kavi's *Rāga-taraṅgiṇī* (*c.* 14th century).

The rāgiṇī Hijeja [Hejujji], an imported melody, now affiliated with Indian rāgas, is also believed to have been so called after the name of a city in Persia.[1]

Of other examples of the Sanskritization of names of non-Indian or non-Aryan melodies, the most important is Velāvalī. In its original form, which we find twice mentioned in the *Abhilāṣārtha-cintāmaṇi* (Ch. 66, 67), it is *vela-ūllī,* apparently a Dravidian word. Toḍi, sanskritized as Tuḍikā (Toḍikā), is originally derived from Tuḍḍī. Āśāvarī, and Dhannāsikā (Dhanāśrī), meaningless as Sanskrit terms, probably conceal within their modern forms, their original non-Aryan names. Similarly, 'Bhāvanā-pañcama' mentioned as an *upa-rāga* in *Saṅgīta-ratnākara,* is a respectable form of Khammāj rāgiṇī), to be distinguished from 'Khaṃvāvatī', (see notes on Plate CXIV) is first described by Śāraṅga-deva as 'Khambhā-iti' (Vol. I, p. 212) and, then under the respectable name of 'Staṃbha-tīrthikā' 'the sanctified water from the pillar.[2] Names which had no chance to put on respectable garbs of Sanskrit names, are exemplified in Chevāṭī,

(1) In Persia, * * * "the modes are chiefly denominated like those of the *Greeks* and *Hindoos,* from different regions or towns; as among the *pardahs* (*maquams*=rāgas), we see *Hijāz, Irák, Isfahán* and among the *shôbahs,* or secondary modes, *Zabul, Nishapur,* and the like. In a Sanskrit book, which shall soon be particularly mentioned, I find the scale of a mode, named *Hijeja,* specified in the following verse:—*Māṃsagraha sa nyāso' c'hilo hijejastu sāyāhṇe.* The name of this mode is not *Indian;* and if I am right in believing it a corruption of Hijāz, which could hardly be written otherwise in the *Nagari* letters, we must conclude that it was imported from *Persia.*" 'On the Musical Modes of the Hindoos' by Sir William Jones, (S. M. Tagore's Reprint, 1882, pp. 134-135).

(2) The familiar rāgiṇī known under the popular name of Jhīnjhoṭî (jhijhiṭ) has for its Sanskrit equivalents: 'Jijāvanta' 'Jhinja-vatī. Likewise, Māru, a prākrta word has Māravikā as its Sanskrit form.

Gollī[1] Kaccoli, Geranjī and various other non-Aryan names, which should provide, for our philologists, new and rich fields of research.

Some of the names are derived from their associations with the season, and seasonal rites, or saturnālias. To this class belong the Megha-rāga, the melody of the rains, Vasanta, the melody of the spring, the Hiṇḍola, associated with the Swing Festival, and the Śrī-rāga, associated with the harvesting season. The text of *Saṅgīta-Sudhā* (early 17th century) alludes to the traditional association of this melody with Lakṣmī, the goddess of Fortune. 'As it is known to all, it brings fortunes.'[2] Prathama-mạñjarī (lit. 'the first shoots') probably borrows its name from its association with early spring. Other melodies associated with the spring and the summer are, Cūta-mañjarī, (lit. 'the Mango-blossom'), Āmra-pañcama ('the mango with the fifth note').

The ancient sub-divisions of the rāgas into a sub-group of Kriyāṅga rāgas, have left their traces on some of the melodies—*e.g.* Guṇakriyā=Guṇakirī (Guṇa-kelī); Rāma-kriyā =Rāma-kirī, Rāma-kri (Rāma-kelī); Nāda-rāma-kriyā= Nāda-rāma-kri; Devakriyā=Devakri; Śiva-kriyā=Śiva-kri.[3] When music, and rāga-gītis, originally associated with the stage and the drama, derived assistance and prestige from the cults and cult-worships, the melodies borrowed some more new names. Thus, Bhairava, and Bhairavī (probably associated generally with the Bhīrava clans) became the medium of singing solemn hymns to Śiva. Kedāra (a name of Śiva), Śaṅkarābharaṇa ('the ornament of Śaṅkara') and Hara-Śṛṅgāra ('the passion of Śiva'), are apparently names given by devout Śaiva worshippers. Ghaṇṭā-rava, (lit. 'the voice of the bell') is apparently associated with the worship

(1) Gollī is sometimes met with in the form Gaulī from which the transition to the Sanskrit name Gaurī (to be distinguished from Gauḍī) is easy.

(2) "*Atha Śuddha-rāgāḥ Śrī-rāgāḥ*: 1: *** *Vīre rase'sau viniyojanīyo Lakṣmī-pradaḥ sarva-jana-prasiddhaḥ*": 130. *Saṅgīta-Sudhā, Journal, The Music Academy,* Vol. III, Nos. 1, 2, 1932, p. 37. Śrī-kanṭhī, now obsolete, is another melody associated with Lakṣmī.

(3) In an intermediate stage, the names of *Kriyāṅga* melodies take the forms of Guṇa-kṛti, Rāma-kṛti, Deva-kṛti, and so on.

in the temple. Kānaḍā came to be associated with the cult of Kṛṣṇa (Kānar, the Hindī-prākṛta form of Kṛṣṇa). The more significant example of a melody associated with Vaiṣṇava worship is the Naṭṭa-Nārayaṇa (the 'Dancing Viṣṇu').

Many a flower appear to have lent their names to old melodies:—Kusuma(flower), Kamala (lotus), Nilotpalī(blue lotus), Utpalī (lotus), Kumuda (lily), Kaumadakī (appertaining to the lily), Kuraṅga-mālikā (the deer-flower), Mālati (jesamine).

Various rāgiṇīs have borrowed names from birds and animals: Kokila (cuckoo), Māyurī (pea-cock), Nāga-dhvani (the voice of the snake), Haṃsa-dhvani (the voice of the swan), Vaḍa-haṃsī (the big swan), Kurañjī-Kuraṅgī, (antelope), Vihagaḍā=Vihaṅgaḍā (the bird).

Sometimes, individual musicians, princes, chiefs, kings and patrons of music, have recorded their names in melodies created by them, or varieties and innovations introduced by them. The earliest example is the name of the melody Bhāṭiyārī, ('Bhartṛharikā', according to the text of *Saṅgīta-Sudhā* [early 17th century]. It is traditionally derived from Bhartṛhari, the famous prince-poet, the author of the *Śatakas,* who is believed to have lived in the middle of the seventh century.

Of master musicians naming melodies after their own names, the typical example is that of the three masters patronised by Raja Mān Thomar of Gwalior, each of whom contributed one variety of mallār, called after them, Bukshoo-ki-mallār," "Charjoo-ki-mallār," and "Dhondee-ki-mallār." The "Bāhādurī-Toḍī" is named after Sultan Bāz Bahadur of Mālwā, (1556-1570) who became their later patron.

The Sharqī kings of Jaunpur (1394-1479 A.D.) were patrons of art and architecture. The popular melody still current under the name of 'Jaunpurī Toḍī', originated from that area.

With the name of Miyān, Tānsen, the famous Court-musician of Akbar, are associated two melodies: 'Miyān-ki-mallār' and 'Darbārī'. Likewise 'Vilāskhānī-Toḍī' has been ascribed to Vilās Khan who has been identified as one of the sons of Tānsen.

The Sanskrit names and their prākṛta and Hindi variations as well as their vulgarized forms have led to some confusion as to the identity of the names of the melodies and their proper designations. These variations have been given, as far as possible, in the descriptive notes on the Plates. But some of the parallel names may be cited here by way of illustrations: Bhairava=Bhairon; Varāṭī=Varāḍī; Deśākhyā=Desākh; Deśī=Deś; Āśāvarī=Āswāri; Mallārikā=Malhār, Malār; Gūrjjarī=Gujrī; Deva-Gāndhāra =Deo-gāndhār; Travaṇā=Trapaṇā, Trivanī; Triveṇī Hām-virī=Hāmmīr; Aḍḍānā=Ādāna.

Bungling copyists have contributed their share to the confusion of names. Thus Paṭa-mañjarī, before it emerged in its present form, passed through the following stages, Prathama-mañjarī (*Saṅgīta-makaranda*, p. 19), Phala-mañ-jarī, Prati-mañjarī (*Rāgārṇava*).

An example of deliberate transformation is offered in the name Madhuma-vatī (*Rāga-sāgara*) which subsequently figures as Madhu-mādhavī, associated with Kṛṣṇa (Mādhava).

The study of the names, as we have seen, yields important data for the origin and the history of the rāgas. But, they have also their practical uses in correctly apprehending the identity and *rasa*-values of fundamentally different rāgiṇīs, current under similar or analogous names, and liable to be confused by novices and untrained musicians. We have in current practices a group of identical or analogous names which under misleading designations stand different and generically distinct melodies, different in structure, and in emotional significance, which must be carefully distinguished from each other. Under misleading similarity of names, pairs, or groups of melodies embody different personalities, with widely different *rasa*-values.

In the illustrations, and in the descriptive plates, these pairs of "opposites", masquerading under similar names have been juxtaposed, and their different pictorial portraits have been exemplified. It will be sufficient to cite here the groups of the analogous names: thus Toḍī (Plate XV) and Tuḍi (Plate XXI) represent differing conceptions Kānoḍā, wife of Dīpaka (Plate L) is different from Kānoḍā, wife of Mallāra (Plate LI): Rāmakirī, wife of Bhairo (Plate XXXII) differs in conception from Rāmakirī, wife of Mālava (Plate XXXIII,

Fig. A), and also from Rāmakelī, wife of Karṇāṭa (Plate XXXIII, Fig. B): Deśākh (Plate XXXIV), Deśī (Plate XLIII) and Deśakāri (Plate LXXV) represent different melodies; two different melodies are indicated under the analogous names of Lalita (Plate XXXVI) and Lalitā (Plate XXXVII, Fig. D); the verses and pictures illustrating Kedārikā (Plate XLVI) and Kedārī (Plate XLVII) offer divergent portraits; Naṭa (Plate XLIV), Naṭikā, Nāṭa (Plate XLV) and Naṭṭa-nārāyaṇa (Plate LXXIX) embody divergent personifications, and differing emotive values; Sāvirī (Plate LXLVI) and Sāverikā (Plate LXLVII) under analogous names conceal different identities.[1]

(1) In a series of articles published by the author in the Bengali journal *Saṅgīta Vijñāna-Praveśikā* (Vaiśākh Āṣāḍh, Śrāvaṇa 1341) Calcutta, the topic has been elaborately discussed.

TIME THEORY

One of the characteristic peculiarities of Indian melodies is their traditional association with particular seasons of the year, and with particular hours (watches) of the day and night. According to the Indian theory, there is some inherent quality in some rāgas which allocate them to particular season, and attune them to the peculiar atmosphere of nature prevailing during a given season, the melody interpreting the spirit of the season, and the seasonal atmosphere echoing sympathetically to the character and essence of that melody. Very antagonistic views have been held by Indian musicians and theorists as to the validity or scientific basis of the so-called relationship between the spirit of a season and its appropriate melodic interpretation, but the theory has been handed down from a period of respectable antiquity. Curiously the earliest texts throw no light on the subject. The works of Dattila, Bharata, and Mataṅga offer no clue for this tradition. And it is not until we come to Nārada's *Saṅgīta-makaranda* (a Northern text, probably datable about the 8th-9th centuries) that we come across written authority for this traditional association of melodies with particular seasons and hours of the day. It is quite possible that the assignation of rāgas to particular seasons may be older than the *Saṅgīta-makaranda.* The seasonal festivities are of great antiquity. The Spring Festival (with its variations for festivals assigned to special flowers e.g. *Kaumudīmahotsava*—the great festival of the *Kumuda* flower) is, as we know from ancient dramatic literature, very ancient and was accompanied by gambols at the swing (*hindola*), very picturesquely described by Rājaśekhara (*circa* 9th century) in his *Karpūra-mañjarī* (ii. 30). It is quite possible that the Vasanta and the Hindola rāgas were melodies specially associated with the spring festivals. The Hindola is the earlier melody, from which the Vasanta has been derived.[1] Some of the texts identify the two melodies as one.[2] The Solstice-feasts had their appropriate rituals and festivals, with appropriate music, lute-playing, the dramatic appearance of loose women, and the turn of the sun dramatized by discus-play an' by mounting of the swing. "Each of the two solstice-festivities had its *proper* divinity and *melody*, and the melody of the summer solstice was accompanied by drums, to imitate thunder, while that of the shortest day was accompanied by the rattle of war-cars, representing an attack on the evil spirits of winter. The dancing girls round fire, with full water-jugs, and their singing ('a joyous song') were additional popular elements."[3] In this way, the Megha-rāga may have become the 'proper melody' of the rainy season, the Vasanta probably became the 'proper melody' of spring. Hindola, which, literally, means 'the swing', was, probably, associated with, the primæval non-Aryan 'Festival of Swing', and, was, later, appropriated by, and affiliated with, the *'Dolotsava'*, or *'Dola-yātrā'*, or the *Jhūlana* festival of the Kṛṣṇa-Rādhā cult, one of the most popular religious festivals in the North-west. Bhairava (Bhairon) was, probably, related to some festival connected with the worship of Śiva, formerly held in the month of Āsvina (September-October) but now amalgamated with the worship of Durgā (*Śāradīyā Pūjā,* literally the Autumnal Festival). Śrī-rāga (lit. meaning Lakṣmī, beauty, riches, the presiding deity of the harvest) may easily be connected with the harvesting season in the winter when the crop is cut, raised, and garnared. In most places in Northern India, the worship of Lakṣmī (*Śrī*) is timed to synchronise with the collection of the harvest in early winter. Śrī-rāga may, therefore, have been the 'proper melody' associated with the harvest festivals in winter. The melodies Bhairava, Hindola, Vasanta and Śrī-rāga must have

(1) *"Iti Hindolaḥ|| Vasantastat-samudhbhavaḥ|| Pūrṇastallakṣaṇo deśi-hindolo'pyeṣa kathyate||* 96 || *Saṅgīta-Ratnākara,* Vol. 1, p. 197.

(2) *Hindolaḥ*: *"Ayameva Vasantākhyaḥ prokto rāga-vicakṣaṇaiḥ"| Saṅgīta-Samaya-sāra,* p. 17.

(3) 'Hindu Festivals and Fasts,' Hastings' *Encyclopædia of Religion and Ethics,* Vol. p. 868b.

been the oldest primary rāgas, originally borrowed from the season festivals. The relation of Mālava-Kaiśika (Mālkous) to a particular season is difficult to explain. Pañcama was originally associated with Autumn and was later replaced by Mālava-Kaiśika. Someśvara is the earliest authority to codify the tradition of allocating the six rāgas to the six seasons. According to this authority, quoted in *Saṅgīta-darpaṇa* (1) Śrī-rāga is the melody of the Winter (2) Vasanta of the Spring season (3) Bhairava of the Summer season (4) Pañcama of the Autumn (5) Megha of the Rainy season and (6) Naṭa-nārāyaṇa of the early Winter.[1]

The allocation of the six rāgas to the six seasons was never perhaps an invariable injunction and the practice must have varied time to time throughout the ages. Thus, according to the *Saṅgīta-kaumudī*, Vasanta is to be sung during the period between the festival of Śrī-Pañcamī (now identified with the festival of the worship of the goddess Saraswatī) and the great festival of Durgā, and Mālava belongs to the months between the festival of Indra up to the time of the worship of the Regents of the Four Quarters. Various authorities have given varying suggestions for the seasons for the melodies, certain practices are proper to certain regions, and the singers should honour local or regional practices.[2]

(1) "*Śrī-rāgo rāgiṇī-yuktaḥ śiśire gīyate vudhaiḥ*|
Vasanta sa-sahāyastu vasantarttou pragīyate|| 27 ||
Bhairavaḥ sa-sahāyastu ṛtou grīṣme pragīyate|
Pañcamastu tathā geyo rāgiṇya saha śārade|| 28||
Megha-rāgo rāgiṇībhir-yukto varśāsu gīyate|
Naṭṭa-nārāyaṇo rāgo rāgiṇya saha hemake|| 29 ||
Yathecchayā vā gātavyā sarvvarttusu sukha-pradāḥ|| 30
Yathecchayā vā gātavyā sarvvarttusu sukha-pradāḥ|| 30
Iti rāgāṇām ṛtu-nirṇayaḥ| *Iti Someśvara-matam*" |
Quoted in *Saṅgīta-darpaṇam*, Calcutta Edition, p. 75.

Although the six rāgas are assigned to six different seasons, there is no immutable rule, or prohibition to sing any of them in seasons not assigned to it. As the last line suggests, 'singers have the option to sing any of the rāgas in all seasons, for the sake of pleasure.'

(2) "*Śrī-Pañcamīṃ samārabhya yāvat-Durgā-mahotsavaṃ*|
Tāvad Vasanto gīyata prabhāte Bhairavādikaḥ||

Whilst associated, on the one hand, with the seasons, the rāgas are also related to specific hours of the day, or night. Each rāga is connected with a special mood, or passion, and it is therefore fitting that each melody should also have a special time appropriate to it. Considerable mystic significance is ascribed to the singing of a particular rāga in its appropriate hour and some music scholars have recently discovered some physiological basis in the structure of the rāgas which seem to offer some rational explanation for assigning particular melodies to particular hours.

It is in the *Saṅgīta-makaranda* that we find, for the first time, a classification of melodies according to their proper hours for singing. In this text, melodies are divided into solar or daytime rāgas, and lunar (*candramāṃsja*) or nocturnal rāgas. According to this text (Ch. III, 10-23), the time-table of the melodies is indicated below:

Morning melodies: Gāndhāra, Deva-gāndhāra, Dhannāsī, Saindhavī, Nārāyaṇī, Gurjarī, Vangāla, Paṭamañjarī, Lalita, Āndola-śrī, Saurāṣṭreya, Jaya-sāksikā, Malhāra, Sāma-vedī, Vasanta, Śuddha-Bhairava, Velāvalī, Bhūpāla, Soma-rāga.

Noon-day melodies: Śankarābharaṇa, Pūrva (?), Valahaṃsa, Deśī, Manoharī, Sāverī, Dombulī Kāṃbhojī, Gopīkāṃbhojī, Kaiśikī, Madhu-mādhavī, Vāhuli (two varieties), Mukhārī, Maṅgala-kauśika.

Madhyāhṇe tu Varāṭyādeḥ sāyaṃ Karṇāṭa-nāṭayoh|
Śrī-rāga-mālavādestu gāne doṣo na vidyate iti||
Indra-pūjāṃ samāsādya yāvad-dik-devatārccanaṃ|
Tāvadeva samuddiṣṭaṃ gānaṃ vai Mālavāśaryaṃ||
Evaṃtu vahudhā-cāryyair-gāna-kālaḥ samīritaḥ|
Yasmin deśe yathā siṣṭar-gītaṃ-vijñas-tathācaret"||
Saṅgīta-Kaumudī (quoted in S. M. Tagore's *Saṅgīta-sāra-saṃgraha* p. 112).

The following version is offered in Locana Kavi's *Rāga-taraṅgīni*, on the authority of Tumburu:

Śrī-Pañcamīṃ samārabhya yāvatsyāt śayanaṃ Hareḥ|
Tāvad-Vasanta-rāgasya gānamuktaṃ maniṣibhiḥ||
Indūtthānaṃ samārabhya yāvad-Durgā-mahotsavaṃ|
Prātar-geyastu Deśākho Lalitaḥ Paṭa-mañjarī|| Poona Edition, p. 12.

After-noon melodies: Gauḍa and the derivatives therefrom.

Noctural melodies: Śuddha-nāṭa, Salanga, Naṭī, Śuddha-varāṭikā, Goula, Mālava-gauḍa, Śrī-rāga, Aharī, Rāmakṛti, Rañjī, Chāyā, Sarva-varāṭikā, Dravatikā. Deśī, Nāga-varāṭikā, Karṇāṭa, Haya-gauḍī.

Singing melodies in hours not appropriate to them are discouraged and this text asserts that, 'melodies are liable to be killed if sung during in-appropriate hours, and whoever listens to them (at wrong hours) courts poverty and shortens his span of life.' Exceptions are made on the following occasions viz., marriages, gifts, and hymns to deities when, singing unassigned melodies, excepting Bhairavī, does not amount to an offence.[1]

In the *Saṅgīta-ratnākara*, the theory of assigning times, or hours to the melodies is not alluded to, or discussed. Nevertheless, the hour and the season for singing most of the grāma-rāgas, and some of the Deśī rāgas are casually indicated. Curiously, although the Megha-rāga is described, its appropriate season, or hour is not indicated. The following time-table is derived from the text of Śāraṅga-deva:

First watch of the day (Winter) ..	Śuddha-Kaiśika. Bhinna-Kaiśika.
First watch of the day (Summer) ..	Bhinna-Pañcama, Madhyama-grāma-rāga, and Śuddha-pañcama.
First watch of the Noon-time melody (Rains) ..	Ṣaḍja-grāma-rāga.

(1) "*Rāga-velā-pragānena rāgāṇāṃ hiṃsako bhavet|*
YaḥS śṛṇoti sa dāridrī āyur-naśyati sarvadā|| 24 ||
Vivāha-samaye dāna-devatā-stuti-saṃyute|
Avelā-rāga-mākarṇya na doṣo Bhairavīṃ vinā"|| 26
Saṅgīta-makaranda. (G.O.S. XVI, p. 15).

According to *Sangīta-mālā*, attributed to Mammaṭa, Vasanta, Rāmakirī, Gujjarī and Surasā can be sung at all times without any offence :

"*Vasanto Rāma kirīca Gujjarī, Surasāpica|*
Sarvasmin gīyate kāle naiva doṣo' bhijāyate"|| cited in Tagore's *Saṅgīta-Sāra* Saṃgraha, p. 113.

MĀLAVĪ (MĀLAVA-GAUDĪ RĀGINĪ)

First watch of the day (Autumn ..	.. Bhinna-ṣaḍja.
Early part of the day	.. Śuddha-ṣaḍava, Bhinna-kaiśika-madhyama.
Second watch of the day	.. Gauḍa-kaiśika-madhyama.
During the noon ..	.. Gauḍa-pañcama (summer), Gauḍa-kaiśika (winter), Hindola (spring) and Takka-Kaiśika.
During the afternoon	.. Vesara-ṣaḍava, Mālava-pañcama, Souvīra and Takka (Rains).
Last watch of the day	.. Bhoṭṭa, Mālava-kaiśika (winter), Travaṇā.
First watch of the evening	.. Bhinna-tāna, Śuddha-kaiśika-madhyama.

The day and night are divided into 8 parts or watches (*praharas,* or *yāma*), each of the duration of three hours each.

Locana Kavī (1375-1400 A.D.) in his *Rāga-taraṅginī* cites two different traditions, one ancient, based on the authority of Tumburu, another of later times (*arvācīna*) probably based on the practices current in his time.

Morning melodies ..	.. Deśākha, Lalita, Paṭamanjarī Vibhāṣā, Bhairavī, Kāmoda, Guṇḍakarī.
Morning-time melody	.. Varāḍī.
Evening melodies	.. Karṇāṭa, Mālava, and Naṭa.

The remaining melodies can be sung at any time, except that the melodies Naṭa, Gauḍī, Varāḍī, Gurjarī, Deśī are forbidden during the early part of the day, and that Bhairavī and Lalita should not be sung in the afternoon. Further exceptions are offered during the night after the tenth watch. Lastly, it is asserted that on the stage, and under royal command, singing a melody at inappropriate hours does not amount to an offence.[1] The author sums up the authority

(1) "*Daśa-daṇḍāt-paraṃ rātrou sarveṣāṃ gānamīritaṃ*|
Raṅga-bhūmau nṛpājñāyāṃ kāla-doṣo na vidyate"||

of Tumburu by suggesting that the melodies appear pleasant and attractive when sung in appropriate hours, and that the rules have been framed on the basis of the structure of the notes.[1]

II. Bhairava belongs to the hour before dawn (*brāmhe muhūrte*); Rāmakirī to the time of the first flush of the dawn; Velāvalī, to the early morning. Then comes Subhagā (?). After the early morning come Ṭoḍī, Saṃkarā, and Varādī. To the third watch of the day belongs Āśāvarī. To the noon belong Kāphī and Sāraṅga. Naṭa and Mālava are to be sung during the afternoon. The evening is the time for Gaurī. At the beginning of the night, Kalyāṇa should be sung, and Kedāra should be sung late at night. Karṇāṭa belongs to the second watch of the night, while, Ādanā belongs to the third watch. Sourāṣṭra is assigned to the afternoon, Pañcama to the morning, while Mallāra belongs to the hours of the cloudy sky.

Pundarīka Viṭṭhala, does not treat the topic separately. But in his *Rāgamālā,* and *Sad-rāga-candrodaya,* he indicates, —the appropriate time for each of the rāgas described by him, and from these indications the following time-table has been derived:

Early Morning Melodies ..	Śuddha-vaṅgāla, Karṇāṭa-vangāla, Mallāra, Vasanta, Madhu-mādhavī, Kāmbhojī, Suhavī.
Sunrise Melodies ..	Śankarābharaṇa, Turuṣka-Toḍī.
Morning Melodies ..	Toḍī, Lalita, Bhairava, Bhairavī, Tuḍikā, Vibhāṣā, Gurjarī, Pañcama, Gouṇḍakriti, Dhannāsī, Deśākṣī, Nārāyaṇa-Gouḍa, Velāvalī, Madhyamādi, Bhupālī (?), Sāverī, Hindola, Sāmanta, Vahulī.
Noon-tide Melodies ..	Śuddha-nāṭa, Sālanga-nāṭa, Deva-kriti,

(1) "*Yathā kāle samārabdhaṃ gītaṃ bhavati rañjakam|*
Ataḥ svarasya niyamād rāge'pi niyamaḥkṛtaḥ||
Rāga-taraṅginī, p. 13.

	Deśikāra.
Afternoon Melodies ..	Vāhulī, Sāranga, Jayata-śrī.
Sunset Melodies ..	Gauḍī, Revaguptī, Śrī-rāga, Kāmod, Ābhirī, Travaṇī, Kalyāṇa, Śuddha-Gauḍa, Devakri, Sālanga-nāṭa (?), Karṇāṭa.
Evening Melodies ..	Kalyāṇa, Śrī-rāga, Guṇa-karī, Kāmbhojī, Gauḍa, Drāvida-Gauḍa, Sourāṣṭrī, Chāya-nāta, Sāmanta, Pāḍī, Nāda-rāma-kriyā, Varālī, Ravaṇa, Jijā-vanta (Jhijhint), Hamira-nāṭa, Sāverī, Vihāgaḍa
Nocturnal Melodies ..	Kedāra.
Melodies suitable for all hours[1] ..	Mukhārī, Kuranjī, Rāma-kri, Vaṅgāla, ĀŚāvarī (?), Prathama-manjarī, Deva-gāndharā, Mālava-śrī, Bhairavī, Saindhavī, Naṭṭa-nārāyaṇa, Hijeja, Śuddha-varāṭī, Deśī, Paraja-Vangāla, Śyāma, Takka, Mālaśrī.

The Śuddha-nāṭa offers some difficulties. In the *Sadrāga-candrodaya* (p. 18) it is assigned to the middle of the day[2] while in the *Rāgamālā* (p. 22), it is assigned to the evening.[3] Likewise, Bhūpālī, considered as an evening melody in current practice is assigned in the *Sadrāga-candrodaya* to the morning.[4] Similarly, Bhairavī regarded as a morning melody (*prabhāte*) in the *Rāgamālā* is assigned to all hours in the *Sadrāga-candrodaya*.[5]

(1) *'Sadā,' 'satatam,' 'nityam,' śāśvad, 'sadāhar-niśim,' 'divā-niśam,' 'anavarata-nāda'.*

(2) *"Syāt śuddha-nāṭo'hani tūrya-yāme"*|| *Sadrāga-candrodaya,* p. 18.

(3) *"Sandhyāyām rāja-mārge sāradi hayagati rājate śuddha-nāṭaḥ"*,| *Rāga-mālā.*

(4) *"Bhūpālikā prātarasou vigeyā"*|| *Sadrāga-candrodaya,* p. 19.

(5) *"Sadā Bhairavikā geyā"*|| Ibid.

Rāmāmatya, without commenting on the topic, indicates the appropriate hours for some of the melodies in his *Svara-kalā-nidhi* (Ch. V) from which the following time-table has been derived:

Early morning:	Mallārī, Velāvalī, Sāverī.
Morning:	Lalita, Dhannyāsī, Nārāyanī, Karnāṭa-Vangāla, Vasanta-Bhairavī, Bhūpalī.
Former part of the day (*pūrva-yāme*):	Deśākṣī, Baulī Gauṇḍakriyā.
Afternoon:	Śudda-rāma-kriyā.
Latter part of the day (*paścime-yāme*):	Naṭī, Sāraṅga-naṭa, Bhairavī, Karnāṭa-gauḍa, Hejujji Madhyamādi, Revaguptī.
Fourth or last part of the day (*carame-yāme*):	Sāmanta, Śuddha-Vasanta, Kedāra-Gauḍa, Nāda-rāma-kriyā, Pāḍī.
Evening:	Mālava-Gauḍa, Śrī-rāga, Kaṃbhojī, Rīti-Gauḍa, Saurāṣṭra,
Sung at all hours (*sarva-yāme*):	Varālī, Mukhārī Mālava-Śrī, Hindola, Sāmavarālī, Nāga-dvani, Soma-rāga, Ghaṇṭā-rava, Bhinna-ṣaḍja.

A peculiar suggestion is that Bhairavī should be sung during the latter part of the day, which seems to mean, the afternoon.[1]

Somanātha (1609 A.D.) in his *Rāga-vivodha* (Ch. V) devotes ten verses to the time-theory which we cite here from the translation given in Mr. M. S. R. Aiyar's Edition (Madras, 1933 p. 27):—"The Timings of the Rāgas."

"7-10. The Rāgas beginning with Śaṅkarābharaṇa should be sung at daybreak; the Rāgas beginning with Jaithaśrī, in the morning; the Rāgas beginning with Ṭoḍi, in the dawn; the Rāgas beginning with Goṇda, in the noon;

(1) "*Sampūrṇo Bhairavī-rāgaḥ sanyāsaḥ śāṃśako mataḥ*||
Ṣaḍja-grahas tathā geyo yāme'hnaḥ paścime ca saḥ"|| 25 ||
Svara-kalā-nidhi, Aiyar's edition, p. 35.

the Rāgas beginning with Bahulī, in the afternoon; the Rāgas beginning with Saurāṣṭra, in the evening; the Rāgas beginning with Suddha-nāṭa, in the dusk, and the Rāgas beginning with Karnāṭa, in the night. And finally the following Rāgas may be sung always:—Mālā-śrī, Dhavala, Mukhārī, Rāmakriyā, Pāvakā, Saindhavī, Āsāvarī, Gāndhāra, Māravī and Paraja. The above-mentioned Rāgas deserve to be sung successively in their respectively appointed times."

In verses (37-166) further indications are given as to rāgas to be sung at different parts of the day, or night.

In the *Saṅgīta-darpaṇa* (c. 1625 A.D.), the following time-table of the melodies is indicated:

Morning (3 hours from daybreak)[1]:	Madhumādhavī, Desākhya, Bhūpālī, Bhairavī, Velāvalī, Mallārī, Vallārī (? Vaṅgālī), Soma Gurjjarī, Dhanāśrī, Mālavaśrī, Megha-rāga, Pañcama, Deśakārī, Bhairava, Lalita, Vasanta.
Morning (after the first watch):	Gurjjarī, Kauśika, Sāveri, Paṭa-mañjarī, Revā Gunakirī, Bhairavī, Rāmakirī, Saurāṭī.
Day-time (after the third watch):	(Gauḍī), Trivanā, Naṭṭa-kalyāṇa, Sāranga, Natta, Naṭas (all varieties), Karnāṭī Ābhīrikā, Vada-haṃsī, Pāhāḍī.

None of the melodies is specially assigned to the evening hours, but it is generally asserted that 'these melodies (that is to say, the last group assigned to the hours after the third watch) are pleasant to hear up till mid-night.'[2] 'The melodies are to be sung at appropriate hours, following ancient traditions, except that in performances under royal com-

(1) "*Prātarārabhya praharaṃ yāvadityarthaḥ*" (S. M. Tagore's note, in his edition of *Saṅgīta-darpaṇa*, p. 73).

(2) "*Ardha-rātrāvadhi-jñeyā ete rāgaḥ sukhapradāḥ*" (*Ibid*, p. 74).

mand, time is of no consideration.[1]

In an excellent paper[2] read before the Fourth All-India Music Conference at Lucknow (1925), Pandit V. N. Bhatkhande, expounding the time theory of rāgas, has pointed out the two-fold division of the rāgas into (i) Pūrva rāgas i.e. rāgas fit to be sung between mid-day and mid-night and (ii) *Uttara rāgas* i.e., rāgas fit to be sung between mid-night and mid-day. The significance of this classification with reference to the time theory is thus explained by him: "Now it will be observed that in the case of rāgas falling under the first division (*Pūrva rāgas*) the *vāḍī* note will be one of the following notes: sa, ri, ga, ma, invariably, and that in the case of the rāgas falling under the second division (*Uttara rāgas*), the *vādī* note will be one of the following notes: ma, pa, dha, ni, sa. The whole scale for this purpose is supposed to be made up of two "Aṅgas," (parts), namely, the Pūrvāṅga, and the Uttarāṅga. The Pūrvaṅga extends from 'Sa' to 'Pa', and the Uttarāṅga from 'Ma' to 'Sa'. In other words, then, in the case of the Pūrva rāgas, the *vādī* note always falls within the Pūrvāṅga and in the case of the Uttara rāgas, the *vādī* note always falls within the Uttarāṅga. From this you will see, that the proper location of the *vādī* note will enable you to determine whether a particular rāga is to be sung between mid-day and mid-night, or between mid-night and mid-day."[3] The relation of the time to be assigned to the Pūrvāṅga rāgas *inter se* is determined on another principle deduced from the structure of the rāgas. For this purpose rāgas can be divided into three groups: (i) Group taking sharp-ri, -ga, and -dha. (ii) Group taking flat-ri, and sharp-ga and -ni. (iii) Group taking flat -ga and -ni.[4]

(1) "*Yathokta-kāla evaite geyāḥ pūrṇa-vidhānataḥ||*
Rājajñayā sadā geyā na tu kalaṃ vicārayet"|| 26 ||
(*Ibid*, p. 74).

(2) 'The Modern Hindusthānī Rāga system and the simplest method of studying the same' published in the Report of the *Fourth All-India Music Conference,* Lucknow, Vol. II, 1895, pp. 114-147.

(3) *Ibid*, p. 134.

(4) "*Ri-ga-dha-tīvrakā rāgā varge' grime vyavasthitāḥ|*
Sandhi-prakāśanāmānaḥ kṣiptā varge dvitīyake||
Tṛtīye nihitāḥ sarve ga-ni-komala-maṇḍitāḥ||"

It will be seen that the rāgas belonging to the first group, are sung between 7 P.M. up to mid-night, and between 7 A.M. and mid-day. While the rāgas of the second group are sung between the 4 P.M. and 7 P.M. and 4 A.M. and 7 A.M. These correspond to Pūrva-rāgas to be sung in the evening, the Uttara-rāgas to be sung in the morning. They are designated *'Sandhi-prakāśa' rāgas* (i.e. melodies which unify the two other groups). For the rāgas, belonging to the third group, come between the first and the second group.[1]

Thus, the *vādī* note will determine whether a rāga belongs to the Pūrva, or Uttara group, and an analysis of the note-structure will determine during what quarter of the day or night, a particular rāga is fit to be sung. Another determinant element is offered by the use of the note sharpened 'ma' (*tīvra madhyama*). "Most of the rāgas taking a *tīvra ma* in their construction are rāgas assigned to the period between sunset and sunrise. The note Madhyama (f), therefore is looked upon as an *'Adva-darsíka'* or guiding note.[2] This function of the note 'ma' (f) is very picturesquely illustrated by Vyankatamakhi in his *Catur-daṇḍi-prakāśikā*: 'Just as by a drop of curd, a jar of sweet milk is converted to the quality of curd, so by the introduction of the note 'ma', a Pūrva rāga melody is turned into an Uttara-rāga melody.'[3] Pandit Bhatkhande cites Pūrvī and Bhairava; Kalyāṇa and Bilāwala as practical illustrations of this principle. Thus, the

[Report of the Fourth All-India Music Conference, 1925, Vol. II, p. 134.]

(1) According to an anonymous writer, (*Leader*, October, 1925), some ancient authority (not cited) the use of the notes Ri (d) and Pa (g) are forbidden early in the morning. According to him, the prolonged use of Ri at that time produces fatal results and that of Pa damages the teeth.

(2) "*Madhyamenānurūpeṇa yato' sāv-adhva-darśakaḥ*||"
[Report, Fourth Music Conference, Vol. II, p. 131.]

(3) "*Katāha-saṃbhṛtaṃ kṣiraṃ*
kevalaṃ dadhi-vindunā|
Yathā saṃ-yojyamānaṃ tu dadhi-bhāvaṃ prapadyate|| 65
Tathaiva pūrva-melāste madhyamena mi-saṃjnikāḥ|
Kevalenāpi saṃ-yuktā bhajantyuttara-melatāṃ"|| 65
Catur-daṇḍi-prakāśikā, Poona Edition, p. 24.

Bhairava *ṭhāṭ* can be changed into the Pūrvī. *ṭhaṭ* by the substitution of *tīvra madhyama for Śuddha-madhyama.* So, we find that the melodies of the Bhairava group e.g. Bhairva, Yogīyā, Vibāsa, Gunakarī etc., take the *Śuddha-madhyama* and are sung in the morning; while those belonging to the Pūrvī group, viz., Śrī, Gaūrī, Jeta-Śrī, Puriyā-Dhānesvarī, Mālavī, Travanī, use the *tīvra madhyama* and are sung in the evening. The *Sandhi-prakāśa rāgas,* assigned to the period of time which represents the junction (*Sandhī*) of the day and night, use both the madhyamas; one group is sung just before sunrise (e.g. Lalita, Pañcama, Bhāṭiyāri, Rāmakeli etc.) while the other group, (Pūrvī and its cognates) are sung just after sunset.

It follows, therefore, as a result of the analysis of the note-structure of the rāgas, that "Rāgs taking both Ri and Dha komala, Rāgs with both Ri and Dha Tīvra, or Ga and Ni Tīvra, and Rāgs containing both Ga and Ni Komal, will succeed, one after the other, in order of time."[1]

Classification of Rāgas:

Since, rāgas connote different and differentiated states of feelings, or emotive flavours (*rasas*), Indian theorists lay great stress on their relative difference in note-structures, corresponding to their relative emotive significances. A correct apprehension of the form of an individual rāga, therefore, involves an accurate understanding of its differences from cognate and other forms of related rāgas. The grouping and classification of rāgas, according to some principles or other, have, therefore, provided important chapters in all ancient text-books. These principles have varied from time to time, and have led to a bewildering variety of catalogues, groups, and classifications. For the purpose of convenient comparisons, we have set out a large variety of groups, or classifications in tabulated forms, arranged as far as practicable in a chronological sequence in the Appendices, (a list of which is summarised on the page opposite). It is not always possible, without accurate informations as to the note-structures of rāgas current at different periods of evolution, to discover the principles on which rāgas have been grouped, or classified. Various principles of

(1) S. N. Karnad: "Time Theory," Report of the *Fourth All-India Music Conference, Lucknow,* 1925, Vol. II, pp. 202-08, at p. 205.

grouping have been evolved and followed during a long course of evolution which can be usefully studied in the Appendices.

The earliest classification of the rāgas has been based on the number of notes used in their structures, according to which they fall under (1) *Oḍava* (five-notes), (2) *Khāḍava* (six-notes), and (3) *Sampūrṇa* (seven-notes) classes, or types. Dattila, the earliest musical authority of some reasonable authenticity, gives another principle of classification (later followed by several text-writers). He catalogues the melodies under 18 *jātis* (species) of which seven are named after the seven notes and the remaining eleven according to their component notes. This is followed by Bharata, who basing the classification under *jātis*, evolve from the *jātis*, a group called grāma-rāgas, which are generic rāgas themselves, derived from the jāti-rāgas. As the two groups of rāgas are classed under two grāmas (scales), seven under ṣadja-grāma, and eleven under Madhyama-grāma, they came to be designated as ***grāma-rāgas***.

As has been pointed out, "Songs (*gītis*) have been sung long before the rāgas as such were formulated" (Fox-Strangways). By the time of Mataṅga, the songs, or melodies (*gītis*) were grouped under seven classes of which the fifth, viz. the *rāga-gīti* was the most significant, the group of melodies being recognised by the name of 'rāgas'. They were seven in number, some having proper names derived from the names of early tribes, or from ancient culture areas. As new melodies were discovered or accepted they were affiliated to one or other of these seven *rāga-gītis,* which were regarded as root-rāgas, and the new melodies were accepted as *bhāṣās* or derivatives of the root-rāgas, or major melodies. As other new melodies were discovered, or evolved,—they were accepted as *bibhāṣās* (derivatives of *bhāṣās*) and as *bhāṣāṅgas, kriyāṅgas,* and *rāgāṅgas.* The relation of *rāgas* and *bhāṣās* and *bibhāṣās* are akin to the later classification of *rāgas* and *rāgiṇīs.*

We have another system of classification, into *śuddha* and *vikṛta* jātis (species) according to the use made of *śuddha* (pure, natural, normal) notes, or *vikṛta* (chromatic) notes. This is referred to both in Bharata (Kāvya-mālā edition, p. 308) and in the *Saṅgīta-ratnākara* (Poona edition

p. 74-76).

Somewhat akin to this classification,—is another classification of rāgas into *'Śuddha'*, *'Sālaṅka'* and *'Saṅkīrṇa'*. A *Śuddha* rāga was understood to represent a melody which follows its own individual structural form, without carrying the suggestion of any other melodies. *Sālaṅka* sometimes called *Chāyā-laga,* carrying the 'shadows', or reflections of other melodies) rāgas are those compounded of two distinct rāgas. It is a 'mixed' melody, a compound, or an amalgam of two rāgas, a 'hybrid'. In *Rāga-taraṅginī,* a chapter is devoted to describing the component modes of hybrid melodies. Some masters e.g. those in the course of Mān Thomar, specialised in evolving new types of hybrid melodies by combining well-known modes. This combination of melodies is technically called 'crossing of modes' (*rāga-śaṅkara*). Hence, a mode derived by crossing more than two melodies can to be known as *sankīrṇas* (crossbreeds). This principle of classification survives in the *Nāṭya-locana,* which cites 44 melodies of the Śuddha type, 16 of the Sālaṅka type, and 22 of the 'Sandhi' (probably an equivalent of *Saṅkīrṇa*) types.

Then followed the principle of classifying the rāgas according to structural affinity, or resemblance of note-structure. This sometimes involves grouping of similar melodies under one group, or genus, a group of rāgas. The Northern and Southern systems followed different methods, if not, different principles of classification.

When we come to Nārada's *Saṅgīta Makaranda,* we have the beginning of the Northern system, in which the major rāgas are treated as 'masculine' melodies and minor melodies are treated as 'feminine' melodies, affianced, or affiliated to the major melodies. Thus Nārada gives two different schemes, in the first of which he enumerates eight major melodies with three minor melodies assigned to each, and in the second, he enumerates six major melodies with six minor melodies (female rāgas) assigned to each, the earliest enumeration of the traditional "thirty-six rāgiṇīs."

The Northern and the Southern systems of classification, originaly, involved no fundamental difference of principles. In the Southern system, the derivative melodies were called *'janyas'* or derivatives of the major melodies which were called *janakas* or 'fathers' (later called *melakas*, or unifiers). In the Northern system, the minor melodies were picturesquely called 'wives' of the major melodies, and the later derivatives, designated as sons (*putras*), just as in the Southern system the *'janyas'* are in the position of the sons of the *'janakas'* (the fathers).

The Northern system is followed in the following texts: (1) *Saṇgīta Makaranda* (Appendix 4), (2) *Saṅgīta-ratnamālā* (Appendix 5), (3) *Mānasollāsa* (Appendix 8), (4) *Rāgārṇava* (Appendix 12), (5) *Rāga-sāgara* (Appendix 11).

The Southern, or the Carnatic system is followed in the following texts: (1) *Saṅgīta-ratnakara* (Appendix 9), (2) *Saṅgīta-taraṅginī* (Appendix 16), (3) *Svaramela-kalānidhi* (Appendix 17). (4) *Rāga-Vivodha* (Appendix 20), (5) *Caturdaṇḍi-prakāśikā* (Appendix 24), (6) *Saṅgīta-sudhā*.

In the Southern system, the secondary, or minor melodies (*janyas*) are formed, principally, by using in a new combination five or more of the notes used in the primary, or major rāgas (*janaka*), variations being obtained from the primary rāgas, by omitting certain notes in the ascent, or descent.

DEIFICATION AND VISUALIZATION OF MELODIES

There is a doctrine inherent in the Indian theory of melodies which helps one to understand the fundamental psychic values of rāgas, and to apply them to requirements of particular emotional situations, or interpretations. It is believed that each rāga, or rāgiṇī has its peculiar psychic form, corresponding to its sonal body over which the former presides as the nymph, deity, or the devatā (presiding genius, or god) of that particular melody. This deity, or image-formed dwells in the super-terrestrial regions,—the world of musical symphonies,—from which it can be invoked and induced to descend to earth through the prayers of the musical performer with the aid of a definite symphonic formula peculiar to each melody. This idea is, evidently, coloured with the doctrine of image-worship as known in the Hindu-Brahmanical religious thought. By the earnest prayers and spiritual exercises (*sādhanā*) of the worshipper (*sādhaka*), the divinity comes down and incarnates in the form of the image for the benefit of the worshipper. Each image has its definite means of approach, the *vīja-mantra,* a method of prayer through the 'seed-formula', and the deity only answers to prayers couched in the mystic words, or letters prescribed for each, each letter-formula having the mysterious power,—the inherent quality of invoking a particular deity. The application to the theory of Indian music, this doctrine of image-worship, i.e. the idea of invoking the presiding deity, or the spirit of the divinity by means of a dhyāna-formula,—an evocative scheme of prayers for contemplation,—has led to the conception of the forms of rāgas and rāgiṇīs in dual aspects viz., as audible Sound-Forms, and as visible Image-Forms—*nāda-maya rūpa* and *devatā-maya rūpa.* This doctrine, inherent in the theory of rāgas, is casually alluded to in the earlier texts, but is not clearly enunciated in any text before the *Rāga-vivodha* (Pañcama viveka), where, after indicating the appropriate hours of melodies, the author describes the two-fold forms (*rūpa*) of melodies[1]:—"That is called *rūpa* which by being embellished with sweet flourishes of *svaras* (notes) brings a rāga vividly before one's mind. It is of two kinds—*Nādātma* (one whose soul or essence is sound), and *Devamaya* (=*devatā-deha-mayaṃ,* one whose soul, or essence is an image incarnating the deity), of which the former has many phases, and the latter has only one" (M. S. R. Aiyar's translation; the words in bracket have been added for elucidation). The author then describes his symbols (*saṅketa*) for his notations, and describes the melodies in terms thereof, and thereafter remarks:[2] "Having (already) expounded the many sound-forms of those rāgas, we will now proceed to relate in proper sequence, the image-forms of each and every one of them."

According to one text[3] 'the images (*vigraha*) of the melodies emanate from the Supreme Deity (Brahma) and their function is to worship the Supreme Deity.'

According to the doctrine, it is believed that the presiding deity,—the spirit, or *ethos* of a rāga or rāgiṇī can be induced to come down and incarnate (*'avatīrṇa'*—lit. 'made to descend') in its physical sound-form (*nāda-maya-rūpa*). If the presiding spirit cannot be induced 'to descend', the rendering, or interpreting of that particular melody cannot be pronounced to have been successfully achieved. A successful interpreter of a particular melody is complimented with the phrase that he has succeeded in pursuading the deity of the rāga or rāgiṇī to descend (*avatīrṇa*) and to reveal its visual image or picture (*tasvīr*), and to live in his vocal song, or his instrument of performance. No amount of

(1) "*Su-svara-varṇa-viśeṣaṃ rūpaṃ rāgasya vodhakaṃ dvedhā*|
Nādātmaṃ deva-mayaṃ tatkramato'-nekamekaṃ ca"|| 11
Rāga-vivodha, Pañcamo Vivekaḥ.

(2) "*Uktaṃ rūpamanekaṃ tattadrāgasya nāda-mayamevaṃ*|
Atha devatā mayamiha kramataḥ kathaye tadaikaṃ"|| 168
Ibid.

(3) "*Rāgāḥ ṣaḍatha rāgiṇyah ṣaṭtriṃśaccāru-vigrahāḥ*|
Āgatā Brahma-sadanāt Brahmāṇaṃ samūpāte"|| *Saṅgīta-Dāmodara* [quoting *Pañcama-saṃhitā*].

mechanical reproduction of its symphonic structure can put life into the melody and make it alive. And unless it is alive in the song, or instrument, it does not fulfil its purpose. A râga or rāgiṇī is something more than its physical form,—its symphonic structure,—its 'body'. It has a 'soul' which comes to dwell and inhabit in the 'body'. In the language of of Indian poetics, this 'soul'—this principle is known as the *rasa,* flavour, sentiment, impassioned feeling, or simply, passion, or aesthetic emotion. It is this emotive principle, the presiding sentiment, or passion, which is evoked by the peculiar combination of the notes, the *svaras.* For, according to the Indian theory, each *svara,* or note has a peculiar emotive value, symbolised by its presiding deity (*svarāṇāṃ devatā*), and has its interpretive seer, sage, or expounder (*ṛṣi*).[1] Particular notes (*svaras*) have peculiar quality of interpreting particular emotions. Thus, the notes 'sā' and 'ri' (*c* and *d*) are said to be appropriate for interpreting the emotions of heroism, wonder, and resentment; the note 'dha' (*a*) is suitable for emotions of disgust, and terror; the notes 'ga' and 'ni' (*e* and *b*) are suitable for emotions of sorrow, and the notes 'ma' and 'pa' (*f* and *g*) are suitable for emotions of humour and love.[2] And it is the *vādī-svara,* the speaking or the dominant note which determines the character of the *rasa,* or the flavour or the emotion of the melody. The *devatā* or the image-form is the *svarūpa,* or the incarnation of the *rasa* of the rāga. A successful performer (*sādhaka*) must be familiar with the image-form as well as the sound-form. The one is the means to the achievement of the other. And educated interpreter makes the spirit of the melodies live, while an untrained one is

(1) "*Dakṣo'triḥ Kapilaścaiva Vasiṣṭho Bhārgavastathā*|
Nāradas Tumburścaiva ṣaḍjādīnāṃ ṛṣiśvarāḥ|| 37 ||
Vahnir-Brahmā Śāradā ca Śarva-Śrī-nātha-Bhāskaraḥ|
Gaṇeśvarādayo devāḥ ṣaḍjādīnāṃ tu devatāḥ||38||
Nārada's: *Saṅgīta-makaranda* (G. O. S. p. 4).

Another version of this enumeration of *svara-devatās and ṛṣis* is given in *Saṅgīta-darpaṇa* (Calcutta Edition, p. 381, verses 88-89).

(2) *Sa-rī vīre'dh-bhūte raudre dho-vībhatse bhayānake*|
Kāryyauga-nī tu karuṇe hāsya-śṛṅgārayor-ma-pau"|| 91 ||
Saṅgīta-darpaṇa, p. 38.

supposed to kill, or slaughter it. A perfect mastery of the technique is necessary to call up the picture in all its characteristic outlines, features, and limbs, its shades, and colour-schemes. An indifferent technician is apt to distort the features and limbs of the deities of the melodies. This is well illustrated in the legend of Nārada, the great mythic interpreter of Indian music. During his early practices of the science, when Kṛṣna wished to convince him that the former's musical practices had not yet given him the necessary technical perfection, Nārada was taken to a celestial region where he found several wounded nymphs and angels, weeping in great misery, for, their limbs had been distorted and mangled. When Nārada enquired of the reason of the pitiable plight of the nymphs,—he was informed that they were the melodies (rāgas and rāgiṇīs) whose limbs have been broken by Nārada's unskilful attempt to render their true and accurate forms, in the course of his clumsy practices. The suggestion was that if one desires to invoke the spirit of the rāgiṇīs to descend from their celestial abode and live in their physical sound-forms, the latter must be delineated with loving tenderness, scrupulous care, reverence, and devotion,—with all the accuracy of technical performance, as well as of spiritual vision. As the Kinnara (fairy) in one of the old tales of the Jātakas says: "To sing ill is a crime."

It has already been indicated that the sound-form of a rāga is the medium—its kernel, or, body, so to speak, through which the spirit of the rāga manifests itself. The objective of the rāga is the *rasa*—the aesthetic emotion, the theme, the subject-matter,—the *motif* of the melody. As the soul must inhabit a body, so every *rasa* is incarnated in the *rūpa* (form) of particular rāga or rāgiṇī. To invoke the *rasa,* one must mediate upon the *rūpa.* Each particular form of rāga—is suitable for the expression of a particular type of *rasa,* that is to say, each rāga is associated with and is the medium of a particular *sentiment,* or *emotion—its* characteristic and definite *ethos.* A musician should, therefore, have a knowledge of the relation of the rāgas to their associated *rasas*—the form of a rāga being a perfected vocabulary, or phrase to express in a significant and an impressive manner a particular class of emotion. From very early times, a knowledge of this *form* and its *contents,* was considered a *sine quo non* of musical education. It is necessary to realise what the *Devatā,* or the image of the deity of a rāga stands for. Unlike the conception of the innumerable divinities in the Hindu Brahminic or Buddhist-tantric (Mahāyānist) pantheons, the musical divinities—the presiding genuises of the rāgas are not conceived and symbolised in individual image-forms or icons. The *devatās,* no doubt, stand as the symbols or the personifications of the essential *rasa*—the theme, or objective of each rāga. But their plastic representation invariably takes a *dramatic* rather than an *iconic* form, a dynamic as opposed to a static visualisation. In the iconography of images, it was necessary to distinguish the bewildering conceptions of Brahmanic gods—by devising differentiating features of heads, arms, weapons (*āyudha*), vehicles (*vāhanas*), and poses (*mudrās*). In describing, or symbolising the character of a *rasa,* it was possible to suggest the same by an individual icon, or image. *Rasa* is a state of the mind—its expression can only be effective and adequate in a dramatic form,—it lives in an environment and in relation to other realities,—in moods and in phenomena. The *rasa* of the presiding principle of a rāga is rendered through *actions*—rather than in *images* through symbolised icons. The *Devatās* of the world of music—have also their *dhyānas*—contemplative prayer-formulas,—but they usually take a dramatic pattern,—rather than the static iconic phrase—of the religious images. They are the picturization of emotions in a concrete and plastic form answering to, rather than symbolising, the abstract states of the mind. They are depicted in an appropriate dramatic and emotional setting—the *surrounding* circumstances which give rise to the various emotion. In a general sense, music is the universal language of emotions. Music of all races and countries is made the vehicle of human feeling. The Indian system cannot claim a special feature in this respect. All systems of music have evolved, according to each racial temperament, different melodies connoting joyous, sad, or heroic feelings. All phases of Western music have airs or "tunes" answering to various moods of the mind. The Indian melodies have similar connotations. The Vasanta rāga is the human reaction to the joy of life in Spring, Megha-rāga, to the advent of the rains,—with all the exuberance of desire and opportunity for enjoyment. Puravī,—the evening melody, is the lamentation of nature for the parting day. Āsāvarī is the melancholy pleading of a grievance for a just redress. Bhairavī—is the melody of love and devotion. Madhumādhavī bespeaks the peace of love and contentment. Lalita stands for unsatiated love, and the sorrow of separation at day-break. Ṭoḍī—is the surrender of animal life to the magic and enchantment of the beauty of nature. Naṭa—is the symbol of the heroic or martial spirit in man. And so on. We have a complete vocabulary in terms of significant melodies—to express the whole gamut of human feeling in all shades and varieties of moods, skilfully woven with the moods of nature. The special feature of the Indian system of melodies arises from the fact that while in Western music—there is room for more than one moods in the same composition,—each Indian melody has for its theme one definite mood—which must not be departed from, or variegated, or tinctured by the shade, or colour of any other feeling. Each melody is, as it were,—dedicated to its own theme,—its *ethos,* its presiding genius,—its *devatā.* And it is by the prayer of the musician,—the singer, or the interpreter,—who has to immerse and identify himself in the theme,—that the *devatā*—the spirit of the melody is made visible (*mūrtimanta*) in the symphonic form,—the *nādamaya rūpa.* Before he can call up the *devatā* of any rāga—by his prayers,—the interpreter (the worshipper of the rāga) has to visualise the image in his mind. For this purpose,—the *dhyānas* for contemplations appear to have been formulated.

Iconography of Rāgas:

These *dhyāna*-formulas in the shape of Sanskrit verses and quatrains represent the *devatā-maya-rūpa,* the image-forms of the rāgas and rāgiṇīs. They are the sources and the bases of all pictorial representations of the Indian melodies—the well-known 'Rāga-mālā' pictures. In these verbal descriptions—the essential character,—the spirit,—the *rasa,*—the *emotional objective* of each rāga, or rāgiṇī is indicated. Very often symbolistic details of the colour of the dress,[1] the nature of the complexion of the *dramatis*

(1) It was at one time believed that the scheme of colours—in the distinct varieties of the colour-notes of the different parts of

personae of each representation are significantly indicated. In many of these personifications,—particularly those which have the many phrases of human love for their theme,—the principles of old Indian love-lore, and erotics, (*rasa-śāstra*) have been applied—and the personages have been conceived in terms of the classic conventions of 'love-heroes' and 'love-heroines' (*nāyakas* and *nāyikās*)—in all the rich variety of their moods and types. The introduction of these poetical ideas has not only enriched the significance of the musical expressions,—but has, also, helped to achieve a happy and a subtle unification of literary and musical ideas. It is a profoundly expressed truth—that music begins where the language of words fails. It is equally true that in some sense, music is a much more definite language than the language of words. And very properly, music has jealously guarded the frontier of its kingdom from the attack, or intrusion of the language of words. There is an interminable controversy—as to what extent the words of a song embarrass the expression of pure musical values. The intrusion of literary ideas in the world of music cannot but be disastrous to musical expression, and, as is well-known, the literary criticism of music is one of the most tragic things of life. The imageries and ideas borrowed from Indian poetics and love-lore and incorporated in the contemplative verses (*dhyānas*) describing the Indian rāgas, stand, however, on a very different footing. They are, by no means, a description of the musical values but an indication of the *rasa*—the nature of the emotions for which the melodies stand. They are not, strictly speaking, literary explanations but a co-relation and a paralellism with imageries which arose out of the experiences of life common to musicians and poets. It is really in the pictorial versions

a rāgiṇī picture had a significant correspondence to the distinctive notes which made up the structure of the particular melody, the seven colours answering to the seven notes of the musical scale. The theory is very tempting, particularly with reference to the limited palettes of the early rāgiṇī 'primitives', but it is impossible to demonstrate that the artists of the rāgiṇī pictures were guided in their choice of particular colours used by any consideration of the structural, or sonal composition of the melodies they illustrated.

that an attempt has been made to interpret the presiding *rasa* of every rāga in elaborate forms in appropriate environment and atmosphere, with illuminating vision and sympathetic intuition. To those educated in the language of music—and the significance of a musical vocabulary,—these literary, or plastic aids might appear redundant, or useless. At any rate, these *dhyānas* and their pictorial illustrations must be taken to date from a period later than that in which the melodies were discovered, or revealed and were understood by contemporary culture in their fullest significance through the medium of the musical language itself without any adventitious aids from other languages. They may have become necessary for the purpose of keeping in tact—without any risk of confusion—the individual entity of each rāga, and for the purpose of systematising them in a graphic form for educational purposes. It is a notorious fact that from the time musical practitioners neglected the *rasa* or emotive aspect of melodies,—indicated in the iconology and the pictorial illustrations, there has been considerable confusion in interpreting the peculiar genius of each rāga—in terms of its characteristic symphonic values. The psychology of rāgas—being the very basic of Indian music, an understanding of the emotive significance of each rāga was an essential part of the education of an Indian musician, from very early times.

It is not possible to indicate, in the present state of our knowledge, when the iconography of the rāgas was first evolved and the prayer-verses formulated. All the Sanskrit verses surviving to-day, appear to be very late compositions. The existing body of *dhyāna* texts show that they were composed at the time when all the three schools of Brahmā, Nārada and Hanumāna were known and practised. For we have different verse-formulas for all the rāgas according to the three schools. Where the conception of a particular rāga in any two schools is identical,—a similar or closely analogous iconographic formula is used. The verses relating to the original six classic rāgas and 36 rāgiṇīs may be very old,—but as new rāgas came into vogue, Sanskrit verses indicating their character were composed at very late times. For instance, the Turuṣka-Gauḍa—which is very well known to have been introduced after Āmīr Khusrau (14th century) has been honoured by a contemplative verse in Sanskrit.[1] The fashion of composing these verse-formulas appears to have survived much later.

History of the Iconography of melodies.

There is no doubt that the two phases of a melody, the sound-form, and its corresponding image-form, were recognised from early times, though we have not yet come across any reference to this dual aspect in the texts earlier than the *Rāga-vivodha*. The *devatā,* the presiding genius of each rāga is, indeed, referred to in many of the old legends, and also indicated in earlier texts, though the images, or pictures of the melodies are not described in any of the earlier texts.

(1) "*Vīre ca raudre ca Turuṣka-Gauḍo*
Niṣāda-jāṃśo ri-pa-varjitaśca|
mūrtistu nivandhāntare|
Turuṣka-Gauḍa āruhya haya-pṛṣṭhe' ruṇa-dyutiḥ|
Śaṅkha-kanṭhopanītaśca soṣṇīṣaḥ kavacā-vṛitaḥ||
S. N. Tagore, "*Saṅgīta-sāra-saṃgraha,*" p. 106.
Translation:

Turuska-Gauḍa is employed in heroic and martial sentiments. The expressive note is *ni,* and the antiphonic notes are *ri* & *pa.*

The image is thus described:

'Turuṣka-Gauḍa has a complexion rosy as the dawn,
He is mounted on a horse, clad in armour and carries a turban.'

The corresponding Hindī verse furnished by Harivallabha does not agree with the above in iconographic conception: [Turuṣka-Gauḍa is a melody different from Turuṣka-Toḍī]:

"*Aṅga lasai bhukhana vasana Turakhāneki rīt|*
Kahe Turaka-Toḍi hai pive surā kari prīt"||
Translation:

'Bedecked with jewelleries and dressed in Turkish modes (he) drinks with great zest. Such, it is said, is Turaka-Toḍī.'

RAGAMALA TEXTS

In connection with the various archaic melodies (*grāma-rāgas, rāga-gītis*) described in the *Bṛhad-deśī,* the *rasa*-value, and their applications (*viniyoga*) with reference to a situation in a drama, are indicated for each melody described. Unfortunately, the presiding deities for the melodies are not indicated by Matanga, though he cites the presiding deity for each musical note (*svara-devatā*). In the present state of our knowledge of the earlier texts, it is impossible to date the time when the presiding principles of melodies were first revealed, discovered, or recognised. In some of the contemplative verses of prayer-formulas (*dhyānas*) for the melodies, Kohala, (an ancient authority earlier than Matanga and Dattila) is cited as an authority for images, or pictures of particular rāgas.[1] But unless the actual texts of Kohala are discovered and investigated, it is impossible to attach any evidentiary value to this ascription. The earliest avail- Kohala:

(1) Thus the verse describing the 'picture of Gauḍī ends by saying 'Gaudi is thus spoken of by Kohala ("*Gauḍiyamuktakila Kohalena*"). This may be an irresponsible or apocryphal ascription for the purpose of lending a spurious halo by invoking the name of an ancient authority.

The verse describing Gauḍî is cited in three places, with various readings, in the *Saṅgīta-darpaṇa* (Tagore's Edition, p. 83) in the *Anūp-saṅgīta-vilāsa* (p. 160), and in the *Saṅgīta-sāra Saṃgraha* (p. 70). In the last version—the last line reads "Gauriyamuktāti—Kutūhalena" (see Plate XXIII).

"*Niveśayantī Śravane' vataṃsaṃ| Āmrānkurarṃ kokila-nāda-ramyaṃ|*
Śyāmā madhusyandi-su-sūkṣa-nādā| Gauriyamuktā kila kohalena"|| *Saṅgīta-darpaṇaṃ,* p. 83.

14

able indication as to the presiding deity of each melody is in the text of the *Sangīta-ratnākara* (13th century). The jāti-rāgas are not assigned to any presiding spirits, but the rāga-gītis described in the rāga-vivekādhyāya are invariably assigned to its protective divinity. Thus the Suddha-sādhārita melody has for its god, the sun (*ravi-daivatā*), the ṣaḍja-grāma rāga has for its god, Bṛhaspati (*guru-daivatā*), Śuddha-kaiśika, has for its lord, the Earth (*bhauma-vallabha*): Mālava-kaiśika is to be sung for the pleasure of Keśava (*Keśava-prītyaye*) its protective deity. Bhinna-ṣaḍja, has for its deity the four-faced god Brahmā (*caturā-nana daivatā*). Takka (Taṅka) rāga is sung for the pleasure of Rudra (*mude rudrasya*). Hindola has for its lord the god Makara-dhvaja, the Indian Cupid, the dolphin-bannered god (*makara-dhvaja-vallabha*). Kakubha is assigned to the god of Death (*Yama-daivataḥ*); and so on. Though the protective deities are indicated, their pictures, or images are not described in the text of Śārangadeva in any prayer-formulas in the shape of descriptive verses (*dhyānas*) such as we find in the later texts.

Raga-Kutūhala: Thus, the Bhinna-ṣaḍja, an archaic melody, is described in a prayer-formula in the text of *Rāga-kutūhala,* which from the point of view of musical iconography, must be regarded as one of earlier texts.[1] As *Rāga-kutūhala* quotes the opinion of *Śangīta-ratnākara,* it must be later than the 13th century. ("*Rāga kutūhala*: *Caturdhā*: *Gurja-rikā Ratnākara-mate,*" *Anūpa-sangīta-vilāsa.* P. 124).

But the earliest available text dealing with the iconography of rāgas is the one known as *Rāga-Sāgara,* the colophon of which describes it as a dialogue between Nārada

(1) *Kṛpāṇa-saṃbhinna-riputtamāngaḥ*
Kṛta-prahāro'pi muhur-muhusca|
Pino rañe bhāti gavasti-sūraḥ
Sa Bhinna-ṣaḍjaḥ kathito munindraiḥ"|| 180 ||

(*Rāga-Kutūhala,* cited in Bhavabhatta's *Anūpa-saṅgīta-Vilāsa,* Joshi's edition, p. 112. Similarly another archaic rāga, Pañcama-ṣāḍava is described in a verse from *Rāga-Kutūhala,* cited in the same text at page 122, and Takka-Kaiśika, at page 139. Another ancient melody Chevāṭī is described in the same text in the following verse:

and Dattila.[1] It is not possible to assign the development of the iconography of rāgas to the time of Dattila, whose name is apparently invoked here for lending an air of antiquity to these dhyāna-formulas given in this text, under the chapter *rāga-dhyāna-vidhānaṃ.* Whether Dattila is the author of this text or not, there is no doubt, from the raga-system given in the text and the classification of the melodies into eight major rāgas with 3 derivative rāginīs for each (See Appendix 11), that the text indicates quite an early stage in the classification of the rāgas. This system is certainly earlier than all the systems with six major rāgas, with five, or six rāginīs each.

The dhyānas given in this text are simple in conception, diction and style, and appears to be earlier than all the known anthologies. This will be apparent if we compare some of the dhyānas in this text, quoted below, with those collected in the *Sangīta-sāra-saṃgraha*[2] and which are cited on the descriptive texts attached to the plates in this work.

"Contemplation of Bhairava: The sea of notes and microtones, with the nectar of all varieties of rhythms and time-measures, the fulfilment of the desire of the worship of Śiva, with the body always besmeared with ashes, decked with matted locks, with the shine of the young moon on the

Padmābh padma-patrākṣī saṅketa-sthāna-māśritā|
Kāntena tanvati hāsam Chevāṭī parikīrtitā|| 445 ||

Ibid, p. 158.

'With the complexion of lotus, eyes like lotus-petals, awaiting at the place of tryst for her beloved, delicate and smiling, such is Chevāṭī known by reputation'.

(1) We owe the discovery of this text to V. Raghavan who gives a short notice of it in his paper 'Some names in Early Sangita Literature' (Journal, Music Association, Madras, Vol. III, Nos. 1-2, 1932, p. 18). The text is available in two copies in the Madras Oriental Mss. Library, Catalogue Vol. XXII, No. 13014, 13015.

(2) Though the *Saṅgīta-sāra-saṃgraha* by Sir S. M. Tagore is a very late anthology, its collection is based on numerous authoritative texts, e.g. *Pañcama Samhitā* (Nārada), *Saṅgīta-ratnamālā, Saṅgīta-Dāmodara, Saṅgīta-Kaumudī, Saṅgīta - Nārāyaṇa, Saṅgīta Pārijāta.* And most of these texts are not readily available some being in Mss. S. M. Tagore's anthology has been used in this work and cited on the descriptive plates.

head, with skulls as decorations, I adore Bhairava, the skilful Dancer."[1] (Compare the texts cited on Plates I-III).

"Contemplation of Bhūpāla: Seated on his throne, fanned with fly-whisks by fawn-eyed (damsels), I always adore, in my heart, Bhūpāla, along with his group of associated (melodies".[2] [This melody—though akin to the picture of Varāṭī (Vide Plate XI) seems to be different from the melody known as Bhūpālī described on Plate LXXVI.]

"Contemplation of Phaṭa-manjarī: Shining in the bower of vine-plant, decked with a crown and armlets set with sapphires, I always adore the melody Phaṭa-manjarī, attended with a couple of damsels on either side."[3]

"Contemplation of Mālava-rāga: With his hands on the two breasts of a beautiful damsel, with his beautiful cheeks shining with swinging ear-pendants, kissing fervently the faces of the young damsel, I am (thus) contemplating in my heart—the melody of Mālava."[4]

(Compare the texts and the illustrations cited on Plate XIV).

"Contemplation of Rāma-Kriyā: Seated in heroic posture, holding a bow and arrows, golden in complexion, I

(1) *"Śruti-svara-manhodahiṃ sakala-tāla mānāmṛtaṃ*
Śivārcana-manorathaṃ bhāsita-lepitāṅgaṃ sadā|
Jaṭā-mukuṭa-bhāsuraṃ śaśi
śiśu-prabhā-maulinaṃ
Kapālā-bharaṇaṃ bhaje naṭana-kausalam bhairavaṃ"
Rāga-Sāgara, tritīya taranga, Madras Ms.

(2) *Siṃhāsana-madhi-vasitaṃ cāmara-lasitaṃ kuraṅga-nayanābhyāṃ Parivāra-vala sametaṃ manasi dhyāyāmi satataṃ Bhūpālaṃ"|| Ibid.*

(3) *'Drāksā-latāgāra-nivāsa-bhāsuraṃ*
Mānikya-keyura-kirīta-śobhitaṃ
Nārī-yugenā-śrita-pārsva-yugmaṃ
Dhyāyāmi rāgaṃ Phaṭa-manjarī sadā|| Ibid

(4) *"Sundarī-yuga-kucāñcita-hastaṃ kuṇḍal-ollisata-cāru-kapolaṃ|*
Gāḍha-cumvita-nitamvinī-vaktraṃ bhāvayāmi hṛdi Mālava-rāgaṃ||
Rāga Sāgara (Madras Ms.).

always adore the goddess Rāma-kriyā."[1]

(Compare the text and the illustration cited on Plate XXXII-A).

"Contemplation of Ghurjarī: Covered with a white mantle (armour) playing with her companions with balls in her hands, swaying in a dance (?) I worship, in the region of my heart, Ghurjarī".[2]

(Ghurjarī appears to be a different melody from Gurjarī cited on Plates LXXII, LXXII).

"Contemplation of Toḍī: With a glass cup filled with the wine called *kādaṃvarī,* with her beautiful face supported by her left and with her right-hand carrying a portion of the silken scarf of her lover, I also think of Toḍī, in my heart."[3]

(Compare with this the illustration of Turuska-Toḍī cited on Plate XX).

"Contemplation of Madhumāvatī: Holding a cup of honey, accompanied by her confidentès, rosy like the *javā* flower, wearing a pure bright yellow garment (welcoming the gathering clouds), caressing, by the other hand, peacocks (?) I always recall in my heart the proud Madhumāvatī Madhu-mādhavī)".[4]

(Compare with this the texts and illustrations cited on Plates LXXX, to LXXXIII).

Apparently, Madhumā-vatī is the earlier torm of the name of Madhumādhavī and this may be another indication

(1) "*Vīrasāne nivasantāṃ śara-kodaṇḍa-dhāriṇīṃ|*
Jamvu-phala-nibhāṃ devīm dhyāye Rāma-kriyāṃ sadā"||
Ibid.

(2) "*Sveta-kavacā-vṛtāngī kanduka-hastāṃ sakhi-janen khelantīṃ|*
Saṃvara-dimvaka-lalaṃ mānasa-deśe ca Ghurjarīṃ bhajāmi|| Ibid.

(3) "*Kādamvarī-rasa-vi-pūrita-kāca-pātraṃ*
Viṇyasta-vāma-kara śobhita-cāru-vaktraṃ|
Savyena nāyaka-paṭāgra-daśām (?) vahantīṃ
Toḍi sadā manasi me paricintayāmi|| Ibid.

(4) "*Gṛhita-madhu-pātrikām paṭa-sanātha-nāthālikāṃ*
Javā-kusuma samāruṇāṃ vimala cāru-pītāmvarāṃ|
Dvitīya karasādrita (?) prakaṭa samvarā damvarāṃ
Smarāmi Madhumāvatīṃ manasi me sadā māninīṃ|| Ibid.

of the early date of this text.

As compared with the *Sangīta-ratna-mālā* (which according to the citation in the *Sangīta-nārāyana* is attributed to Mammaṭacārya, the famous rhetorician of the 9th century), the text of the *Rāga-sāgara* appears to be earlier. This may be seen by comparing the two contemplative verses (*dhyāna*), describing the melody Deśī:—

"Contemplation of Deśī: Living in a hut of *Uśira* grass, holding a wreath of flower in her hand, of a very fair complexion, clad in attractive robes, I contemplate on the youthful Deśī.[1]

The visual picture of the melody is thus given in *Ratna-mālā*: "With the slow movement of a king of elephant, with eyes like that of a fawn, with a complexion like the lotus, with heavy hips, with her plaits dangling like a serpent, with a frame quivering like a delicate creeper, this comes into view, the rāginī Deśī, sweetly smiling. This is Deśī.[2]

Pancama-sāra-Samhitā: The practice of composing rāga-mālā verses, descriptive of the images of rāgas, and suggesting their emotive atmosphere and values must have been current long before the middle of the 15th century. In a Ms., dated 1440 A.D. of the Pancama-sāra-saṃhitā by Nārada, a complete series of descriptive verses are given of six rāgas and thirty-six rāgiṇīs. (See *ante* P. 24).

It is difficult to suggest if pictorial illustrations, answering to these descriptive word pictures, had been painted very much before the sixteenth century, the estimated date of the earliest rāga-mālā pictures. Although no pictorial versions as early as the fifteenth century have yet come to light, there is nothing improbable in such pictures having been painted contemporaneously with the written verses.

(1) "*Usirā-gāra nivāsāṃ kusuma-mālānca* karām sugaurāngīṃ|
Rucirāṃvarāvṛtāṃ tāṃ Deśīṃ dhyāyāmi yuvatī-kara-susaṅgīṃ|| *Ibid.*

(2) "*Murtistu Ratna-mālāyāṃ*|
Gajapati-gati-renī-locanendi varāngī
Pṛthula-tara nitaṃva-laṃvī-veṇī-bhujangā|
Tanutara tanu-vallī vīta kauśambha-rāgā
Iyamudayati Deśī rāgiṇī cāru-hāsā"|| *Iti Deśī*| (Cited in S. M. Tagore's *Saṅgīta-saṃgraha*, p. 95).

The earliest landmark during the Moghul period is the work called Rāga-mālā by Meṣakarṇa, composed in 1509 A.D. (1431 śaka). It belongs to the period before the revival of Indian music under Akbar. A typical verse from this text describing Bhairava-rāga is translated below:

Rāga-mālā by Mesa-karna:

'White in complexion, clad in white, carrying the crescent, and the horn and wearing a garland, Bhairava is born from the mouth of Śiva, and carries the poison on his neck and his eyes are red. He (also) carries the trident, the skull, and the lotus, and wears jewelled pendants on his two-ears and matted locks. This (melody) is sung by the gods in the morning in autumn.[1] A name of a musical iconographer is alluded to in a single verse. In the *Saṅgīta Mahodadhi,* itself a treatise of uncertain date, the verse describing the rāginī Mallārikā (See plate LXVIII) contains a passage: "She is Mallārikā called by Nṛpa" (*Mallārikeyaṃ Kathitā Nṛpeṇa*"). This seems to suggest that there was a musical authority named Nṛpa who had provided outlines for the portraits, or images for visualising some of the melodies. No other reference to Nṛpa has been traced, and it is impossible to say anything about this iconographer, on the basis of this single allusion.

Nrpa:

The next important text on the iconography of rāgas in the Raga-mālā by Pundrika Viṭṭhala composed in 1576 A.D. during the reign of Akbar, if not under royal auspices. An instructive comparison may be made by considering the verses describing the melody Śuddha-Bhairava, with the verse cited above:

Rāga-mālā by Vitthala:

"Born of the first face of Śiva, with 'ga' and 'ni' in vikṛta forms, using three phases of the note 'sa', carrying matted locks, clad in white, besmeared with ashes, with three red eyes, with a horn to his lips, pendants on the two ears, with the crescent on the locks, Śuddha-Bhairava, the protector of

(1) *Śubhrānga śubhra-vāsa śirasi śasī-dhara* śṛnga-vādyasca hārī
Śambhar vakṛājāto dhṛta-gala-garalo Bhairava rakta-netraḥ|
Dhatte śūlam kapālaṃ jalajaṃ maṇi-maye kundale karaṇa-yugme
Tāram jūṭaṃ jaṭānāṃ śāradi sura-gaṇair-giyate prataresaḥ||
Meṣkarṇa's *Rāga-mālā*, Asiatic Society of Bengal. Ms.

the bull is playful in the morning, in the winter."

Verses from this text are quoted in describing Praja (Plate CVII) and Devakri (Plate CIII). Images of some melodies not described elsewhere, are given in this text e.g. Vāhulī, Suhavi, Jijāvanta (jhijhit ?) and Takka. The last melody is visualised as follows:—'Addicted to dancing, patient (?), with the notes 'ga' and 'ni' in vikṛta or sharpened forms, with two additional *śrutis,*[1] a full-toned melody, having the note 'sa' as its initial, medial, and terminating notes. Dressed in patterned robes, wearing a be-jewelled string on his breast, and a fine crown on his head, Takka is a passionate person, of white complexion, and his body besmeared with sandal-paste, carrying flower globes in his hand, like a clever messenger of love, he roams (i.e. sung) at all times.'

Some of the melodies described have very curious designations. Vāhulī is said to be a Maharaṭṭa lady (? *Marahaṭṭa-vanitā*), and Deśī is said to be a grand-daughter of Ahaṅga (? *Ahaṅgasya papautrī*).[2] Puṇḍarīk Viṭṭhal's descriptive verses are more iconological, and hieratic, and very rarely indicate the emotive significance of the melodies in dramatic conceptions such as met with in the verses of Nārada and others.

The text *Catvāriṃśatchata-rāga-nirūpaṇaṃ* attributed to Nārada belongs to about the same time. The author adopts the descriptive verses given in earlier texts, but also provides verbal visualizations for many minor melodies not cited elsewhere. Thus Vaulikā, and Ārabhī, wives of Śrī-rāga, are thus described:

"Carrying peacock's feather, fond of sweets, dark in complexion and having an attractive figure, Vaulikā shines."

"Always attended by her lover, covered with *nava-*

(1) According to the technical meaning of the word 'gati' used by Puṇḍarīka, it refers to a note which moves from its normal and natural 'śuddha' position to a vikṛta or sharpened form by adding *śrutis* to its normal form. As Mr. Bhaṭkhande has pointed out, "Each 'gati' will be measured by a śruti; for instance 'gāndhāra' rising one *śruti* will be called 'trigatikā'; when it rises two *śrutis,* it will be supposed to have gone up to two 'gatis' and so on."

(2) Āhaṅga may be the *prākṛta* form of *Ābhaṅga.*

mālikā flowers and engaged in drinking, sweet-speaking Ārabhī is thus described."

Other verses from this text are cited on Plates.

(LXXXIII, LXXXIV, LXLIV, LXLVII, LXLVIII, CI, CIII-F, CX).

Like Puṇḍarīk Viṭṭhala, Somanātha, offers in his *Rāga-vivodha* a series of original verses, describing 52 melodies. His descriptions are very terse, and sometimes enigmatic and unintelligible, but for the annotations that he himself provides on these texts. That the verses are not adequately descriptive is proved by the fact that in many cases the author has to indicate in his commentary—the name of the *nāyikā,* to suggest the emotive essences of the melodies described. Of the melodies visualised in the *dhyāna-formulas,* some are of peculiar interest, such as, the Pāvaka rāga, and the Mukhārī.

'Dressed as a cow-herd, playing on the flute, and always in a playful mood, and his body decorated with patterns, Pāvaka rāga is beautiful in bluish complexion.'[1]

'Blue in complexion, under the grip of passion, being unable to bear any separation from her beloved, Mukhārī is a very clever lady, having jewelled covers for her breasts, and carrying a lute in her hand.'[2]

Other verses from this text are cited on Plates LXL, LXLI, LXLII, LXLIV, LXVIII, CII, CV, CVII, CX, CXIII.

Sangīta-darpana:

Dāmodara Miśra, follows the School of Hanumāna in his *Saṅgīta-darpaṇa,* which is a compilation rather than an original treatise. He cites descriptive verses for 36 melodies according to the system of Hanumāna. The dhyāna formulas are identical with those given in the *Nārada-Saṃhitā* and other texts.

Bhāva-bhatta:

Two of the works of Bhāva-bhaṭṭa (1674-1701 A.D.) namely: *Anūpa-saṅgīta-vilāsa* and *Anūpa-saṅgīta-ratnākara*

(1) "*Gopāla-veṣa eṣaḥ kvanayan-veṇuṃ sadā mudā krīḍan|*
Citrāṅga-rāgo-bhāvaḥ Pāvaka-rāga'sito lālitaḥ"|| 214 ||

(2) "*Śyāmā kāmākrāntā kānta-viyogā-sahā Mukhārīyaṃ|*
Maṇi-maya-sukucāvaraṇā vīṇā-pāṇiḥ pravīnoccaiḥ"|| 212||
Rāga-vivodha, (Poona edition, p. 105-106).

(both of them compilations, which liberally quote earlier authorities), contain quotations from earlier rāga-mālā texts. Of these, *Rāga-kutūhala,* and Viṭṭhal's *Rāga-mālā,* have already been discussed. He however cites some anonymous verses, giving the *dhyāna* formula of three of the early grāma-rāgas, two of which are of interest, as will appear from the examples cited below:

"Śuddha Khāḍava: 'Seated at the foot of a tree, with his mind under control, (yet) smiling in company with his beloved, his head covered by a coronet, Śuddha Khāḍava is thus described."[1]

"Gāndhāra-pañcama: 'Of golden complexion, having golden (pendants) on his ears, and smiling in company with his beloved, Gāndhāra-pañcama is under the protection of the shade of a deodāra tree."[2]

Some of the early Rāga-gītis and Bhinna-gītis (a group of melodies as old as Kaśyapa) are visualised by anonymous descriptive verses in this text. Of these the typical examples are those describing Takka-Kaiśika, Souvīra, Souvīrī, and Bhinna-pañcama:

Takka-Kaiśika: "A youth of bluish complexion, with his body besmeared with saffron, awaiting at the trysting-place, at the bidding of his beloved, smitten with desire, such is Takka-Kaiśika."[3]

(1) *"Taru-mūle sthita-cetāḥ priyayā saha saṃhasan|*
Vṛto-ttamāṅga-mukuṭaḥ śuddha-ṣāḍava īritaḥ"|| 288 ||
Anūpa-saṅgīta-vilāsaḥ, p. 130.

(2) *"Svarṇa-varṇa-karṇaḥ priyayā saha saṃhasan|*
Deva-pādapa-śuṣkāyāṃ (? su-cchāyāṃ) śrito
Gāndhāra-pañcamaḥ" || 331 || *Ibid,* p. 137.

The verse for Madhyama-ṣāḍava is a fragment:
"Śūraḥ khaḍgaṃ·dadhat-savye kare vāme sucarmakaṃ ***
ṣaḍavo madhyamādikaḥ"|| *Ibid,* p. 179.

(3) *"Śyāmo yuvā kuṃkuma-lipta-dehaḥ| saṅketa-mākhyāya-kṛta-pratīkṣaḥ|*
Priyā-janasya smara-pīḍitasya| Takko' yamuktaḥ kila kaiśikākhyaḥ"|| 345||
Anūpa-saṇgīta-vilāsa, page 139.

Sauvīra-rāga: "Seated on pure petals of flowers (?), he is an anchorite of great power, in a mood of peace, very thin and delicate in his body, known by the name of Sauvīra-rāga."[1]

Sauvīrī (bhāṣā): "With eyes like lotuses, with her desires fulfilled, but again bent on desires, in a mood of peace, and having the effulgence of the lotus, such is Sauvīrī known by reputation."[2]

Bhinna-pañcama: "Of yellow complexion, with hairs of russet hue, he strikes great terror in his enemies in battles, taller than the tallest, he carries strings of skulls on his breast, incessantly loud and terrific laughters emanate from his throat to resound in the skies,—Bhinna-pañcama has thus been indicated by the learned."[3]

The picture of Turuṣka Toḍī (described by Puṇḍarīk as Yāvanī Toḍikā) cited by Bhāvabhaṭṭa, is worth quoting:

'Very much current in the country of the Turks, carrying white and other coloured flowers, draped in brilliant red costume, Turuṣka Todī is thus spoken of by the sages.'[4]

Sangīta-mālā:

The latest datable treatise to contain *rāgamālā* texts in Sanskrit, visualising the melodies is that represented by *Saṅgīta-mālā* by an anonymous author; it is represented by

(1) "*Nirmala-kamala-dalāntaḥ śāntodāttaḥ tapasvitāpannaḥ*|
Kṣīṇaḥ kṣīnatarair-nāmnā dhīraḥ Sauvīra-rāgo' yaṃ"|| 356 ||
Ibid, p. 141.

(2) "*Bhogonmanāḥ punaḥ prāyo bhuktā rājīva-locanā*|
Śāntā padma-dyutiḥ seyaṃ Sauvīrī parikīrtitā"|| 359 ||
Ibid, p. 141.

(3) "*Pītaḥ piṅgala-mūrdhajaḥ kṛta-mahā-śaṅkā raṇe vidviṣām*|
Stavdhāntaḥ paramonnataḥ paramataḥ vakṣ-kapālāvalī||
Kanṭhe vibhraddabhra-bhīti-jananīmuccocca-hāsaṃ muhuḥ|
Kurvanneṣa nirūpito budha-janair-Bhinnādimaḥ Pañcamaḥ"|| 366 || *Ibid,* p. 142.

(4) "*Turuṣka-deśa-pracura-pracārā*| *Sitā'sitā puṣpa-varaṃ dadhānā*|
Surakta-vastreṇa vibhūṣitāṅgī| *Turuṣka-Toḍī Kathitā munīndraiḥ*"||298|| *Ibid.* p. 132.

a single MS. dated 1778, so that the work may be a few years earlier, say about the 1750 A.D. The work follows a system of six rāgas with five rāgiṇīs each. (See Appendix 3). The descriptive verses are elaborate and not only give a visualized picture of each melody but also its note-structure, and an indication of its appropriate hour of singing. Each verse is followed by a note in Hindī under the title of *Sāhitya gūḍhārtha* (i.e. implicit rhetorical significance of each melody) in which the nāyikā (the heroine), the nāyaka (the hero) and the *rasa* (emotive flavour) of each melody are specified, and is accompanied by two or three examples of old songs in which each melody has been appropriately sung.

Some typical examples from this text are quoted below with paraphrases in English.

'Gauḍī Rāgiṇī: The fair damsel has defeated the cuckoo by the flourish of her word surpassing nectar; she had decked her ears with new sprays of mango-blossoms, having a complexion like the beautiful blue cloud, her handsome body is robed in white silk; her lotus-face subdues the pride of the Moon, (for) the creator used all his skill and art in creating her form with great care; her grace and beauty are attractive alike to the eyes and the mind; (its structure is) Sa ri ga ma pa dhā ni, with *ṣaḍja* as its initial note. Gauḍikā is sung at the end of the day in autumn.'

'Rhetorical interpretation: The heroine is a married spouse of the middling type, she is in the fullness of her youth, and (for the time being), separated from her lord who has gone abroad. The hero is a tender-hearted young man. The prevailing emotive flavour is unsatisfied love-longing. This melody should be applied to emotions of this quality.'[1]

(1) "*Sudhādhika vacacchaṭā vijita kokilā sundarī|*
Navāmra-dala-śobhinā vilasitā'sukarṇe nica||
Sunīla-jalada-tviṣā su-vapuṣā vasanāṃśkaṃ|
Sitaṃ ca śaśi darpahaṃ vadana-paṅkajaṃ vibhartī|| 27 ||
Prayatna-parinirmitā vividha sādhanair-brahmaṇā|
Mano nayana-hāri sad-viha dhatī hi lāvaṇyakaṃ||
Sarī-gama-pa-dhā-nikā bhavati ṣaḍjā|

Dīpaka-rāga: 'Born from the eyes of the sun; by the effulgence of his complexion scolding the flower of the pom-megranate; ravishingly graceful as he rides on a rutted elephant; accompanied by female attendants, carrying round his neck an incomparable necklace of pearls. The melody is centred on the note ṣaḍja, it is sung at noon-tide in summer season.

'Rhetorical interpretation: The hero is a wily and faithless person. The heroine is a married spouse of the middling type,[1] in the fullness of her youth. The prevailing emotive flavour is enjoyment of love-passion. This melody should be applied to emotions of this quality.'[2]

Other examples from this text are quoted in the descriptions of Vasanta (Plate LXI), of Bhūpālī (Plate LXXVI) and of Taṅka (Plate LXXVII).

Rāga-kalpa-druma:

The encyclopædic anthology, *Rāga-kalpadruma* (c. 1843 A.D.) does not claim to be any original presentation of the topics treated in the volumes. The *rāga-mālā* texts cited in this work are borrowed from *Saṅgīta-mahodadhi*, *Saṅgīta-nārāyaṇa* and sundry other texts, and principally from the

Sārade-ntime divasa-yāmake subhaga-gīyate Gauḍikā|| 28 ||
Sāhitya-gūḍhārtha: Nāyikā-svīyā-madhyā-
prāruḍha-yauvanā-prāyuḍha-yavanā-proṣita-bhartrikāhai|
Nāyak iskā dhīra-lalita.|
Ras: Vipra-lambha sṛṅgāra | *isī raskī cije isme*
gānī cāhiye"|

Text published in Kannoomall's *Sāhitya-saṃgīta-nirūpaṇa*, Delhi, 1917, p. 55).

(1) The word in the text is '*svīyā*, which is probably used as an antonym to '*parakīyā*' (another's wife).

(2) "*Raver-netrod-bhūtaḥ sva-tanu-mahimā dāḍimva-kusumaṃ*
Tiras-karvan-matta-dvirada-madhi-rūḍho'ti-lalitaḥ||
Yutaḥ strībhi muktā-phala gaṇāñcita-hāra-matulaṃ
Dadhat-kaṇṭhe ṣaḍje sthita iha dinārdhe tapa ṛtau|| 47 ||
Sāhitya gūḍhārtha: Nāyak:—Śaṭha| *Nāyikā:—iskī svīyā-madhyā prarūḍha jāuvanā hai*|
Ras-isme sambhoga śṛṅgāra| *Isme isī ras saṃvandhī cīje gānī cāhiye*"| *Ibid*, p. 72.

Saṅgīta-darpaṇa.

Tagore's Sangīta-sāra-samgraha: S. M. Tagore's *Saṅgīta-sāra-saṃgraha,*—which has been largely used in citing the texts quoted on the descriptions of the Plates of the present work, is also a compilation, which gives a large variety of *rāga-mālā* texts according to the three schools. The descriptive verses cited are quoted from *Nārada-saṃhitā, Rāgārṇava, Saṅgīta-ratnamālā, Saṅgīta-darpaṇa,* and *Saṅgīta-nārāyaṇa.*

Hindī Rāgmālā Texts: Having taken a bird's eye-view of the available texts of *rāga-mālās* in Sanskrit, we will proceed to make a show survey of Hindī texts, with the data so far available. It must have been realised from very early times in the practice of the rāgas, that the Sanskrit texts of the *rāga-mālā* could only be accessible to a very few of the practising musicians learned in Sanskrit literature, who could study the theory of the musical science from the original texts. The necessity of translating the Sanskrit texts into a popular vernacular must have been felt, with the growing popularity of music during the period immediately preceding the advent of the Moghuls. The Hindī Language had already lent itself to a complete *vulgarization* of the classical 'Sanskrit' culture in terms of a popular folk-psychology, accessible to the general public to whom the academic classical culture was a *terra incognita.* With the development of a wide-spread interest in musical culture and development, a group of Hindī poets devoted themselves to unlock the key to the Sanskrit musical texts and to render them in easily accessible popular versions in Hindī quatrains and couplets (*copaī* and *dohās*). In this way, short popular recensions in Hindī verses opened to all and sundry the secrets of musical theory and sciences hitherto locked up in learned treatises in Sanskrit. This duty of popularising the academic knowledge and culture for popular apprehension was undertaken by well-known and talented poets, and also by lesser luminaries. One would expect Tānsen, (*c.* 1520-1589 A.D.) the great exponent of Indian music, and a Hindī poet of some distinction (who composed several Dhrupada songs in old Braja bhāṣā), should have been the first composer of *rāga-mālā* texts in Hindī as foundations for pictorial illustrations. Unfortunately, his hand as an iconographer has not been discovered in any Hindī compositions visualising the melodies. Of poets of distinction who condescended to write these popular guide-books on music, the most famous name is that of Deo-Kavi, a bright luminary in Hindī Literature. But he seems to be forestalled by another poet, of considerable talent, but whose name and fame was not hitherto known to the history of Hindī Literature. This was the poet Harivallabha, the author of an elaborate treatise on Indian music. His work introduces a new name in Hindī literature, as he is totally ignored in all known anthologies and histories of literature.

Hari-vallabha (C. 1625-1643)

This musical poet is represented by an elaborate treatise which he himself describes as a vernacular version of *Saṅgīta Darpaṇa,* written in an obscure form of old Hindī. The work survives in four manuscripts, the earliest, in the collection of the British Museum[1] and bearing a dated colophon: 'Finished vernacular version of *Saṅgīta darpaṇa* by Harivallabha Saṃvat (1710 (=1643 A.D.), the second day of the black fortnight of Phālgun (February-March) written by copyist Sāranga".[2] The second manuscript written by Khemankar Miśra at Shāhajahānāvād (Delhi) is in the collection of the Sarasvatī-bhavan Library, Benares, and bears a colophon which purports to bear date Vaiśākh Sudi 7, Saṃvat year 1748 (=1691 A.D.)[3] The third manuscript, undated, is in the collection of the Asiatic Society of Bengal.[4] The fourth manuscript is a magnificent *editio princeps,* finally written and illustrated with numerous pictures of the rāgas, now in the collection of Mr. P. C. Nahar, Calcutta. It contains a dated colophon which runs as follows: 'Finished

(1) Add. 26, 540 (Blumhardt's *Catalogue,* 1899, p. 20, (30).

(2) "*Iti bhāṣā saṅgīt-darpaṇ-ka*|| *kṛtā Harivallabhena*|| *Saṃvat* 1710.
Varṣe phālgun vadi duni dine sāraṅga lekhakena likhitaṃ"||

(3) Ms. No. 3 of 23. "*Śaṃvat satrahasau varṣa vīte aṭha tālīs*|| *mādhava sudi tithi saptamī vāra varani vāgīs*|| *Gauḍ Hariyānyā jagad vidita misra Kṣemaṅkara nām*|| *Sāhijahānā vādme likhavāī sukha kām*"|| In this Ms. the *rāgādhyāya* is missing.

(4) No. 791 (7) Hindī Ms. No. 1.

chapter on dancing,—the vernacular version of the essence of music by Harivallabha Saṃvat 1855 (=1798 A.D.) first Śrāvan (July-August), black fortnight, the auspicious twelfth moon, Thursday, written by Brāhmaṇ Giridhāri for the benefit of Babu Meghraj in the District of Murshidabad at Azimgunge near the bank of the Ganges, copy finished."[1] The work is in five sections, or chapters: (i) Musical notes (ii) Melodies (iii) Compound melodies (iv) Musical measures and (v) Dancing. The chapter on melodies *(rāgādhyāya)* appears to be based partially on the Sanskrit text *Saṅgīta-darpaṇa* by Dāmodara Miśra (described above pp. 32, 62) and which seems to lend its name to the Hindī work, which appears to have borrowed its materials freely from other and older texts.[2] As the colophon at the end of each section suggests, Harivallabha gave in a vernacular version the substance of musical data abstracted from authoritative treatises.[3] Any how, the date of the work cannot be earlier than 1625 A.D., when Dāmodar Miśra's work was composed.

Confining ourselves to the chapter of *rāgādhyāya,* we find Harivallabha, following Hanumāna, describing six rāgas and thirty rāgiṇīs. He first indicates the note-structure of the melodies and then gives a visual picture of the same in very rhythmic and melliflous verses of *Kavittas,* generally

(1) *"Iti srī Harivallabha kṛta vākhā prakaraṇa saṅgīta-sāra nṛttyā-dhyaya samāpta| Saṃvat 1855 ādika sāvan mās kṛṣṇa pakṣa puṇya tithou dvādasī guru vāsara likhitaṃ Giridhāri Brāhman ciranjīv Bābu Beghrāj-ji hetārthaṃ Moksudāvād-madhye nikaṭa Gaṅgā-tīre Azimgunj madhyhe likhi sampūrṇaṃ."*

(2) The printed text of *Saṇgīta-Darpaṇa* (Tagore's Edition, Calcutta 1881) only gives the text up to the *rāgādhyāya,* and does not give the complete text which must have included the chapters on Measures and Dancing.

(3) *"Harivallabha bhākhā raceyo sava saṅgīta ke sār|*
Tāme sampūrṇa bhayo nṛtya vicār apār"||

'Harivallabha has composed in vernacular the essence of the principles of music, of which the incomparable dissertation on dancing forms the final, or terminating portion.'

TODĪ RĀGINĪ

containing in its last line *(bhanitā)* the name of the poet. As will appear from the descriptive verses quoted on the plates in the second volume from the text of Harivallabha (with variant readings according to the Asiatic Society and the Nahar Mss.), the poet does not slavishly follow the original Sanskrit verses, but gives an amplified and original version of the 'picture' of each rāga, though following the main outlines of the Sanskrit models. The descriptive picture for each melody is preceded in the first instance by the note-structure of the melody. This is well illustrated from typical pages reproduced from the Nahar Ms. on Plates LXVI, LXXXVIII-B, LXL-B, LXLV-C, and CII-A. Considering the fact that the poet had to conform to the conventional pattern of the 'picture' of a rāga as laid down in the Sanskrit text, he has displayed not only great technical skill in smooth and attractive versification, but has also given proofs of considerable poetic imagination, both in ideas and diction, and his alliterations are mostly made of significant choice of musical words and not of mere mechanical assemblage of a cheap jingle of empty vocables. Harivallabha's chapter on melodies include (over and above the thirty-six rāgiṇīs of Hanumāna) a number of *sankīrṇa* (composite melodies) and *upa-rāgiṇīs* (additional melodies not affiliated to the six rāgas). Some of these are cited with quotations on the Plates LXXXVIII-B, LXL-B, LXLII-B, LXLV-C, & CII.-A.

Earlier Hindī Texts:

It is a matter of some conjecture, if the verses of Harivallabha represent the earliest *rāga-mālā* texts in Hindī versions. For, if the couplets *(dohās)* quoted on the back of the series of rāgiṇī pictures in the Museum of Fine Arts, Boston (No. 17.2371 to 17.2385) and on the back of analogous examples in the Ghose Collection in Calcutta are proved to be contemporaneous with the pictures which have been dated about 1600 A.D., then the texts endorsed on these early *rāgiṇī* series must be older than Harivallabha.

The fact that none of the verses of Harivallabha has been found quoted on any rāgiṇī pictures, would suggest that texts composed by other hands had already acquired popularity which could not be displaced by the higher literary merits of Harivallabha's compositions. Dr. Coomaraswamy considers the Hindī texts quoted on the earliest rāgiṇī paintings mentioned above, as of the same date as the paintings themselves. "We know nothing of descriptive *Rāgamālā* poems older than those found on the paintings themselves, and these are apparently in a Bundeldkhaṇḍi dialect which is related to the language of the *Padumāvatī* of Malik Muhammad Jaisī, which can hardly be older than the beginning of the sixteenth century."[1] The careless and perfunctory style of the writing of these texts endorsed on the back of these early Rāgamālā pictures (designated as S. 1 and S. 2 in the Boston Museum, *Catalogue* Part V, p. 72) do not encourage the suggestion that the writings and, therefore, the texts are as old as the pictures. But certain significance attaches to the fact that the same couplets are quoted on Mr. A. Ghose's Mālkousa Rāga (Plate XIV-B) as on the analogous example of the same rāga in the Boston Museum (see the two identical texts with minor variations quoted on Plate XIV). The identity of this *dohā* quoted on two examples of analogous illustrations of nearly the same date suggests that both these pictures were based on the same text, that is to say, the text existed before those miniatures were painted.

Lachiman:

Now, the dohā quoted on a Vibhāṣā rāgiṇī in the Boston Museum (Plate LXXXV) appears to be the concluding couplet of a string of verses, quoted on a Vibhāṣā rāgiṇī in the Fogg Art Museum (Plate LXXXVI). The author of these verses, as appears from this text and the text quoted on Plate LXXVIII, was a poet of the name of Lachiman: 'Lachiman (the poet), describes king Vibhās' *("Lichiman varnai bhūpa Vibhās")*. 'This is suggested by Lachiman' (*"Karai Lachimana iha upadeś,"* describing the Pañcama rāgiṇī). Three poets of this name are known to Hindī Literature, *(Miśra-Vandhu-Vinod, Pariśiṣṭh,* p. 1566), but we have no sure evidence to identify the author of the verse in question. The style of our Lachiman is very terse and sometimes inclined to be archaic and obscure in idea, reminding one of the obscure diction of Keśavadās' *Rasikapriyā* (c. 1591). The merits and demerits of the style are best studied in considering the translation of the *dohā* describing Lalita [identical couplets quoted on examples in Ghosh Col-

(1) Coomaraswamy: *Catalogue of the Indian Collections,* Boston Museum, Part V, Rajput Painting, 1926, p. 43.

lection and in the Boston Museum (Plate XXXVII)] which in Dr. Coomaraswamy's translation does not reveal the emotive flavour of the melody, and which in our version, appropriately illustrates the situation of a *Khaṇḍita nayikā,* ('one whose love has been dishonoured by the lover spending the night with another and returning in the morning') as shown in the two illustrations cited on the plate. 'It is *not* the visit of the enemy to the hero's wife while the hero is abroad' as suggested (Coomaraswamy's *Catalogue,* Part V, p. 72), on a wrong interpretation of the meaning of the terse and obscure text. 'His lips are red with chewing betel-leaf [*Rāgai (not Bāgai) birā*], his robes are fragrant, or luminous with sandal *(āgar dūti),* the dishevelled state of his whole body shuts out the god of Love' [*"rupu vāriyatu main(u)"*]. These details suggesting a night passed with another lover justifies the interpretation of a *Khaṇḍitā-nayikā,* who is unable in her resentment to utter any words —'after seeing such a sight how can the elephant-gaited one speak' (*"phiri kaisai kahi sakai gaja gāminī sau bain).*"

Deo-Kavi (1673-1745 A.D.):

The most famous name in Hindī Literature which figures in *rāgamālā* texts is that of Deo-Kavi. "According to native opinion he was the greatest poet of his time and indeed one of the greatest poets of India." He was a Sanādh Brāhmaṇa of Etawah, born in Saṃvat 1730, and is believed to have died in 1802 Samvat. He wrote in pure Braja-bhāṣā and some of his verses are believed to be the finest productions of the poetic art. His poetic career began at the age of sixteen (c. 1689 A.D.). He wrote a short treatise on Music entitled *Rāg-Ratnākar,*[1] specially devoted to a classification and description of the rāgas with five rāgiṇīs each. To each melody is devoted a short descriptive couplet *(dohā)* followed by a *savāyiā* giving a more detailed picture with suggestions for appropriate season and time for singing, and, sometimes, some details of the notes composing the melody. As will appear from an example to be cited below, the image

(1) Printed in the collected edition of his works published by the Nāgarī-pracāriṇī Sabhā, Benares, 1912. This edition and the printed text of Bhanu Kavi, *infra,* call for a modification of Dr. Coomaraswamy's assertion that "Apparently, no printed texts of *Rāgamālā* poems exist."

of each rāga is first indicated in bare outlines in a couplet *(dohā)* followed by a more elaborate description in the form of a quatrain *(savāyiā)*:

Lalita *(couplet)*: "Lalita is of a delicate frame of golden complexion, she wears ornaments and robes made of gold; coming out of her chamber in a spring morning, she waits, her mind full of the expectation of her lover. *(Quatrain)*: Dressed in yellow, she carries a garland of fresh *campaka* flower, mingled with blossoms of mango and *aśoka;* she has decked her complexion of gold with ornaments of gold, her voice is mistaken for the song of the cuckoo in spring mornings. The Moon leaving the celestial abode (and assuming the form of her face) has secured the rare ambrosia of her sweet and juicy lips. Lalita is seeking union with her beloved (alternately—the melody seeks the notes 'dha', 'ni', 'sa', 'ga' and 'ma') and coming out of her abode is looking out for him."[1]

Anonymous Text: British Museum Ms. Add. Or. 2821:

We now come to a stage of rāga-mālā illustrations when the texts instead of being quoted on the reverse side of the miniatures (as in the early primitive series which carry on the back, the text of Lachiman) began to be superscribed on the face of the miniatures themselves at the top, in a rectangular space, allotted for the purpose. In the earlier

(1) "*Lalita (dohā): Lalita lalita suvarna varana suvarana bhūṣana vās|*
Madhu-prabhāta gṛhason nikasi thāḍī jiya piya ās|| 37 ||
(Savaiyā): Pīta dukūla dhare nava campaka-phul gare mile amva asokai||
Sonese aṅgani soneke bhūṣana prāta-vasanta pikī dhuni dhokai|
Oḍī sudhā madhurādhara mādhavī pāyo sudhādhara cchāṇḍi surokai|
Cāhati hai dha ni saṅgama ko lalitā gṛhatain cali tāhi vilokai||" Rāg-ratnākar, p. 10.

The word '*oḍī*' has also a *double entendre,* suggesting that it is a pentatonic (*oḍava*) melody, omitting 'ri' and 'pa'. Likewise, the words '*cāhati hai dhani saṅgama*' has a double meaning suggesting that the melody requires the notes 'dha' 'ni' 'sa' 'ga' and 'ma' in its structure.

illustrations, though a small space is left at the top, it is not large enough for quotations of *dohās,* much less of *savaiyās* or *kavittas,* and is used for superscribing the name of the rāga, and the number indicating the place of the rāgiṇī and nothing more (see Plates IX, X). At a later stage, it became the practice to write out the whole text descriptive of the rāgiṇī on the illustration itself, as if to allow connoisseurs to compare and verify if the illustration accurately justified the idea and the situation pictured in the text. Generally, the space for the text for the superscription, pictured at the top, was coloured yellow, so as to offer an effective background against which the text could be easily read. The earliest example for this new practice is represented by two miniatures of Vibhāṣā, and Madhumādhavī in the Museum of Fine Arts, Boston (No. 15.51, and 15.53, here cited on Plates LXXXVII.—A; and LXXXII.—C) which have been roughly dated about 1630 A.D.

The rāga-mālā texts superscribed on these two miniatures are identical with the texts in the almost complete series[1] of rāgiṇī illustrations in the British Museum Collec-

(1) The series is complete excepting the Dīpaka rāga which is missing, but examples of illustration of Dīpaka in similar style, and with identical text, occur in the collection of Mr. Ajit Ghosh, Lala Shambhunath, and other collections. Next in date to the two examples in the Bostom Museum, superscribed with this text, come the three examples analogous in style and with identical text in the Tagore Collection, Calcutta, and the example, Vangāla Rāgiṇī in the author's collection (Plate VIII, B). From a study of the relative styles of these various series bearing identical texts, they seem to answer to the following chronological sequence: (1) Vibhās and Madhumādhavī No. 15. 51, 15. 53, Boston,—C. 1625 (2) Dīpak-rāga (Plate 20, *Year Book of Oriental Art,* 1925),—C. 1630-1640, (3) Three examples, viz. Varāṭī, Vaṅgālī and another in Tagore Collection, Calcutta, C. 1650, (4) Vaṅgāla rāgiṇī, Author's Collection (Plate VIII, B of this work),—C. 1650, (5) Dīpak rāga (Plate LVIII, A), and Kāmode (Plate XLVIII, B),—C. 1660, (6) Lala Sambhunath Collection (Plates XIV, C; XV, B; XXVII, C; XXXVI, C &c.),—C. 1675 (7) British Museum series Ms. Add. Or. 2821—C. 1700 (8) Lipperheide Library, Berlin, (Plates XII, C; XXII, D; XXVI, D;)—C. 1800.

tion being Ms. Add. Or. 2821, nearly all of which have been cited in the plates volume of this work. The text by an anonymous poet, quoted in this series, has been the most popular text used by illustrators of rāgamālās, through several centuries. If the estimate of the date of the two miniatures in the Boston Museum (15.51, 15.53) is correct, the text of this anonymous poet must be earlier than 1630, that is to say, earlier than the text of Harivallabha, discussed above. The popularity of the anonymous text, (which could not be superceded by the numerous series of illustrations, which bear quotations from it, viz. (1) British Museum Ms. Add. Or. 2821, (2) Lala Sambhunath Collection, Jaipur, (3) Jaipur Museum Collection, (4) Ajit Ghose Collection (stray examples), (5) Collection of Mr. S. Gangoly, Baroda, stray examples (Plate LXXXI), (6) Author's Collection, (stray examples), (7) Lipperheid'sche Bibliothek, Berlin, 1474 (stray examples), and numerous stray examples in various private collections. In one or two instances *dohās* from this anonymous text have been cited on the back of the early rāga-mālā pictures e.g., Vasanta rāgiṇī, Metropolitan Museum (Plate LX, B). This would lend support to the assertion that in some cases, at least, the texts were added later. The text on the back of the Vasanta rāgiṇī which we reproduce on the page opposite is so clumsy and careless as to preclude a supposition of its being contemporary with the miniature. One peculiarity of the text under discussion is its independent and original treatment of the themes. While the versions of Harivallabha keeps to the main outlines of the pictures and also, invariably, to the significant vocabulary of the Sanskrit text, as we have pointed out, the anonymous text shows a complete detachment from the Sanskrit models, though conforming to essential iconographic details and particulars of emotive significances. There is no verbal correspondence with the vocabulary of Sanskrit text such as we meet with in the text of Harivallabha. This may be easily demonstrated by considering the three versions (one Sanskrit and two Hindī texts) cited in the descriptions to Vangāli rāgiṇī (Plate VIII). It will be seen that Harivallabha not only reproduces the imageries but actually borrows several words from the Sanskrit model (*triśūla, karaṇḍa, vāma-hasta, taruṇārka-varṇa*), which the anonymous text absolutely ignores. The author gives an independent version, altogether allowing his own imagination to weave pictures, imageries and details to realise the main essences of the themes. Thus, in calling up the picture of a Yoginī, a female ascetic, performing asterities, the poet makes her sit on a rug of deer-skin in a shining temple, or a monastery, situated in a lonely forest, where the ascetic has retired, away from the haunts of men. The picture of the forest called up by the poet includes the necessary details of a group of frisking monkey,[1] and a live lion seated near her *(maṭha siva tala siṃhaju vaiṭhāi)'*. None of the Sanskrit texts suggests a lion—which is the poet's own independent contribution to complete the picture of a lonely forest. The lion is not an essential iconographic detail required by the original *dhyāna*-formulas, but an innovation of the poet whom the artist has slavishly followed. It follows, therefore, that the illustrators had for their literary guidance the Hindī version of this anonymous text, and not the Sanskrit text of the authoritative treatises. Indeed, with rare exceptions,[2] the illustrations invariably quote Hindī, but not Sanskrit texts. The popular demand for the Hindī texts naturally called for poetic efforts on the part of several versifiers who came forward with original *dohās* and *savayiās* giving graphic word pictures of the emotive and dramatic features of the melodies for the benefit of the pictorial artists.

We, therefore, come across various other groups of texts, some composed by poets whose names are attached to the poems, while others are by anonymous poets. A series of thirty-six illustrations in the British Museum (Or. Add. 26550 folios 1-36) are superscribed with texts in Braj-bhāṣā, written on a yellow grounded scroll enclosed within a decorative panel. The author of these verses has since been identified[3] as a poet of the name of Lāl, as his name occurs in the verses on the folios 10, 11 and 12 des- Lāl Kavi:

(1) A group of monkeys occurs in the version of Vaṅgāla rāgiṇī in the Collection of Lala Sambhunath not, here, reproduced.

(2) Sanskrit texts are superscribed on the following examples: Ṭoḍī (Plate XV-C), Sāraṅga (Plate LXXXVIII-A).

(3) Blumhardt (*Catalogue of the Hindī, Panjabi, and Hindustāni Ms. in the British Museum,* 1899, p. 61) mistook an adjective describing the heroine, viz, *obhirām* as the author of the poem.

cribing Mālaśrī, Rāmkelī and Guṇakelī. 'Lāla says: she is the rāginī of Malkous' ("*Lāla kahai Mālakosaki rāgiṇī*," P. XXXII). Other examples from this text (not containing the author's name) are quoted on plates descriptive of Bhairava (Plate III), of Gurjarī (Plate LXXII), of Pañcama (Plate LXXVIII), of Seta-malār (Plate LXX), of Vilāvala (Plate XXXVIII), of Dīpaka (Plate XLI), of Mālaśrī (Plate LIV), of Śrī-rāga (Plate LIII), of Naṭa (Plate XLIV). That Lāl Kavi's text won some amount of popularity with the illustrators is proved by the fact that his *Kavittas* are quoted in more than one series of miniatures. Thus, we find, they are quoted on another series of miniatures in the British Museum (Pers. Ms. Or. 8839, bequeathed by Baroness Zoucha and presented by Lord Curzon), late in style, and with oblong panels, flanked with square knob-decorations containing the text, one of which (with an illustration) is cited here (Plate XXIII). Indentity of the texts in the two series is further supported by the verses cited for Kakubha (Plate XXVII). The same text is also quoted in an analogous series, also late in style, in the British Museum (Pers. Ms. Or. No. 8838, presented by Lord Curzon, 13th October, 1917) of which an example, Megha-mallāra (f. 31) is cited here (Plate LXIV, C). Yet a third series appears to quote the same text, as will appear from a stray example, a Kedāra rāgiṇī, cited here, from the author's collection (Plate CIII—H). As will appear from the last line of the illegible text, it contains the name of the poet.

As may be judged from examples cited on the above plates and the simple diction of the verses, free from obscurities, this series of Hindī texts remind one of the grace and beauty of the text of Harivallabha, with whom Lāl Kavi appears to have occasional correspondence in ideas and in words. Without a comparative study of the style and of philological and phonetic pecularities, it is difficult to say if the author of this rāga-mālā text is identical with the court poet of Bundela Rājā Chhatraśāl who espoused the cause of Aurangzib and fought against Dara Shuko at the battle of Dholpur (1658 A.D.).[1] The style of the miniatures

(1) Lāl Kavi wrote a ballad on this battle in Kanauji dialect

of the *rāga-mālā* pictures (B.M. Add. 26550) is very clumsy and mechanical and cannot be earlier than the middle of the 19th century. Lāl Kavi's text is of iconographic value as it helps to identify certain versions of rāgiṇīs different from other pictorial patterns. The literary merit of his verses may be judged from a typical quatrain describing Bhairava rāga (Plate III) and the one describing Pañcama rāgiṇī quoted on Plate LXXVIII.

Peāray Rangalāl:

Particular interest attaches to an incomplete series of six rāgiṇī pictures in the British Museum (Add. 21934, Blumhardt, *Catalogue*, 95, p. 62). In the first place, these miniatures are signed by artists of whom we get the following names: Pañcama (the 4th rāgiṇī of Vasanta rāg) by Sītaldās (Plates LXXVIII, D); Gaurī (the 4th rāgiṇī of Śrī-rāg) Girdhārī Lāl (Plates XXIII, A); Devagāndhārī (the 1st rāgiṇī of Śrī-rāg) by Sītal Dās (Plates LXLI, D); Śrī-rāga (the 3rd rāga) by Bāhādur Singh (Plates LII, C); Hindola (the 5th rāga) by Bāhādur Singh (Plate XXXI, A); Megha-mallār (the 2nd rāga) by Sītal Dās (Plate LXLI, D); Śrī-rāga (the 3rd rāga) by Bāhādur Singh (Plate LII, C); Hindola (the 5th rāga) by Bāhādur Singh (Plate XXXI, A); Megha-mallār (the 2nd rāga) by the Sītal Dās (Plate LXV, B). The versions of these melodies as illustrated in these miniatures are peculiar conceptions different from their usual types, and they offer very valuable examples of these peculiar versions. In the second place, each of these six miniatures bears on the top in a rectangular space allotted for the purpose, a Hindī verse, descriptive of the rāgiṇī, composed by a poet named Peāray Raṅgalāl, whose name is given in the last line. In the quatrain for Gourī cited on Plate XXIII—A, he signs his name, simply, as 'Raṅgalāl'. If he is the same poet as is noticed in *Miśra-vandhu-vinode* (p. 762) he lived about Saṃvat 1807 (1754 A.D.) and wrote his poems under the patronage of Surajamul Raja of Bharatpur.[1] The style of the pictures which follows the

entitled. *'Chhatraśāl kī laḍāī'* (Blumhardt, *Op. Cit*, p. 35). He also wrote a poem describing the love of heroes and heroines (*nāyikā*) called "Viṣṇu-vilās".

(1) Without a careful comparison of phonetic and stylistic peculiarities it is not possible to identify the *protegé* of Surajmull with Peāray Raṅgalāl, the author of this rāgamālā text.

manners of the late Moghul miniatures does not take us earlier than the nineteenth century. Probably these examples are copies of earlier versions. The illustrations were evidently painted to justify the peculiar versions indicated in the Hindī texts. The style of Peāray Raṅgalāl, in spite of the pretentious and long-winded rhythm of his verses, is somewhat heavy, artificial and turbid and lacks the grace and easy flow of the earlier rāga-mālā texts. We have no certain data as to the date of this text, unless we can identify him with Raja Surajmall's court-poet.

Vrajanāth: Two stray examples of rāgiṇī miniatures, Gunakalī (Plate XXIV, C) and Deśākhī (Plate XXXV) in the Collection of Mr. P. S. Nahar, furnish two interesting quartrains, one of them bearing the name of the poet Vrajanāth. It is a name known to Hindī literature and he is probably the same poet as is cited in *Miśra-vandhu vinode* (Vol. II, p. 167). He was born in Saṃvat 1780 (1727 A.D.) and his literary activity dates from Saṃvat 1810 (1757 A.D.). He was the author of a treatise on Rāgamālā, from which apparently the verses quoted on the reverse of the two miniatures have been quoted. The Miśra brothers characterise him as a poet of average merit (*sāḍhāran śreṇī*). To judge from the two *coupaīs* available to us, the poet appears to have been capable of giving vivid descriptions, in strong and effective diction, not entirely devoid of some charm and an easy flow.

A complete set of rāga-mālā text is cited on a complete series of pictures which, at one time, belonged to a dealer in Jaipur (here cited as 'Jaipur Private Collection'). This series (cited here in twelve examples: Plates II, VII, XII, XIII, LVI, LVII, LVIII, LXII, LXXV, LXXVI, LXXVII) of miniatures are not of much aesthetic merit, (though the treatment of the trees is quite distinctive), being apparently copies of better versions. But their interest lies in the fact that they have helped to fill up one or two gaps which occur in the available series of complete illustrations. As a rule, complete series of rāgiṇī pictures are now almost impossible to obtain. This series (the present *provenance* of which is unknown) offers an illustration of Taṅka rāgiṇī (Plate LXXVII) of which only one other illustration has been traced. The author of this text, who has composed the descriptions in *modaka chanda*, gives his name twice, once in the *copāi* and once in the terminating *dohā* describing Deskārī rāgiṇī (Plate LXXV, D): 'Paidā says: She is fond of pleasing her lover'; 'To be sung in the fourth hour, so says Paidā.' After giving a description of each melody, the poet indicates in the closing couplet, the note-structure of the melody and the appropriate time and season for its singing. The style of the poet is simple and devoid of flourish, or ornamentations. The quality of his verse may be judged from a typical *copāi,* describing Māru rāgiṇī (Plate LVII). He seems to have been a mediocre versifier, not having found a place in anthologies and his name is not noticed by any compilers of Hindī poems.

Anonymous text:

An anonymous Hindī text, is quoted on a series of rāgamālā pictures formerly in the Mouji Collection (Bombay) now dispersed. They were published, along with the miniatures, in a series of articles in a Gujerati Journal[1] from which we cite here, two typical quotations, describing Dīpaka and Deśī:

"Mounted on an elephant, surrounded by a bevy of young damsels, with gaits of elephants, his complexion is rosy, his robes are scarlet, he carries garlands made of pearls. His dress is beautiful, his hair dishevelled, he sings in auspicious words like the bee in a grove, such is Dīpaka to be understood.[2]

"Dressed in blue, and of shining complexion, she is standing near her lord, carrying a fan, full of desire for dalliance. She is burned by passion and has a voice like the cuckoo which captivates the heart of her beloved. Proud of her youth, and full of joy, she is called Deśī rāgiṇī"[3]

(1) "*Suvarṇa-mālā,*" a quarterly journal, in English and Guzerati, edited and published by Pursuttom Visraṁ Mouji, 1923-1926.

(2) "*Sauhata gaja pīṭha parana āvṛta gana (gaja)-kāmanī*
Āruna tana lāla vasana māla mugatakī vanī|
Vesa subhaga kesa khulita gāvata subha vāniyen
Kunjana madhi guñja madhupa Dīpaka yaha jāniyen"||

(3) "*Nīla vasana goura ṣutana sovata patīpain* (?) *kharī*
Āmrana tana pāṇi añjana cāha ramanakī bharī|
Rūpa rasika gāvana pīka prītama manamohanī
Jovana mata rījhata cita Desi kahata rāgaṇī||" *Suvarṇa-mālā* Vol. I, No. 4, p. 32-33, 1924.

Both the text and the miniatures are late versions not ante-dating the middle of the nineteenth century.

Rāg-kutūhal by kavi Rādhā-krsna:

To the third quarter of the eighteenth century belongs an interesting Hindī text which provides some very attractive verses for rāga-mālā illustrations. It is a short treatise called *Rāga Kutūhala* composed by a Gauḍa Brahmin of Jayanagar named Rādhā Kṛṣṇa (Kavi-Kṛṣṇa), under the patronage of Prince Bhīm Singh of Unyiār-gaḍ (Jaipur State). It bears a colophon[1] dated Saṃvat 1853 (1781 A.D.). It gives a general survey of the theories of Hindu music and also describes the 'pictures' of the melodies ("*Kahaun rīti saṅgīta kī, rāga-rūpa darasāi*"). It survives so far as we can gather in a single manuscript,[2] which has not yet been published. The rāga-mālā text of this poet has, however, been utilised and published by Bhānu-Kavi in his *Kāvya-prabhākar*. And we have quoted several verses from this text (Plates VII, X, XIII, XIX, XXV, XXVIII, XXX, XXXII, XXXIV, XXXVII, XXXIX, XLIII, XLIV, XLIX ,LXI, LXIII, LXIV, LXVII, LXXVI, and LXXVII) to indicate the high merit of these rāga-mālā verses. The composition of this text proves that the demand for rāga-mālā texts and pictures had continued unabated, at any rate, as late as the end of the eighteenth century. We have not, however, been able to trace any, miniatures which have utilized the excellent verses of Rādhā Kṛṣṇa. Whether they have offered materials for pictorial illustrations or not, the verses are very distinguished compositions of their kind and are marked by qualities of ideas, imageries, and dictions very rarely met with in the average level of rāga-mālā texts. We

(1) "*Saṃvat guṇa sara vasu mahī mās anūp|*
Sudi pācai ravi-vara-yuta bhayou prantha sukha-rūp||"

(2) The work is described from a Ms. by Kunwar Brajendra Sinha of Dholpur in an article entitled "Rāg-Kutūhala", published in the Hindī Journal *Sarasvatī*, November 1933, pp. 425-26. I am indebted to the writer of the article for other informations connected with this text. He has cited from *Rāg-Kutūhala* six descriptive verses on the iconography of Bhairava, Mālkous, Des, Bhūpālī, Deśkārī, and Śyām. On comparison of these verses with the text borrowed in *Kāvya-prabhākara*, we find slight variations in readings which suggest that Bhānukavi had used some other Ms. of the text.

have, therefore, frequently quoted from this text for the purpose of affording comparison with the earliest and the latest poetical efforts on this topic, though the quotations have been made under the erroneous assumption that they are works of Bhānu Kavi, the author of *Kāvya-prabhākar*. As typical examples of the qualities of his verses one may particularly study the *savaiyās* on Toḍī (Plate XIX) and Kakubha (Plate XXVIII) which are marked by remarkable depth of feeling and also by considerable technical skill.

We quote here from the text of *Rāg-Kutūhala* two more verses, not cited on the descriptions of the plates:

"Bhairava: On his matted locks the Ganges sparkle and play; his large forehead is clasped by snakes; his three eyes offer emancipation from all woes; and round his face the earpendants dangle; his body, smeared with ashes, carries ornaments provided by snakes; and his hands carry the trident, and the drum which he beats; it is the incomparable picture of Sadā-Śiva (a gracious aspect of the God). The melody of Bhairava shines as a great masterpiece (picture)."[1]

'Śyām: Her body shines with the beauty of clouds; she has snatched away the picture of the figure of Kṛṣṇa (Ghana-śyām). The glitter of her yellow robes is full of beauty; she has decked her brow with specks of saffron. The damsel dallies in sweet smiles which raise new desires in one's heart. Such is the great melody Śyām, carrying a wreath of jewels round her neck,—a captivating beauty,—as the incarnation of Cupid.'[2]

(1) "*Sīsa jaṭā sira saṅga umaṅgati, bhāla visāla mayaṅka virājai|*
[v.r. pīta jaṭā sira gaṅga umaṅgata (Kāvya-prabākara)]
Locana tīni lasain dukha-mocana, ānana kānana kuṇḍala rājai|
Aṅga vibhūti dharai ahi-bhuṣana, sūla liye kara damarū (v.r. bhairava) vājai
Rūpa anūpa Sadā-śiva-mūrati, Bhairava-rāga mahā chavi chaājai||"
Rāg-kutūhala (*Sarasvatī*, Nov. 1933, p. 426).

(2) "*Śyām: Tan syām-ghaṭā abhirāma lasai,*
Ghana-syām ghaṭā-chavi chīni laī|
Ati sobhita pīt dukūlani kī duti,
Kum-kuma-vindu lilāṭa daī|

If we judge by a comparison of the verse describing Mālkous rāga as cited from *Rāg-Kutūhala* with the verse cited by us from a Ms. of the text of Harivallabha (Plate XIV: Hindī text: Harivallabha As. So. Ms.) we find that Rādhākṛṣṇa has sometimes adopted the text of Harivallabha. In the case of Mālkous, the verses are identical except in the two concluding lines.[1]

Gangādhar:

A late text of Rāgamālā which we owe to an author named Gangādhar, is a small treatise of 27 verses. It was composed in Samvat 1855 Chait vadi 2 (April, 1798 A.D.).[2] According to the system followed, the author accepts the following major rāgas: Bhairava, Mālkous Hindola, Dīpaka, Śrī-rāga and Megha-rāga. The rāgiṇīs are those given in the scheme of Hanumān (Appendix 7). Each of the six rāgas are described in a *dohā* followed by a *savaiyā,* while the rāgiṇīs are described in short and simple *dohās.* We cite here four illustrative examples:—

"Now, the image of the melody Mālkous: Malkous wears

Mṛdu hāsa-vilāsa karai vanitā,
Ura main umagai abhilāṣa naī|
Vaha syām visāl garai mani-māl,
Manohara mūrati main-maī||"..*Ibid,* p. 426.

The above verse is not cited in Bhānu-Kavi's *Kāvya-prabhākar.*

(1) "*Mālkous: Tana jovana jora marorani soun*
Rasa-vīra chakeo mana dhīra dharai|
Kara-mai karavāl liye chavi soun
Paṭa lāla pravālakī joti harai|
Rati koka-kalā paravīna mahā
Dṛga dekhata rūp anupa bharai
Yahi Mālai kos udata kiye
Aravindo-prasūna kī māla gai"|| *Ibid,* p. 426.

(2) It has been printed as the second part of Rāga-ratnākar, a collection of Hindī Hymns published by Khemraj Kṛsna Das in the Vyankatesvara Press, Bombay 1893. In the colophon which gives the date, the author states that with six rāgas and 30 rāgiṇīs they make up 36 melodies. But Miyā Tānsen has sung about 111 melodies'. The writer is indebted to Rai Bahadur Bishan Swarup of the discovery of the treatise, and the name of the author, which is not given in the work itself but is gleaned from a reference in another work dated 1874.

a robe of blue, he holds a white staff in his hand. He wears on his shoulders a string of pearls, he is accompanied by a number of lady companions. Dressed in blue robe, his shining complexion puts to shame the prince of Kausaka(?) With garlands on his shoulders and a white staff in hand he is the very picture of the purity of the flavour of Love. He overpowers the heart of women, and by his beauty attracts the gaze of all. At early dawn he is up and seated. Hero and Lover, he is contemplating on his colourful exploits of love."[1]

"Now the image of Madhu-mādhavī: Golden in complexion, with eyes like lotuses, the damsel is of incomparable beauty. She is seated laughing with her beloved—such is the picture of Madhu-mādhavī."[2] Now the image of Hindola-rāga: Hindola is robed in yellow, he is seated at the centre of the swing. The confidanté are swinging him with passion, singing and singing with smiles.

"Who has made this masterpiece of beauty, seated on the swing in a mood of passion, as it rocks to and fro? The ladies are swinging him, singing songs with gusto and without reserve. Their shining complexions enhanced by their yellow robes flash like lightening. All the young damsels indulge in the sport, carried away by hilarious mirth and passion."[3]

(1) "*Atha Mālkous rāg-ko-svarup: Dohā:*
Mālkous nīle-vasan, sveta-charī liye hāth||
Mutiyanakī māla gare, sakala-sakhī-hai sāth|| 42 ||
Atha saviyā: Kausakako apanāno-bhalo tanu goura virājata hai paṭa-nīle||
Māla-gare kara sveta charī-rasa-prema chakeyo chavi-chaila-chavīle||
Kāminike mana-mohata hai sabhake mana bhāvata rūp rasīla||
Bhora bhaye uṭhi vaiṭhyo hī bhāvata nāgara nāyaka ranga rangīle|| 43 ||

(2) *Atha Madhumadhāvī-svarup: Dohā:*
Kāncan-tanu-locana-kamala, nāgari-mahā-anūp|
Piya-pai vaithi-hansata-hai, Madhu-mādhavī-svarup|| 40 ||

(3) "*Atha-Hindola-rāga-svarup: Dohā:*
Pīta-vasan-Hindolake, haiju Hiḍole-māhi||
Sakhī-jhulāvai-cāvason, gāya-musakāhi|| 49 ||

Sangīta sara.

The Hindī authors we have discussed do not exhaust all the poets and versifiers who have provided rāga-mālā texts for the pictorial artists. We have only been able to notice those who have been cited on rāg-mālā pictures.

The compilation of music data, offered by Maharaja Sawai Pratap Sinha Deo of Jaipur (1779-1804) in his Hindī work entitled *Sangīta-sāra,* gives the iconography as well as the note structure of a large variety of rāgas. The iconographical notes giving the image (*svarūpa*) are in prose, and are mere paraphrases of well known Sanskrit texts as will appear from the specimens cited below. The author has cited several new rāgas of which, four quoted here, may be found interesting.

"Now the picture (image) of Velāvalī is written: For the purpose of meeting her beloved in the trysting-place, she is putting on her jewels, (sitting) on the terrace; and she is repeatedly recalling and invoking her favourite deity—the god of love; her complexion is like the colour of blue lotus. A rāgiṇī visualised as above, one should recognize as Velāvalī."[1]

"Now the picture (image) of Lankā-dahan is written. His complexion is fair, he is dressed in a white robe, he is turning a lotus in his hand, his eyes are large, his tresses are long, he is an adept in the Art of Love, his body is soft, he wears jewels on all his limbs, he carries a staff in his other hand, he is contemplating in his heart on the God Siva, he is associated with his friends. A rāga thus visualized should be recognized as Lankā-dahan."

Savaiyā: Kīnhe-vanāva mahā-chavi sundara bhāvate vaithyo hidolahi dolai: jhūla-jhulāvata ournihūm sava gāvata hai sakhiyān-mukha-kholai: Gore jo gāta dipāta varī dyuti dāminisī mānou pīta paṭolai: Keli karai avalā ālavelī alola-svai-rasa kāma kilolai|| 50 ||

"*Rāg-ratnākar,* pp. 326-327.

(1) "*Atha vilavaliko svarup likhyate*|| *Sanketamai piyake pās jāyveko anganmai ābhūṣan pahare hain*| *Or apano iṣṭa deva jo.*

Kāmdeva tāko bāraṃbār smaraṇ kare hai|| *Nīle kamalako so jāko*

Sarīrako rang hai| *aisī jo rāgiṇī tāhi Vilāvalī jāniye*||

The melody is a hybrid rāga, composed of Devagiri, Kedār and Gārā.[1]

"Now, the picture (image) of Līlāvatī is written: her complexion is red, her eyes are like the petals of lotus, her gait is like that of a rutting elephant, her friend is Indra, she is dressed in variegated robes, she wears ropes of pearls, she carries a lotus, she is immersed in the flavour of love, she is of sixteen summers, she is accompanied by confidantés of the same age, her braid is strung with garlands of flowers, she is wearing a smile. A rāgiṇī thus visualized should be recognized as Lilāvatī."[2]

This melody is a hybrid rāgiṇī, composed of Jaita-Śrī, Lalit and Deskār.

"Now the picture (image) of Tārā-Dvani is written: her complexion is fair, she is dressed in yellow robe, she is

Saṅgīta-Sār, Saptamo rāgādhyāya, Poona Edition, 1912, Part VII, p. 41.

This is an obvious paraphrase of the Sanskrit text, cited on Plate XXXIX.

(1) "*Śiv-jī-nai rāgan-maison vibhāg kariveko apnain mukhason Devagiri kedāro, sankīrna Gāro gāike vānko Lanka-dahan nām kinou|| Atha Lankā-dahanko svarūp likhyate|| Goro jāko ang hai| Svet vastra pahari hai| hāthson kamal phirave hai| Vaḍe jāko netra hai| Vaḍe jāke kes hai| rati-kalāmai pravín hai| Kamal jāko ang hai| Sav angame soneke ābhūsan pahare hai| dusare hāthmai chaḍi hai| manmai Śivko dhyān kare hai| Mitrankarike yukt hai| Eso jo rāg tānhi Lankādahan jāniye||* *Ibid*, p. 133.

(2) *Śiv-jī-nai un rāgan-maiso vibhāg kariveko apanai mukhason Jaita-śri, Lalit, Sankirna Deśkār gaike vānho Lilāvatī nām-kinou|| Atha Lilāvatīko 'svarūp likhyate|| Lāl jako ranga hai|| kamala patrose jāke netra hai| māta hātikisī cāl hai| Indra jāko mitra hai| rang-virange vastra pahare hai| motīnkī mālā garemai hai| hāthmai kamal hai| Śṛṅgār rasmai magna hai| Solā varaskī avasthā hai| apane samān sakhīn karike yukt hai| phūl-mālā sūn guthī jāki venī hai| manda muskān kare hai| Esī jo rāgani tānhi Lilāvatī jāniye||* *Ibid*, pp. 136-137.

besmeared with sandal paste, she has saffron spot on her forehead, her eyes are large, she has tied a pair of amulets on her head, she is contemplating on the God Śiva, she is attended by her confidantés, she wears a rope of pearls on her neck, and various jewels on all her limbs,—she is sporting in company with pea-cocks, she is generous and liberal. A rāga thus visualized should be recognized as Tārā-dvani"[1]

Diwan Lachirām's Buddiprakās Darpan.

A short treatise on Hindu Music, in Brajabhāsā verse by Diwan Lachiram, written in Gurumukhī characters survives in a manuscript[2] bearing a colophon dated Samvat 1880 (A.D. 1823). The second chapter (*prabhāva*) describes the six rāgas and in the following chapter the rāgiṇīs are described with some elaboration. The verses given in this text have not been traced on any rāginī miniatures.

Sangîta sudarśana.

A music-scholar[3] has cited some verses from a Hindī treatise named *Sangīta-Sudarśana* composed by another theorist from the Punjab named Sudarsan-ācārya, who quotes the opinion of another named '*Svara-sāgara.*' According to this text, Mālakous has five wives:—It has been said in the *Svara-Sāgara* that this rāga (malkous) has the picture of an ascetic, it has Visnu as its presiding deity, and, therefore, it is a peaceful and spiritual melody, its principal

(1) *Sivji-nai un rāgan-mai-son vibhāg kariveko apanai mukha-son Śuddha-mallār sankirna-Kedāra gāikc vānko Tārā-dvani nām kīno|| Atha Tārā-dvaniko svarūp likhyate|| Goro jāko rang hai|| or pītamvarko pahare hai|| Candanko anga-rāg lagāye hai| lilāṭmai kesarko tilak lagāyo hai| or vaḍe netra hai| Vāranko juḍā māthe vandho hai| Śiv-jīko dhyān kare hai| mitran karike saran hai| motīnakī māla kanthamai pahare hai| or say anganmai ābhūsana pahare hai| moranke samuhamai vihār kare hai| param udār hai| Eso jo rāga tānhi Tārādvani jāniye||* *Ibid*, p. 176.

(2) Or. 2765, described in T. F. Blumhardt's *Catalogue of the Hindi, Panjabi, and Hindustani Manuscripts* in the Library of the British Museum, 1899, p. 20(31).

(3) Mr. Brajendra Kisore Roy Chowdhury of Mymensingh, cites passages from this work in his articles in Bengali, "Mālkos-Paricaya," published in the Bengali Journal "*Sangīta-Vijnāna-prakāsikā* (Asvin, 1336, P. 411).

queen is Bhaṭāhāri."[1] But the meagre quotation specifying the names of the melodies according to an unknown school of Ganapati, does not give us any idea as to the verses descriptive of the different melodies.

Cunni-Lalji's Nād-vinod.

That the practice of Hindu music had not missed the significance of emotive values and their related pictorial illustrations and musical iconography is proved by the interesting work in Hindī entitled *Nād-vinod*, by Gossain Cunni Lalji published in Samvat 1953 (1896 A.D.). The author cites the standard Sanskrit ślokas descriptive of the rāgas and rāginīs and paraphrases the Sanskrit texts in Hindī prose. He does not offer any independent rāga-mālā texts. His descriptions are illustrated by quaint wood-cuts giving pictorial versions of some of the melodies of which some typical specimens have been cited on Plate CXV.

Bhānu Kavi.

The latest poet who has bequeathed to us a dissertation on Indian music in Hindī is a modern poet of great distinction who wrote voluminous verses on a variety of topics under the pen-name of Bhānu Kavi, and which were collected and published under the title of *Kāvyaprabhākar*.[2] This volume treats of various conventions at topics, which it has been the practice of old Hindi poets to write verses upon. The topics are divided under 15 chapters (mayukhas), the second chapter being devoted to music (*Sangīta*). As explained in the short preface to this chapter, the author's materials are derived from older authorities and treatises e.g. *Mūlādhār, Rāga-ratnākar* and others. Bhānu Kavi, has thought fit to give us a short metrical treatise on music with a complete rāga-mālā text for the current rāga-system. As pointed out above, his verses describing the iconography of

(1) "Svara-sāgarme kahā hai ki yaha rāga sādhu-veś hai, iskā Viṣṇu-devatā hai, ataev yaha śānta sātivk rāga hai iskī Bhaṭha-hārī pāṭa-rānī hai|
Dohā: Bhatha hārī aru sarasvatī rūpa-manjarī vām|
Catura kadaṃvī pācavī rūpa-rasāla nāṃ||

(2) This was printed and published in Samvat 1966 (1909) by Ganga Vishnu Srikrshna Das, Lakhmi-Vyankateswar Press, Kalyan. The Poet's real name is Jagannath Prasad. He received a good education in English and served as a Deputy Collector at the time of retirement.

rāgas (*rāga-rūp*) are borrowed from the text of Rādhā Kṛṣṇa's *Rāga-Kutūhala,* although he does not acknowledge the debt. When we quoted, on the descriptions of the plates, from the *Kāvya-prabhākar* the texts describing several rāgas, it was not known that Bhānu Kavi had drawn his materials bodily from the text of *Rāg-Kutūhala.*

It cannot be claimed that this modern poet, the latest contributor to rāga-mālā texts, wrote his verses to answer the demand of illustrators. For, the demand of rāga-mālā pictures had ceased by the middle of the 19th century. During the centuries, the practice of composing rāga-mālā verses had grown up, and poets accepted this subject as a conventional topic, worthy of poets. And Bhānu Kavi has only touched upon a topic hallowed by ancient poets, without the slightest hope of his verses being put to any practical pictorial uses.

The large body of rāga-mālā texts in Hindī, a fraction of which we have been able to consider here, came into existence in answer to a demand to popularise the currency of the melodies in accurate presentation of their distinctive emotive values, for, they have been used in intimate application to the pictorial illustrations, the pictures justifying the texts as much as the texts justified the pictures, both contributing to an accurate knowledge of the different emotional significances of the different, though sometimes, related melodies. As compared with the brief and miniature forms of the Sanskrit prototypes, the Hindī descriptive texts are not confined to essential iconographic lineaments of the images suggested in the Sanskrit prayer formulas (*dhyāna-ślokas*), but in their popular Hindī versions, these original musical images are each amplified and elaborated in an emotional situation, in an appropriate dramatic form which makes it easier to apprehend their inherent emotive concepts. This may be typically illustrated by comparing the Sanskrit dhyāna and the corresponding Hindī version of the Lalita rāginī (plate XXXVI) in the meagre Sanskrit texts, there is hardly room for anything but a suggestion that the lady, carrying a wreath as a memento of her dalliance over-night heaves heavy sighs ("*viniśvasantī sahasā prabhāte*"), when with the sun-rise her beloved walks out of the love-chamber to attend to the duties of the day. In the Hindī version,—the germ of this idea is elaborated into a dramatic device—in which the forlorn lover left alone in her couch when the sun is up, is plunged in grief ("*Ugata Bhānu cale navakānta tāvai tiya dekhi viyogame bhīṁhī*"). Unable to detain her lover by any plausible excuse She tries to pick up a lover's quarrel, unreasonably taunting him with the false charge that he is going to another lover, whom he loves. And the poet, in order to elucidate the state of the feeling of the lovers parted at day-break, (the appropriate hour for singing the melody), introduces this clever dialogue with remarkable dramatic effect. All this elaboration is implied but not actually suggested in the Sanskrit text, and naturally grows out of the seeds imbedded in the essence of the emotional idea connotated by the melody of Lalita rāginī. Other examples of such happy dramatization of the essential emotive concept, in charmingly picturesque situations of profound feelings of diverse flavours and shades, are strewn over the numerous Hindī texts quoted on the Plates (in Volume II) which the reader may find out for himself.

Persian texts.

While the Hindī versions helped to broadcast the message of Indian music and to a popular realization of the qualities of rāgas among an ever-growing circle of appreciation far beyond the narrow clique of learned experts, it was found that the meaning and significance of the rāgas were inaccessible to a large group of cultured men ignorant of the Hindī dialects. India has hardly seen more sincere and enthusiastic admirers of her music, than the enlightened princes of the Moghul dynasty whose patronage brought about very rich and significant developments in the art and the science of music. But the Moghul patrons took care to ascertain accurately the fundamental principles of Indian musical science, before proceeding to help towards its further growth and enrichment. And for this purpose, more than one authoritative treatises in Sanskrit were translated into Persian as the basis of a scientific investigation.[1] The most typical effort on this line, was the translation of the Sanskrit and Hindī treatises into Persian. The *Rāga-darpaṇa*, the

(1) The investigation has been going on since the days of 'Amir Khusrau (1296-1315 A.D.).

Sangīta Darpaṇa, Sangīta Pārijāta, and the Hindī treatise. *Mān kutūhala* were made available in Persian versions.[1] Led by Akbar, the grandeés of the Imperial Court, (Hindu as well as Mohamedan), became intelligent connoisseurs of Hindī Music, and developed an ardent curiosity to study music from all points of view. The popularity of the rāga-mālā pictures helped to stimulate and satisfy this curiosity, through pictorial and literary forms. The descriptions of the distinctive 'images' (*tasvīrs*) of the rāgas were demanded in Persian versions and musical interpreters learned in the two languages, were not wanting to answer the demand. Various illustrations of rāginīs had already been painted by Mussulman artists. A typical example is the Moghul version of Toḍī rāginī, wrongly attributed to Rizzā 'Abbāsi. Though the attribution is wrong, the example proves the popularity of rāgiṇī pictures amongst Mussalman artists.[2]

The earliest attempts to indicate the nature and quality of the motive of rāgas in Persian versions appear to be represented by interpretive annotations written on rāga-mālā pictures of which some typical examples are borrowed here (Plate CXI, A.B. & C) from the Johnson Albums in the India Office. They appear to be quite early, if not the earliest specimens of their kind. The miniatures B & C (Plate CXI) appear to be earlier than A, and have the explanation in Persian crudely inscribed on the top and at the bottom beyond the borders which frame the pictures. The other examples, Śrī-rāga (Plate CXI-A) is of much more interest as it provides the Persianized version of the Hindī original cited on Plate LII-C, which it copies somewhat crudely substituting an interpretation in Persian in place of the Hindi verses of Pearay Rangalāl. An early series of examples in the Government Art Gallery, Calcutta, are of high aesthetic merit, both in their lovely and native types of figures, and in

(1) The *Mān-kutūhala* was translated by Fakur Ullah; the *Pārijāt* was translated by Deena Nauth in 1724 A.S. (Vide Sir W. Ouseley 'Anecdotes of Indian Music,' *The Oriental Collections*, Vol. I).

(2) Coomarswamy *Catalogue of Indian Collection*, Boston Museum, Part VI, Moghul Paintings, Plate LXI, p. 71.

their deeply felt emotional contents. From this series, four specimens have been borrowed in the second volume (Plates XVI-C: 'Toḍī'; LXI: Vasanta; LXIV-D: Megha-rāga, and CXIV: Khamāic). On this series beyond the ornamental border in yellow, certain Persian texts are inscribed indicating the name of the rāginī, and the rāga to which it belongs. Strictly speaking, the texts are mere labels for identifications, and do not suggest the atmosphere of the melodies, and have no literary pretensions. These labels show the necessity of Persian texts for a class of patrons of Hindu music who had no knowledge of the Hindī language and to whom the Hindi texts conveyed no information. These Persian labels establish a demand for Persian texts for which we have other evidences.

Persian Ragmālā Album.

The most important and authenticated evidence is provided by the unique Persian rāga-mālā album, three pages from which are cited in Volume II (Plate LXXIII-B, Śyām Gujarī, Plate CXII-A, Dīpak rāga, and B, Khokkar rāgini). The album consists of 84 paintings together with descriptions in excellent Persian verses, explaining the illustrations opposite to the text.[1] The colophon, in prose, states that the work was executed under the command of His Imperial Majesty Muhammad Shah and completed at the city of Kabul in the year 1150 Hejiera (1737 A.D.) and presented to the Emperor. The demand for rāga-mālā pictures, appears to have continued unabated to the middle of the 18th century, and also very much later. If we study the text of the Persian versions of the pictures of rāga-mālā, we find that though the identity of the characteristics of each rāga is adhered to in the interpretations, a good deal of the romantic atmosphere and mystical significance inherent in Hindi love-poetry, derived from the *rasa-śāstra* (the canons of erotics) have evaporated in the Persian translation, though the illustrative pictures still retain some of the glamour and *naivetè* of the pictorial concepts. Śyām Gujarī (Plate LXXIII B) perhaps carries the sweetest memory of the fragrance of the best prototypes. The illustrations have no original merit in their

(1) Other pages from the album illustrating 4 rāginīs are reproduced in *Shāmā'a* vol. V, January 1935, p. 154, by Syed Hashmi in an illustrated article: 'Indian Ragamala in Persian.'

style and conception and they can only be judged by the extent of the flavour of the original that they have been able to retain. The Persian verses visualizing Śyām-Gujarī appear to lend the appropriate atmosphere for the melody by calling attention to the enjoyment of nightingale, and to the image of the forlorn heroine, vowed to join her beloved, pouring her sorrows to the peacock, the very picture of intense love-longing. The version of Dīpak is perhaps less happy; but, the whole series of pictures in this album and the charming verses describing them stand for a very sincere and ardent attempt to get at the ideas behind the conception of Indian melodies.

Rāgmālā with Persian inscriptions.

There can be no doubt that many such pictures must have been painted, and many more of such texts may have been rendered in Persian versions. For, we have, at least, one complete set of rāga-mālās with interpretations in Persian superscribed on the miniatures themselves. This is the admirable series in the Collection of the Prince of Wales Museum, Bombay. Their pictorial patterns are adaptations, if not copies, of finer and earlier series in the India Office (Johnson Album, Vol. 43 and Vol. 37) with the descriptive texts, in Persian, superscribed on rectangular panels at the top and at bottom. The correspondence in pictorial motifs and designs are evident from the juxtaposed examples (Plates CVI,-C and D: CVII-A, and B: CVIII-D and E: CX-C and D). On stylistic grounds, the series in the Prince of Wales Museum may be dated about the end of the 17th or the beginning of the 18th century; they, therefore, ante-date the album from Kabul discussed above. The descriptions inscribed on these series indicate the rāga to which each rāginī is assigned and also its appropriate time and season. This is followed by a somewhat bold recital of the details of the atmosphere related to the melody, but without any suggestion for the emotional background. The descriptions were put on more for the purpose of interpreting and enjoying the pictures for their own sake, rather than as graphic diagrams of musical concepts.

Later examples of rāga-mālā Pictures with Persian texts occasionally come to light. An incomplete series is in the collection of a dealer in Bombay from which we have borrowed an example on the plate on the opposite page. It is a very rare illustration of Puhupa rāginī.

Rāgmālā Text in Bengali.

If the beauty of musical concepts levied its tribute from the scholars and poets in Hindī and Persian languages, the votaries of the Bengali language, followed suit. And we have at least one metrical treatise which provides not only a complete rāga-mālā text in Bengali, but also offers a general survey of Indian musical literature and the main essentials of the theory, expounded in simple *payār* (rhyming) verses couched in the archaic language of the time, together with specimens of songs illustrating the melodies.

This laudable effort we owe to the enterprise of a Bengali music-theorist named Radha Mohon Sen who published his treatise in the Bengali year 1225 (1881 A.D.). He gives a summary of the different systems of rāgas according to the School of Hanumāna, Bharata (Brahmā), Somesvara, and Kallināth, and also cites the opinion of *Tuph-e-t'ul Hind* and other Persian treatises. He devotes a section of his work to the contemplative images of rāgas and rāginīs, which offer descriptive word-pictures of the different melodies according to the School of Hanumāna. Though not of much literary merit, the verses in long strings of couplets fulfil their purpose and convey to us the main outlines of the iconographic peculiarity, and the emotive personalities of the melodies. His verses, as a matter of fact, give us attractive physical portraits of the personified melodies rather than any subjective musical values. As will appear from the citations of representative verses from his work, they are based on Sanskrit texts, but are not accurate translation, but only free rendering, sometimes with many omissions, of important iconographic details and frequent additions of original imageries.[1] "Barārī: Barārī is the second rāgiṇī (of Bhairava), a young damsel, who makes the four quarters effulgent with her radiance. Her tresses are new clouds—her robes are white: the flowers of the Wishing Tree are her pendants for the ears. Her face is the Moon without the marks (spots) of the deer. The 'beauty' has golden bracelets on her wrists. The breadth of her waist is very narrow her navel is deep like a lake, and her breasts are firm. The

(1) The original Sanskrit text (Plate XI) has 'deodāra' flowers (*Sura-vṛkṣa puṣpam*) instead of *Kalpa-druma'* flowers.

fragrance of her body is fascinating: the blind bees mistake it as that of lotuses.[1] In a pleasant mood she smiles and indulges in pleasantries with her beloved. The damsel shines as a full-toned melody, the string of notes being Sa, -ri, -ga, ma, -pa, -dha, ni: Her home is in the note 'Sa' she should be sung at the end of the day."[2]

"Madha-mādh (Madhya-mādi): Madha-mādh is incomparable in beauty; her complexion is gold, her robes are yellow. Her frisky eyes are emphasized with pasted collyrium, a wag-tail seems to dance on a golden lotus. A pearl-top at the end of her nose,—resembling a dew-drop on a flower of seasame. Her body is radiant with the paste of saffron, she is a damsel from the family of septa-tonic melodies. She adores her lord like cupid and gives him kisses and embraces. The quarter of her abode is the note *madhyama* (F) the succession of the notes are ma-pa-dha-ni-sa-ri-ga. Suitable for the six seasons beginning with the autumn, she is to be sung in the morning."[3]

(1) The Bengali version misses the fly-whisk (*cāmara*), an important iconographic detail.

(2) "*Barārī| Barārī dvitīyā rāginī-vālā| Rūpe daśa dig kare ujālā||*

Keśa navaghana sveta vasan| Kalpa-druma-puṣpa karṇa-bhūṣaṇ||

Mṛga-cihna-bhinna vadana-śaśī| Kanaka-kankana kare rūpasī||

Mājār valani parama kṣiṇa| Nābhi-sarovar kuca-kaṭhin||

Amodita kare angera gandha| Kamala-bharame bhramar andha||

Mṛdu mṛdu hāsi hariṣa mane| Rasa-ālāpana nāyaka sane||

Jāti sampūrane vihare dhanī| Surāvali sa-ri-ga-ma-pa-dha-ni|| Kharaja surete gṛha-vidhān| Divaser śese karive gān||2||

Radha Mohan Sen: "*Sangīt Taranga*", Bangabasi Edition, 1310, pp. 136-7.

(3) The Sanskrit text cited on Plate VII may be compared with this version.

"*Madha-mādh| Madha-mādha-rūpe nāhi tulanā| Kanaka-varanī pīta-vasanā||*

Cancala nayane dalitānjana| Svarna-padme yena nāce khanjana||

"Sindhuvī (Saindhavī): She was in expectation of her lord, Sindhuvī, has given up that hope. The appointed hour has gone by, still the beloved has not come. This has led to deep resentment; she assumed the robes of an ascetic. Having cast aside her scarlet robes she has assumed russet ones (proper to ascetics). Casting aside jewelleries she has be-decked herself with strings of rosaries (*rudrāksa*: Śiva's rosary) and crystals. She abjured the fragrance of *aguru* (scented wood and saffrons, and besmeared all her body with ashes. Making pendants from Vandhuka flowers, she wore them on her ears. Taking a trident, and the counting-beads in her hands, Sindhuvī is worshipping Śankara (Śiva). A septatonic melody having its abode in the note 'sa', the succession of notes being sa-ri-ga-ma-pa-dha-ni. Proper for the six seasons, beginning with autumn, you should sing it at the end of the day."[1]

Toḍī: The damsel Toḍī, beloved of Mālkausa has a complexion of yellow: with saffron and camphor on her body,

Nāsāgre mukuta-tār tulanā| Til-phule yena sisira-kaṇā
Keśara-carccite tanūra bhāti| Sampūrana-kule avalā jāti||
Patike rati-pati samādare| Cumva alingana-pradāna kare||
Madhyama haila grhera diga| Sreṇī-mata-ma-pa-dha-ni-sa-ri-ga||
Śāradadi sada-ṛtu-vidhān| Prabhāta kālīn karive gān|| 3 ||

Ibid, p. 137.

(1) "Sindhuvī| Pati āsivār āśyaya chila| Sindhuvī se āśā nairaśe dila||
Sanketa-samaya gata haila| Tatrāpi nāyaka nāhi āila||
Tāte mān guru bhāva dharila| Yoginir mata veśa karila||
Lohita vasana dūre tyājila| Geruyā vasana āni parila||
Rudrākṣa sphaṭika gāthiya thare| Tyājiyā bhūṣaṇa bhūṣaṇa kare||
Aguru candana keśara rākhe| Sakala śarīre vibhūti mākhe||
Kundala kariyā vandhuka phule| Parila sundarī śrutira mūle||
Triśūla jāpya mālā kare kare| Pūjen Sindhuvī deva śankare||
Sampūraṇa gṛhe kharaja gaṇi| Sura śreṇi sa-ri-ga-ma-pa-dha-ni||
Śāradādi sadā ṛtu-vidhān| Divasera śeṣe karive gān"|| 4 ||

Ibid, pp. 137-8.

Compare the Sanskrit text cited on Plate XIII.

and dressed in white robe. Her developed breasts are firm, her waist is thin. Her navel is deep, she has the shine of gold. Her tresses are strings of clouds, her face is the full-moon, in which dance her eyes like those of a fawn and in which shine her teeth like a row of pearls. She wears bejewelled ornaments, of incomparable beauty. Venus says to Cupid—'Be sure do not forget me, if you please.' Her patterned beauty, lights up the four quarters: she plays on a vīnā, reposing in a meadow. The strings of the vīnā, shine like the rays of effulgence, discoursing melodious music with the sweet fifth note (G). She practises the form of the melody in her improvization, by hearing the melody, birds and animals are moved to tears. Absorbed in the song, the fawns dance before her, without fear. The melody of Todī belongs to the Septa-tonic variety, and its structure is made up of the notes sa-ri-ga-ma-pa-dha-ni. In the abode of the note Sa(C) it is counted with the winter season, its songs are sung after the first quarter of the day.[1]

"Dīpak: The eyes of the Sun are hot and severe, and there was Dīpak born. His robes are scarlet, and strings of large pearls grace his neck. He rides on a rutting elephant, with young lads and lassies, some on the right, some on the left, some hanging on him. His beloved indulge in pleasantries, and in this manner he roams frequently. I count it amongst the septa-tonic class, the string of notes being—sā-ri-ga-ma-pa-dha-ni. The season is the spring, the

(1) "Toḍī| Mālkausa-priyā Toḍī vālā pīta varaṇā|
Keśara karpūra ange sveta-vastra paraṇa||
Kuca pīn su-kaṭhin, madhya ksin valanā|
nābhi-kūp sarovar, svarṇa-kānti lalanā||"
Kādaṃvinī keśa-pāś, pūrṇa-candra-vadanā|
Tāhāte kuraṅga cakṣu, muktā-pangti-radanā||
Maṇimaya ābharaṇ nāhi tār tulanā|
Rati vale anañgere,—dekho yena bhulanā||
Daś dig ālo kare hena rūp sājanā|
prāntare vasiyā kare vīṇā-yantra vājaṇā||
Vīnār samūha tantra dīpti-rūpe mājanā|
Madhur paṅcama svare rāg bhāg bhānjanā||
Ālāp-cārir vole rāg-rūp-sādhanā|

note 'Sa'(c) is the starting and prevailing note, the rule is to sing it at noon.'[1]

"Megh: The melody Megh is the son of the heaven, or, born of the hills, according to another view. His complexion surpasses the shade of new clouds, he binds a turban round his matted locks, in beauty, he looks like the god—'who vanquishes Cupid' (Viṣṇu). He flashes a keen-edged sword in his hand, he is the jewel on the head of the youthful. His words are strung with the honey of nectar, starting with the note 'dhaivata' (A) A penta-tonic melody made of the notes dha-ni-sa-ri-gā. It is assigned to the months of rain, to be sung during the end of the night.'[2]

Rāg śuni paśu pakṣī save kare kāndanā||
Gān śuni kuranginīgaṇ hayā maganā|
Sammukhe kariche nṛtya, nāhi bhīti-cetanā||
Ṭoḍī-rāgiṇīr jāti sampūraṇe ghaṭanā|
Sā-ri-ga-ma-pa-dha-ni-te rāgiṇīr gaṭhanā||
Kharajer gṛha śiśirādi ṛtu-gaṇanā|
Divā prathama prahara pare gān-racanā|| 6 ||"

Ibid, p. 140-141.

Compare the texts cited on Plates XV to XIX.

(1) "*Dīpak| Ravira nayane prakhara dṛṣṭi| Tathāy Dīpak haila sṛṣṭi||*
Lohita-varaṇa vasana tār| Galāy gaja-mukutār hār||
Ārohaṇa mattavara mātaṅge| samūha taruṇa-taruṇī saṅge||
Keha vāme vasi, dakṣiṇe keha| Keha vā āśraya kariyā deha||
Rasa-ālāpana kare pramadā| Erūpe bhramaṇa karena sodā||
Jāti sampūraṇa bhāvete gaṇi| Surāvali sā-ri-ga-ma-pa-dha-ni||
Grīṣma-ṛtu gṛha kharaja sthān| Madhyāhṇa samaye gān vidhān||" *Ibid,* p. 150-51.

(2) "*Megh| Megh rāga gagana-tanay| matāntare parvvat haite janma hay||*
Nava-megh jiniyā var[illegible]| Jaṭā-jūṭa jaḍāiyā uṣṇīṣa vandhan||
Rūpe yena madana-mohan| Kharatara karavāla karete dhāraṇ||
Yuvaka-gaṇera śiromaṇi| Vākya-śreṇī hena-yena sudhār gāthani||
Karilena dhaivate utthān| Dha-ni-sā-ri-ga pramāṇe oḍote nirmmāṇ||

Enough quotations have been given from the work of Rādhā Mohan Sen, to convey the nature and quality of the rāga-mālā texts composed in Bengali rhyming metre *(payār)* prevalent at the time. He adds many piquant accessories and details which make his portraits of the rāgiṇīs shine out in rich, vivid, attractive, and sensuous colours. No rāga-mālā paintings appear to have been painted in Bengal,[1] so that the text of Rādhā Mohan Sen have had no other uses excepting conveying to practising musicians in Bengal, ignorant of Sanskrit, the systems of the classification of the melodies, and their individual characteristics in pictorial as well as in musical form. "*Saṅgīta-Taraṅga*" appears to have acquired sufficient authority and the author of "*Rāga-Kalpa-druma*" pays it a compliment by quoting passages from this Bengali work in his anthology.

Varasādirtute vidhān| Rajanīra śesa-bhāge karivek gān||"
Ibid, p. 161.

(1) Excepting, of course, the illustrations appearing in the edition of Harivallabha's Ms. in the Nahar Collection which was executed in Murshidabad. [Plates XX, XLII, LXVI, etc.].

PICTORIAL MOTIFS

That rāga-mālā pictures have been painted, (in different parts of Northern India), whether in relation to specific Hindī texts, or independently, throughout the centuries right up to the nineteenth, is amply borne out by the large number of surviving miniatures. The demand for these specimens of "visualized music" must have been continuous, and wide-spread, and, in order to meet the demand, skeleton drawings (*khākās,* pricked drawings), and other outline sketches from the patterns designed by gifted artists were used by lesser artists who found it profitable to meet the popular demand. An interesting series of skeleton drawings (not pricked outlines), from the Tagore Collection are collected on Plate CXIII and other examples are cited on other plates for purposes of comparison (Plates I-A, XIII-B). On the drawings in the Tagore collection are inscribed in Hindī and Persian, the names of the rāgiṇīs, with indications and suggestions for the colour schemes. They must have been the basis of finished miniatures, although no finished specimen corresponding to these particular designs, has yet been traced. The most interesting of these series is the one representing Hāṃvirī (Plate LXLVIII-C) which has helped to identify the well-known miniatures (Plate LXLVIII, A and B), not, hitherto, recognized as illustrations of the rāgiṇī. The drawing for Bhairo (Plate I, A), also helps us to identify an analogous drawing (Boston Museum, CCXI, No. 17.2822) as an illustration of the melody. The example in the author's collection (Plate XIII-B) is perhaps the finest specimen, both in its elaborate pattern and impressive setting.

Sources of Pictorial Motifs.

Materials are not adequate for a demonstration of the processes by which familiar scenes and experiences in life were adopted and developed and utilized into patterns and designs for visualizing the Indian melodies. But one, or two suggestions may be made how characteristic scenes and themes may have been worked out and idealized into a pattern for a rāgiṇī picture. The three examples of Kānaḍā rāgiṇī cited on Plate L, seem to indicate the three stages in which, a hunting melody, originally used by attendant *Shikāris* (hunters) helping a Prince in his elephant-hunts, later developed into the rich but plaintive strain of the melody now recognized under the name of Kānaḍā. Possibly, when the prince killed an elephant, the attendants stood up to salute the hunter and broke into congratulatory cheers, in some crude *minstrel-songs (cāraṇagītis)*, in which the plaintive groans of the dying animal mingled its deeply moving notes of sorrow, which perhaps still linger in its refined, finished, and developed structure, now known to us. In the final 'picture' that it evolved, it obliterated all traces of its origin, and in this developed picture (Plate L-A) it is interpreted as a song of inspiration to Kṛṣṇa (Kānar= Kānorā) as He starts to ride out from His palace to kill the demon gajāsura.[1] The sources of the pictorial motifs have been forgotten, defaced, or obliterated in most cases. But we shall endeavour to indicate the origins of the motif woven into the theme of the Toḍī rāgiṇī. Possibly, the melody came originally from the peasants' field. Very probably, it was a melody sung by the wife, or daughter of the peasant who watched the paddy fields, (as they still do today, from sunrise to sunset, perched on a bamboo frame), chiding away the deer, and other animals which strayed into the fields, in groups, to eat up the standing crop, before it was ready to be shorn. Perhaps, the farmer's daughter, weaned away the encroaching depredator, by the music of her primitive lute, which attracted the deer, and kept them away from mischief. Some such picture, is called up by many stray passages in ancient poetical literature. We seem to have vivid pen-pictures of deer dropping the food they were chewing in the crop-fields in their depredatory raids, under the enchanting strains of music. Thus in Śrī-Harṣ's "*Nāgānandam,*" in the dialogue of Ātreya and Jimūtavāhana

(1) Like Hercules, Kṛṣṇa is credited with a series of brave and adventurous deeds of valour and heroism, one of which is the vanquishing of a demon in elephant's form (*gajāsura*). Another of the exploits of Kṛṣṇa is worked into the theme of Sāraṅga-rāga (Plate LXL).

(Act 1), this appears to be the identical picture suggested: "Ātreya: 'Even the deer prick up their ears, and listen to the strain with their eyes closed, while from their mouth falls the half-chewed grass."[1] That the depredatory deer were attracted by the songs, or the music of the dames who kept watch over the paddy fields, is suggested by a passage in Subandhu's *Vāsavadattā:* "With herds of deer delighted by the songs of happy female guardians of the rice."[2] This seems to be graphically pictured in the miniature (Plate XV-C), where we find the graceful guardian of the paddy-field, attracting the herds by her music, and alluring them away from the young shoots of paddy which will yet take a long time to mature. The partiality of the deer for music, was an old recognized piece of zoological knowledge, and very soon passed into poetic conventions, of which several applications are met with in Sanskrit literature. Thus in *Vāsavadattā,* we read: "With herds of deer delighted by the notes of songs of *kinnarīs* (satyrs) close by."[3] Other examples of the convention occur in the *Kathā-Sarit-Sāgara*[4] and in two passages in Hemachandra's *Pariśiṣta parvan:*[5]

(1) *Nāgānandam* translated by B. H. Wortham, London, p. 28.

(2) *Vāsavadattā* (Gray's Translation, Columbia University, 1913), p. 135-36, Text (at p. 192, line 8) "*Hṛṣta-kalama-gopikā-gīta-sukhita-mṛga-yuthe.*"
On this passage, the commentator Sīvarām (Hall's edition, p. 288) glosses '*kalama-gopikā*' as '*Śāli-saṃrakṣikā*', that is, 'guardians of the paddy fields'.

(3) Gray's translation, p. 126.
Text (at page 187, line 9): "*Samāsanna-kinnarī-gīta (Śravaṇa-ramamāṇa) ruru-visareṇa.*" [266].

(4) In the anecdote of Harivara and Anaṅgaprabhā (Penzer's Edition, Vol. IV, p. 152).
Text: "*Sa tena gīta-śavdena śruteṇa hariṇo yathā| Ākṛṣto' bhyapatattatra rathamunmucya kevalaḥ||*" 197.

(5) "*Pāṭalīputra-nagare yatra yatra jajou sa tu|*
Tatra tatra yayuḥ pourāḥ gītākṛṣṭāḥ 'kuraṅgavat||' 39
(Bib. Indica, Edition, IX, 39).
"*Rājāpi tasyāstādṛkṣa-niḥ kṣobhatvena vismitaḥ|*
Utkarno' bhut kathāṃ śrotuṃ gītiṃ mṛga ivoccakaiḥ"|| 194
Ibid. III, 194.

"Wherever Kunāla went, the citizens of Pāṭalīputra followed *like deer attracted by music.*" "They pricked up their ears to hear his words, *like dear anxious to listen to music.*" These poetic conventions have also their practical application in the methods employed to capture gazelles which is described by Alberuni: "I myself have witnessed that in hunting gazelles they had caught them with the hand. One Hindu even went so far as to assert that he, without catching gazelles, would drive it before him and lead it straight into the kitchen. This however, rests, as I believe I have found out, simply on the device of slowly and constantly accustoming the animals to one and the same melody. Our people, too, practise the same when hunting the ibex, which is more wild than even the gazelle. When they see the animals resting, they begin to walk-round them in a circle, singing one and the same melody so long until the animals are accustomed to it. Then they make the circle more and more narrow, till at last they come near enough to shoot at the animals which lie there in the perfect rest."[1]

This practice of hunting deer by the lure of music is recorded in a picturesque Hindī verse, in the form of the deer's wail in which the animal hungry for the music expresses itself ready to sacrifice its body in lieu of the prize of a musical treat: "When a single leaf rustles, I fly to the island of Ceylon; (but having heard the notes of your flute, I have offered to you my head as a present; you can sell my horns and turn them into coins, and roast my meat to eat, take my skin to make into rugs, but O! do please treat me to the music of your flute!"[2]

Sometimes old legends and folk-stories have been adopted and worked into the themes of rāga-mālā pictures. Thus, an old snake legend has provided the theme for the Āhirī rāginī.[3]

(1) E. Sachau, "*Alberuni's India,*" London, 1910, p. 195.

(2) "*Ek patra yav khaḍkhaḍāye, haṃ bhāge siṃhal ka dvīp|*
Suṅke terā venusvara merā śir diyā vakśiś||
Sing necke kouḍi karanā māś payāyke khāo|
Cāmḍā leke āsan kijīye venukā svar sunāo"||

(3) Coomaraswamy, *Catalogue of Boston Museum, Rajput*

The practice of visualising musical compositions in pictorial forms is no more confined to India. During the last few years a few European artists have made attempts to set down famous master-pieces of music into visualized pictures. The "Twenty-four Preludes" of Chopin have received pictorial interpretations by Robert Spies, an English artist.[1] A few years earlier, Miss Pamela Colman Smith exhibited in London, a series of pictorial drawings, interpreting famous musical pieces, which included Panderwski's "Chant du Voyage", Chopin's "Prelude No. 4", César Franck's "Symphony", Schumann's "Kinder-scenen" and Debussy's "Granada", and other pieces.[2] Yet, another series of illustrations of musical master-pieces were exhibited by Miss Juliet Williams at the Aeolian Hall in 1926, which included visualized versions of Bach's 'Concerto in E', Chopin's "Berceuse", Debussy's "L'Après-midi d'un Faune", and Borodin's "Unfinished Symphony."[3]

Visualization of Music by European Artists.

Dr. Bake has cited the Latin verse composed by Monk Adam of Fulda (15th century) descriptive of the character of different musical modes. "There are even images of the different modes with inscriptions that run: "This mode is the first as far as the singing of songs full of melody is concerned. That which follows is the second in rank and importance. The third portrays the suffering and glorification of Christ. Then follows the fourth mode; its chants portray sorrow." The statuettes represent female figures in different attitudes and of different expressions. Consequently, it is

Painting, Part V, p. 99; *Journal, Punjab Historial Society*, IV, 2, 1916, p. 118.

(1) His illustrations were published, with accompaniment of poems by Laura Vulda, in French and English versions in the monthly journal, now defunct, called *"Kosmos,"* Calcutta, 1916, Second year, No. 18.

(2) Her pictures were described by the Hon. Mrs. Forbes-Sempill in an article published in the *Illustrated London News*, 1927. See also the article 'Seeing sound' in the *Statesman*. Calcutta, 6th March, 1927.

(3) A selection from her pictures are reproduced in the *Sketch*, London, November 10, 1926, at page 278.

only the later development which has estranged us from the basic idea, and makes us stare at the idea of portrayed rāgas and rāgiṇīs in Indian Art. The classical Indian system at its height presents the beautiful spectacle of something absolutely perfect."[1]

(1) Dr. A. A. Bake: "Different Aspects of Indian Music," *Indian Art and Letters* New series, Vol. VIII, No. 1, 1st issue for 1934, pp. 68-69.

CRITICISM

The function that the Indian melodies, as rāgas, have been made to play, namely, of spelling out in the language of symphonic formulas definitive *rasas,* capable of evoking a variety of human emotions has yet to be investigated with reference to the nature of the psychology of musical expression. So much mystery has hovered round the phenomenon of musical expression itself, that until recently no clear conception of the nature of musical utterance has been possible. Great lovers of music have helped to intensify rather than elucidate the mystery. Definitions of music such as that of Cardinal Newman, as "the out-pouring of eternal harmony in the medium of created sound", or of Carlyle, who called "music a kind of inarticulate, unfathomable speech leading us to the edge of the infinite", or that of Lafcadio Hearn—who characterized music as "a psychical storm, agitating to unimaginable depths the mystery of the past within us", can only be regarded as emotional effusions, rather than as scientific enunciations of the nature of musical expression. Even the attempts of expert musicians have not been helpful in unravelling the mystery of the riddle. The technical experts, long persisted in the psychological fallacy, that music had nothing to do with the ordinary emotions of life, but were concerned with emotions peculiar to music itself—i.e. purely musical emotions. According to this view, supported by psychologists like Dr. W. Brown[1] and M. Combarieu, music is a unique kind of thought and musical concept which connotes sensations unattainable in the other medium. Says M. Combarieu: "La musique est l'art de penser avec des sons sans concepts." ['Music is an art of thinking in

(1) Dr. W. Brown: "Music expresses an emotional life peculiar to itself. The emotions expressed are not the emotions of everyday life, nor are they even idealised forms of these emotions." *The Quest,* 1912.

terms of sound without concepts']. The logical implication of this view is that music, unlike painting and sculpture and, like architecture, is incapable of rendering, or expressing a theme, a subject, or a topic. It is one thing to say that music is a language, having laws and logic of its own, and it is quite another, to suggest that music can only deal with matters peculiar to the Kingdom of Sound and is unable to utter, express, or deal with subjects of human emotion, or other thematic materials. According to this doctrine, music is a Non-representative Art,—an Art of production of certain dynamic shades, tempos, phrasings, tone colours—blended into a design of orchestration—having a significance other than that of intellectual, or emotional values. If it arouses any emotion,—the same is not akin to anything that can be imitated, or verbally described. To put it in the language of plastics, music is decorative rather than illustrative. Its patterns have dynamic rather than thematic motifs. There is a certain amount of truth in the doctrines indicated above. It insists, somewhat unduly, on the quality of music as "pure art values"—something akin to 'abstract aesthetic qualities' aimed by exponents of modern paintings in attempting to release the art of painting from the tyranny of subject-matter. The exponents of the modern movements in painting have demonstrated that it is possible—to produce 'pictures' of great aesthetic significance, without recourse to any subject, theme, or anecdote. A picture need not tell any story, or represent any imitation, or description of nature. 'Absolute painting' though they represent nothing,—evokes a disinterested aesthetic sensation,—due to a happy perception and contemplation of special relations, dimensions, proportions, accents, colour values and rhythm inherent in the quality of the design, claiming to attain the condition of music. But this demonstration of the quality of non-representative painting, does not invalidate the capacity of the painter's craft to represent, delineate, or imitate nature, or to render themes of human or emotional significance. And if music possesses, as it indeed does, in a large measure, the power of creating forms of 'pure aesthetic values',—it is not incapable of rendering and expressing concepts evocative of human emotions. Indeed, a school of psychologists, supporting the ordinary popular view, has strenuously emphasized on this function of music and some have gone to the length of declaring that music possesses an emotional power greater than that of speech itself and the expression of human emotion is its essential mission and glory. There is little doubt that music "can suggest and stimulate feelings akin to those produced by the vicissitudes of real life, and it can interest, fascinate, delight, or weary and displease, by what we can only call the purely musical quality of its sound patterns" (Vernon Lee). Musical experience has indeed proved to us that certain musical patterns, can well induce reveries peopled with a whole phantasmagoria of tender, weird, or alarming shapes,—reminiscences which one loves to recall, or shrink from recalling,—longings too unbounded to be called hopes—a submerged world of baffled endeavours, undirected passions, romances lived only in fancy. These take form again and again and become embodied in sound, emerging from the caverns of the mind where they have been biding their time of summons into the light of recognition. This phenomena of the evocation of human passions, sentiments and feelings (*rasas* in term of Indian aesthetics) is explained by psychologists by the theory of 'emotional memory'. As enunciated by M. Ribot, this doctrine claims that emotional states divested of all their accompanying circumstances can leave behind them a memory of themselves. Feelings of love, fear, disappointment, anger, elation, disentangled and disassociated from its cause on the various occasions on which such feelings were experienced, attain an *abstract emotional state,* or *form*—which musical patterns can arouse and through them, by means of association "a kind of emotional reverberation," call up in each hearer his own particular images and ideas which once formed the settings of such emotional states when originally experienced by each individual.

The patterns of Indian musical melodies claim to answer somewhat to these *emotional abstract states* or generalized forms of emotions visualized in dramatic forms with approximate "accompanying circumstances." The melody Ṭoḍī Rāgiṇī [Plates XV-XX] is the emotional symbol of the "feeling of the country side." The human response to the call of nature is embodied in the image of Ṭoḍī, the Indian pastoral symphony *par excellence*. The melody of the early morning—Lalita, [Plate XXXVI] symbolises on the one hand,--the break of the night and the day, and on the other hand,—the separation of the lovers with all its pangs and sufferings told in all the poignancy of the dramatic situation. Here the, 'emotion' as well as its dramatic 'setting' or 'circumstance' or both indicated. In the version of Lalita [Plate XXXVII]—in which the offending lover returns at day-break after spending the night with a rival—the sorrows of love are given in an altogether different 'circumstance', or 'setting'. Vibhāsa [Plate LXXXV], another of the early morning melodies,—pictures pangs of separation—in an analogous, though a somewhat different environment. The cockcrow is the sworn enemy of all love-carousals—and the melody is symbolised in the picture of a lover attempting to shoot the early cock with his bow and arrow. In a version of Lalitā [Plate XXXVII-D]—the feeling of the satiety of love *(rati-tṛpti)* is pictured in the symbol of a beautiful lady who has come out of her love-chamber early in the morning accepting the advent of the dawn as a logical termination of a chapter of love. Rāmakelī [Plate XXXII],—the melody of resentment, claims to concentrate within the orchestration of its peculiar notes—the emotion of an offended lady vainly assauged by her lover. Vasanta [Plate LX] in the dancing rhythm of its symphonic form, suggests the emotion of human-beings on the advent of the new spring. Likewise, —the manly and sonorous symphony of the Megha rāga [Plate LXV]—pictures the majesty of clouds—and the inevitable longings for love-union—that the rainy season invokes. Kānoḍā [Plate LI]—pictured in the image of a young lady—standing at the foot of the *Aśoka* tree—lean as a golden creeper and drenched in tears—is the lamentation of a heroine cut off from her lover by cruel fate. On the other hand, Bhūpālī [Plate LXXVI]—the evening melody,—is the silent joy of the lover as she meets her beloved at the door by her bed-chamber—with her present of flower-garland which she has been weaving for him during the long hours of the separation. In a version of Kāmoda, [Plate XLVIII] the melody suggests the rapture of love-dalliance symbolised in a pair of lovers, who on the pretext of picking lotuses, have selected the loneliest spot by the lotus-pond. And if in some of the morning melodies, passion and the sorrows of separation, receive undue emphasis, this is amply compensated by the conception of Bhairavī [Plate IV],—likewise a morning melody, which,—symbolized in the person of Pārvatî,—worshipping the image of Śiva—in a crystal temple, glorifies the unsullied purity of Love without Desire, and Passion purified by Renunciation. Such are some of the radiant images which flit across the vision of Indian musical imagination. Though rendered in obviously sensuous forms,—they transcend our sense-experience and transport us to a region of super-sensual ecstasy —an atmosphere of sublimated and spiritual emotion.

LIST OF MUSICAL TEXTS

In Sanskrit, Hindi. Persian and Bengali

(Items not otherwise indicated represent Sanskrit Texts).

[This list does not pretend to be anything like a complete Bibliography of Indian Musical texts. It represents texts actually utilised in collecting data put forward in this work].

	Date.
Dattila-muni (mentioned by Bharata, 1-26): DATTILAṂ	Circa 2nd century A.D.
Bharata: NĀṬYA-SĀSTRA, (Chapters 28, 29, 38)	Circa 4th century A.D.
Nārada: NĀRADĪYĀ-ŚIKṢĀ CH. II	Circa 5th century A.D.
Matañga-muni: BṚHAD-DEŚĪ	Circa 5th to 7th century A.D.
KUḌUMIYAMĀLAI INSCRIPTION (PUDUKKOTTAI)	Circa 7th century A.D.
Nārada: SAÑGĪTA-MAKARANDA	Circa 7th to 9th century A.D.
RĀGA-SĀGARA (attributed to Nārada and Dattila)	Circa 8th century A.D.
Mammaṭa: SAÑGĪTA-RATNA-MĀLĀ	Circa 9th to 13th century A.D.
NĀṬYA-LOCANA	Circa 9th century A.D.
Nānya-deva (1197-1133): SARASVATĪ-HṚDAYĀLAṂKĀRA	Circa 1100 A.D.
Abhinava Gupta: ABHINAVA-BHĀRATĪ	Circa 1030 A.D. z
Someśvara deva: MĀNASOLLĀSA or ABHILĀṢĀRTHA CINTĀMAṆI	Circa 1131 A.D.
Śārañgadeva: SAÑGĪTA-RATNĀKARA	1210-1247 A.D.
Parśva-deva: SAÑGĪTA-SAMAYA-SĀRA	Circa 1250 A.D.
RĀGĀRNAVA	Circa 1300 A.D.

	Date.
Śubhaṃkara: SANGĀNA-SĀGARA ..	1308 A.D.
ŚĀRANGARA-DHARA-PADDHATI ..	1363 A.D.
Locana-Kavi: RĀGA-TARAÑGINĪ ..	Circa 1375-1400 A.D.
Nārada: PAÑCAMA-SĀRA-SAṂHITĀ (Asiatic Society of Bengal Ms. Colophon dated 1362 Śaka)	1440 A.D.
Rāṇā Kumbha Karṇa Mahimendra: SAÑGĪTA-MĪMĀMSĀ, SAÑGĪTA-RĀJA	Circa 1450 A.D.
Catura Kallinātha: RATNĀKARA-TĪKĀ	1460 A.D.
Harināyaka: SAÑGĪTA-SĀRA ..	Circa 1500 A.D.
Meṣakarṇa: RĀGAMĀLĀ (Asiatic Society of Bengal. Ms. dated 1431 Saka)	1509 A.D.
Rāja Mānsing Tomār: MĀNA-KUTŪHALA	1486-1518 A.D.
Madana Pāla Deva: ĀNANDA SANJĪVANA	1528 A.D.
Tānsen: RĀGMĀLĀ, (attributed to Tansen), (Hindī)	1549 A.D.
Puṇḍarīk Viṭhṭhala: ṢADRĀGA-CANDRODAYA (Burhān Khān) ..	Circa 1562-1599 A.D.
Puṇḍarīk Viṭhṭhala: RĀGMĀLĀ (Bhandarkar Institute Ms. dated)	1576A.D.
Puṇḍarīk Viṭhṭhala: RĀGMAÑJARĪ (Madho Singh)	Circa 1600 A.D.
Puṇḍarīk Viṭhṭhala: NARTANA-NIRṆAYAṂ	Circa 1610 A.D.
Nārada: CATTVĀRIṂŚACCATA-RĀGA--NIRŪPAṆAṂ	
Rāmāmatya: SVARA-MELA-KALĀ-NIDHI	1550 A.D.
Somanātha: RĀGA-VIVODHA ..	1609 A.D.
Dāmodar Miśra: SAÑGĪTA DARPAṆAṂ	Circa 1625 A.D.
Govind Dīkṣita: SAÑGĪTA SUDHĀ (Composed under the auspices of Raghunāth Nāyak of Tanjore) ..	Circa 1614-1640 A.D.
Hṛdayā Nārāyana Deva of Garwa: HṚDAYA KOUTUKA, HṚDAYA PRAKĀŚA	Circa 1724 Samvat 1646 A.D.

	Date.
Rājā Jagajjotirmalla: SAÑGĪTA SĀRA SAṂGRAHA SAÑGĪTA-BHĀSKARA	Circa 1650 A.D.
Harivallabha: SAÑGĪTA-DARPANA (Hindī) (British Museum Ms. dated 1710 Saṃvat)	1653 A.D.
Venkaṭa-makhī: CATUR-DANḌI-PRAKĀŚIKĀ	1660 A.D.
Ahovala: SAÑGĪTA PĀRIJĀTA .. (Translated into Persian in 1724 A.D.)	Circa 1665 A.D.
Deokavi: RĀG RATNĀKAR, (Hindī), Saṃvat 1780	1673 A.D.
Bhāva-Bhaṭṭa: ANŪPA-SAÑGĪTA-VILĀSA ANŪPA-SAÑGĪTA-RATNĀKARA ANŪPA-SAÑGĪTĀNGKUŚA (Composed during the reign of Mahāraj Anūp Singh)	Circa 1674-1701 A.D.
Subhaṃkara: SAÑGĪTA-DĀMODARA ..	Circa 1690 A.D.
Muḍeveda: SAÑGĪTA-MAKARANDA .. (Composed during the reign of Shāhāji)	1684-1712 A.D.
Puroṣottam Miśra: SAÑGĪTA-NĀRĀYAṆA	Circa 1730-50 A.D.
SAÑGĪTA-MĀLĀ (Copy Ms. dated Samvat 1835=1778 A.D.) .. .. (Published by Lala Kannomal under the title: Sāhitya-Saṅgīta-Nirūpan, Saṃvat 1817, Delhi.)	Circa 1750 A.D.
Saiyid 'Abd-alWali, 'Uzlat: RĀG-MĀLĀ (Hindustānī), dated 25th Muḥarram A.H. 1173	1759 A.D.
Nārāyaṇa Deva: SAÑGĪTA-NĀRĀYAṆA	Circa 1760 A.D.
Tulāji: SAÑGĪTA SĀRĀMṚTA 1765-1788 A.D.)	Circa 1770 A.D
Kavi-Kṛṣṇa: RĀGA-KUTŪHALA (Hindī) (Ms. dated Saṃvat 1853 described in *Sarasvatī*, November 1933, p. 425)	1781 A.D.
SAÑGĪT-SĀR, (Compiled by Maharaja Sawai Pratapsimha Deva, Jaipur), (Hindī)	1779-1804 A.D.
RĀGA-VICĀRA (Bikanir Library Ms.)	Circa 1800 A.D.

	Date.
Mahomed Rezza: NAGMAT-E-ASAPHI (Persian)	1813 A.D.
Rādhāmohan Sen: SAÑGĪTA-TARAÑGA (Bengali)	1818 A.D.
(Published in the Bengali year 1225 Sāl)	1819 A.D.
Diwan Lachhiram: BUDDHI-PRAKĀŚA-DARPANA (Hindī) dated Saṃvat 1880	1823 A.D.
Kṛṣṇānanda Vyāsadeva: RĀGA-KALPA-DRUMA (Hindī)	1843 A.D.
Chhatra Nṛipati: PADA-RATNĀVALĪ (Hindī) (Lithographed in Benares, Saṃvat 1911)	1854 A.D.
Sir Sourindra Mohan Tagore: SAÑGĪTA-SĀRA-SAṂGRAHA (Calcutta, Saṃvat 1932)	1875 A.D.
Gossain Cunni-Lālji: NĀDA-VINODA, (Hindī) (Saṃvat 1953)	1896 A.D.
Bhānu-Kavi (Jagannāth Prasād): KĀVYA-PRABHĀKAR. Dvitīya Mayukh, (Hindī), Saṃvat 1966	1909 A.D.
Pandit Bhāt Khande (Viṣṇu Śarmā): ŚRĪ-MAL-LAKṢA SAÑGĪTAṂ, (Bombay, Śaka 1843)	1921 A.D.
Pandit Bhāt Khande (Viṣṇu Śarma): ABHINAVA RĀG-MAÑJARĪ (Bombay, Śaka 1843)	1921 A.D.

SELECTED BIBLIOGRAPHY

I. BOOKS

RAJA SOURINDRA MOHUN TAGORE: *Six Principal Ragas of the Hindus*, 6 plates, Calcutta 1877. Out of print.

RAJA SOURINDRA MOHUN TAGORE: *The Eight Principal Ragas of the Hindus, with tableaux and dramatic pieces illustrating their character*, pp. 161, 8 plates, Calcutta, 1880. *Out of print.*

J. GROSSET (Lyon): *Contribution à l'étude de la Musique Hindoue*, (Paris, 1888, Leroux). *Out of print.*

B. A. PINGLE: *Indian Music*, pp. XVIII, 341, Index, Byculla, 1898, 2nd Edition. *Out of print.*

ANNE C. WILSON: *A Short Account of the Hindu System of Music*, pp. 48, London, 1904.

RICHARD SIMON: *The Musical Compositions of Somanatha critically edited with a table of notations* (Lithographed Ms. in Nāgarī), pp. 11,33 Leipzig, 1904.

A. K. COOMARASWAMY: *Essays in National Idealism*, Colombo, 1909. Chapter on Music.

MRS. MAUD MANN: *Some Indian Conceptions of Music*, (Proceedings of the Musical Association), London, 1911, 12, pp. 41.

A. C. MACLEOD (Lady Wilson): *Five Indian Songs*, Edinburgh, 1912.

RATAN DEVI: *Thirty Indian songs, with texts and translations* by A. K. Coomaraswamy, London, 1913, 7 Illustrations. *Out of print.* Perhaps Messrs. Luzac & Co. London have copies.

E. CLEMENTS: *Introduction to the Study of Indian Music*, pp. IX. 104, London, 1913. (Longmans Green & Co.).

E. CLEMENTS: *Lectures on Indian Music*, Philharmonic Society, Poona (no date).

A. H. FOX-STRANGWAYS: *The Music of Hindostan*, Oxford, 1914.

K. V. DEVAL: *Theory of Indian Music as expounded by Somanath*, pp. 64, Arya Bhusan Press, Poona, 1916.

Report of the First All-India Musical Conference held at Delhi in

Report of the Frst All-India Musical Conference held at Baroda in 1916, Baroda, 1917.

Report of the Second All-India Musical Conference held at Delhi in 1919. Delhi, 1919.

Report of the Fourth All-India Music Conference held at Lucknow in 1925. Lucknow, 1925.

K. V. DEVAL: *The Rāgas of Hindustan*, Philharmonic Society, Poona, 1918-23, 3 Vols.

H. A. POPLEY: *The Music of India* (Heritage of India Series), Association Press, 3, Russell Street, Calcutta, 1921.

H. P. KRISHNA RAO: *The First Steps in Hindu Music in English* notation, Bangalore.

H. P. KRISHNA RAO: *The Psychology of Music*, Bangalore, 1923. (To be had of author, 6th Road, Chamarajpet, Bangalore).

ATIYA BEGUM FYZEE-RAHAMIN: *The Music of India*, London, Luzac & Co., 1926.

ETHEL ROSENTHAL: *The story of Indian Music and its Instruments*: A Study of the Present & A Record of the Past, (William Reeves), London, 1928.

PANDIT N. V. BHATKHANDE (Vishnu Sarmā): *Hindusthānī Saṅgit Paddhati*, published by B. S. Sukthankar, Vols. I to IV, Poona, San 1914-1932. In Mahratta.

A Hindi translation of this work is in course of publication in the Journal "Sangeeta", Lucknow.

LALA KANNOO MAL: *Kāma-Kalā*, published by the Punjab Sanskrit Book Depot, Lahore, 1931.

M. S. RAMASWAMI AIYAR: *Rāmamātya's "Swara-Kalā-nidhi"* edited with Introduction and Translation, The Annamalai University, 1932.

M. S. RAMASWAMI AIYAR: *Somanāth's "Rāga-vivodha"*, edited with Introduction and Translation, Triplicane, Madras, 1933.

MAHARANA VIJAYADEVJI OF DHARAMPUR: *Sangīt Bhāva* (with pictorial illustrations and notations of rāgas), Bombay, 1933 (Publishers: D. B. Taraporevala & Sons).

RAI BAHADUR BISHAN SWARUP: *Theory of Indian Music*, Swarup Bros. Maithan, Agra, 1933.

II. ESSAYS AND ARTICLES IN JOURNALS, PERIODICALS, ETC.

PANDIT N. V. BHATKANDE: *A Short Historical Survey of the Music of Upper India.* (A paper read at All-India Music Conference, Baroda, 1916) published by "Bombay Samācar," 1917.

PERCY BROWN: *Visualised Music*, Young Men of India May 1918.

JOGENDRA NATH MUKHERJEE: *A Lecture on Rāgas & Rāginīs* delivered at 'Indian Music Salon' held at Government House, Calcutta, on 7th December 1920, published by the Indian Society of Oriental Art, Calcutta, 1921, with illustrations.

P. V. MAUJI: *Rāgmālā*, (a series of articles in English with Sanskrit and Hindi texts, and annotations in Gujarati, accompanied by illustrations of Rāginī pictures, published in the Journal "Suvarṇa-Mālā", Bombay, 1923-1926.

S. G. KANHERE: *Some Remarks on Indian Music*, (Bulletin, School of Oriental Studies, London, Vol. IV, pp. 105-120).

LALA KANNOO MAL: *Notes on Rāginīs*, (Rūpam No. 11, 1922).

PHILIPPE STERN: *La Musique Indoue*, (La Revue Musical, Mai, 1923, pp. 31-36, Paris).

A. K. COOMARASWAMY: *Hindī Rāgmālā texts*, (Journal of the American Oriental Society, Vol. 43, 1933. pp. 396-409).

STANLEY RICE: *Hindi Music*, (The New Criterion, June 1926, pp. 538-551, London).

A. K. COOMARASWAMY: *Dīpaka Rāga*, (Year Book of Oriental Art & Culture, London, 1925, p. 29).

M. RAMAKRISHNA KAVI: *King Nānyadeva on Music*, (The Quarterly Journal of the Andhra Historical Research Society, October 1926, Vol. I, Part 2 pp. 55-63)

M. RAMAKRISHNA KAVI: *Literature on Music,* (*Ibid.,* July 1928, Vol. III, Part 1, pp. 20-29).

M. RAMAKRISHNA KAVI: *Literary Gleanings*: Saṅgītāchāryas: Nānyadeva, Jagadekamalla, Someśvara, Śāraṅgadeva, Pārsvadeva, Devana Bhatta, Aliya Rāmarāya. (*Ibid.,* Vol. IV, Parts 2, 3, & 4, October 1928—April 1929).

BRAJENDRA KISHORE ROY CHOUDHURY: A series of articles in Bengali on the iconography of rāgas with Sanskrit texts in the Bengali monthly Journal *Saṅgīta-Vijñān-Praveśikā* (Bengali years 1335 to 1340).

V. V. NARASIMHACHARY: *The Early Writers on Music,* (Journal Music Academy, Madras, 1930, Vol. I, No. 3, Vol. II, No. 2).

PANDIT V. N. BHATKHANDE: *A Comparative Study of the Leading Music Systems of the 15th, 16th, 17th, and 18th centuries.* (A Series of articles published in "Sangeeta", Lucknow, Vol. I, No. 1, 2, 3, 4, 1930-1931).

T. L. VENKATARAMA IYER: *The Musical Element in Kalidasa* (Journal of Oriental Research, Madras, Vol. IV, Part IV, 1930).

V. RAGHAVAN: *Some Names in Early Saṅgīta Literature,* (Journal of the Music Academy, Madras, Vol. III, Nos. 1 & 2, 1932).

V. RAGHAVAN: *Some More Names in Early Saṅgīta Literature,* (*Ibid.,* Vol. III, No. 3 and 4, 1932).

V. RAGHAVAN: Later *Saṅgīta Literature,* (read before the Music Conference, Madras, December, 1932).

N. C. METHA: *Rāgas & Rāginīs in a Laudian Ms.,* (The Bodleian Quarterly Record, Vol. VI, No. 76, Oxford, 1932).

PHILIPPE STERN: *The Music of India and the theory of the Rāga.* (Indian Art and Letters, New Series, Vol. III, No. 1, pp. 1-9, London, 1933).

W. J. TURNER: '*Visual Music*', (The New Statesman and Nation, London, July 7, 1934, p. 13)

O. C. GANGOLY: '*Rāg Rāginir nāma-rahasya*' [The mystery of the names of melodies], (A series of articles in Bengali published in the Journal *Saṅgīta-Vijñāna-Praveśikā,* Calcutta, Bengali year 1941, Baiśākh to Chaitra).

III. JOURNALS ON INDIAN MUSIC

I. *The Indian Music Journal* (monthly) edited by H. P. Krishna Rao, Mysore, 1911-1912, now extinct.

II. *Sangeeta-Prakāśikā* (monthly), a Bengali Journal, Calcutta (1307 to——), now extinct. A translation in Bengali of the Sanskrit text of Rāga-Vivodha was serially published in this Journal.

III. *Ānanda-Saṅgīta-Patrikā,* (monthly Journal in Bengali, Edited and published by Lady Prativa Chowdhury and Indira Devi, Calcutta (1320——).

IV. *Sangeeta,* A quarterly Journal of Hindustanic Music, published by the Marris College of Hindustani Music, Lucknow. (From 1930, in progress).

V. *The Journal of the Music Academy,* Madras, A quarterly devoted to the Advancement of the Science and Art of Music (From January 1930, in progress).

VI. *Saṅgīta-Vijnāna-Praveśikā* (monthly Journal in Bengali, from 1331 Bengali year, in progress).

SUPPLEMENTARY BIBLIOGRAPHY.

BOOKS:

HEMENDRA LAL ROY: *Problems of Hindusthani Music,* Bharati Bhavan, Calcutta, 1937.

S. SUBRAMANYA SASTRI: *The Sangraha-cuda mani of Govinda.* With a Critical introduction in English by T. R. Srinivasa Iyengar, The Adyar Library, Madras, 1939.

C. SUBRAMANYA AYYAR: *The Grammar of South Indian Music,* 1939. Maharana Vijayadeoji of Dharampur—*Sangit Bhava,* Vol. II (English Gujarati text). B. J. Mody, Sanj Vartaman Press, Bombay, 1940.

G. H. RANADE: *Hindustani Music, an Outline of its Physics,* Poona, 1939.

S. SUBRAMANYA SASTRI: *Sangita-ratnakara* with the commentaries of Chatura-Kallunatha and Simhabhupāla, Bramhavidya, The Adyar Library Bulletin, 1940.

P. S. S. AIYAR AND S. S. SASTRI: *Sangita-Sudhā* of King Raghunatha of Tanjore, Madras, 1941.

K. G. MULAY: *Bharatiya Sangit* (Marathi Text), Yoshoda-chintamani Trust Series, Vol. X, Bombay 1941).

P. SAMBAMOORTY: *South Indian Music,* 3rd Edition, Madras, 1941.

RAMAKRISHNABUA VAZE: *Sangit Kalā Prakash,* Part II (Hindi Text), R. N. Veze, Loka Sangraha Press. Poona, 1941.

C. KUNHAN RAJA: *Sangita-Ratnakara of Sarangadeva,* English Translation, The Adyar Library, Madras, 1945.

V. N. BHATKHANDE: *A Comparative study of some of the Leading Music Systems of the 15th, 16th, 17th and 18th Centuries,* Bombay, 1941.

V. N. BHATKHANDE: *Hindusthani Sangit Paddhati,* 5th Edition (Marathi Text) Bombay, 1941.

SHRIPADA BANDOPADHYAYA: *The Music of India,* A Popular Handbook of Hindusthani Music, with 23 reproductions of Indian Miniature Paintings depicting Ragas and Raginis, D. B. Taraporevala Sons & Company, Bombay.

R. L. BATRA: *Science and Art of Indian Music,* Lion Press, Lahore, 1945.

D. P. MUKHERJI: *Indian Music, An Introduction,* Kutub Publishers, Bombay, 1945.

SHRIPADA BANDOPADHYAYA: *The Origin of Raga.* A short Historical Sketch of Indian Music, Sircar Bros. Daryagang, Delhi, 1946.

ARTICLES:

MISS P. C. DHARMA: *Musical Culture in the Ramayana,* Indian Culture, Vol. IV, 1938. pp. 445-454.

MAHARANA SAHEB OF DHARAMPUR: *Music in India,* Indian Arts and Letters XII, 1938, pp. 61-64.

MUHAMMAD UMAR KOKIL: *Music during the reign of the Sultans of Gujarat* (Gujarati Text). Quarterly Journal of Forbes Gujarati Sabha, Bombay, Vol. III, 1938, p. 398

LAKSHMANA SANKARA BHATTA: *The mode of Singing Sama Gana,* Poona Orientalist, IV, 1939, p. 1-21.

V. K. R. MENON AND V. K. RAGHAVAN: *"Govinda", the greatest musical theorist of South India,* Bulletin Ramverma Research Institute, Trichur, VII, 1939, pp. 140-143.

N. S. RAMACHANDRAN: *The Ragas of Karnatic Music,* Bulletin No. 1, Department of Indian Music, University of Madras, 1938.

P. SAMBHAMURTI: *A History of Sacred Music of India,* K. V. Rangaswami Aiyangar Commemoration Volume, Madras, 1940.

JOHN KAVANAGH: *Indian Music,* Indian Arts & Letters, XIV, 1940, pp. 105-110.

TARUN GHOSHAL: *Hindu Contribution to Music,* Calcutta Review, LXXIX, 1940, pp. 257-266.

K. D. RUKMINIYAMA: *Music,* Journal of Indian History, XX, 1941, pp. 133-34.

DENNIS STOLL: *The Philosophy and Modes of Hindu Music,* Asiatic Review, Vol. 37, 130, 1941, pp. 334-342.

O. C. GANGOLY: *Non-Aryan Contribution to Aryan Music,* Annals of the Bhandarkar Oriental Research Institute.

O. C. GANGOLY: *Date of the Saṃgīta-Rāga-Kalpa-Drumah,* Annals of the Bhandarkar Oriental Research Institute, Poona, Vol. XV, Pts. 1-11, 1934.

O. C. GANGOLY: *Who were the Sātavāhanas?* Journal of the Andhra Historical Research Society, Vol. XI, Pts. 1 & 2, P. 13 —15 (Discussion of Āndhri Ragini).

O. C. GANGOLY—*Dhruvā: A type of Old Indian Stage-Songs,* the Journal of the Music Academy, Madras, Vol. XIV, Pts. I—VI, P. P. 1-7.

O. C. GANGOLY: *The Meaning of Music,* The Hindoosthan, (a quarterly Journal published from Calcutta) January—March 1946, P. 12.

Dr. BANI CHATTERJI—*Applied Music,* a Lecture delivered at the Royal Asiatic Society of Bengal, 8th March, 1948, and Published by Bankim Mukherji, No. 5/1B, Baranashi Ghose 2nd Lane, Calcutta.

APPENDICES

CLASSIFICATION OF RĀGĀS IN THE APPENDICES

1. According to Dattila (Second Century A.D.)
2. According to Bharata's Nāṭya-Śāstra (C. 3rd Century A.D.)
3. According to Bṛhaddeśi by Matanga (Circa 5th to 7th Century).
4. According to Sangîta Makaranda by Nārada (Circa 7th to 9th Century A.D.)
5. According to Mammata (about the eleventh century A.D.)
6. According to Nāṭya-locana (circa 850-1000 A.D.)
7. According to King Nānya deva's Sarasvatī—Hṛdayalāmkāra (circa 1097 to 1154 A.D.)
8. According to Someśvara Deva (circa 1131 A.D.)
9. According to Sangîta-Ratnākara by Śārangadeva (1210-1247 A.D.)
10. According to Sangîta-samaya-śara by Párśvadeva (circa 1250 A.D.)
11. According to Rāga-sāgara, attributed to the joint authors Narada & Dattila.
12. According to Rágárṇava (datable about the 1300 A.D.)
13. According to Pancama Samhitā by Narada.
14. According to Kallinātha, (1460 A.D.)
15. According to Rágamálá by Meṣakarṇa (dated about 1509 A.D.)
16. According to Raga-Tarangini by Locan-Kavi (circa 1375 A.D.)
17. According to Svara-mela-kalānidhi by Rama-matya (1550 A.D.)
18. According to Rāgāmālā by Pundalik Vithala.
19. According to Catvārimśacchata-raga-nirūpanam by Narada (circa 1550 A.D.)
20. According to Rága-vivodha by Soma-nath (1609 A.D.)

21. According to Raga-Darpaṇa by Dāmodara Miśra (circa 1625 A.D.)

22. According to Hrdaya-prakāsā by Hrdayanārāyaṇa Deva (circa Samvat 1724-1646 A.D.)

24. According to Catur-dandi-Prákāsikā by Vyankatamakhi (1660 A.D.)

25. According to Anūpa-Sangîtānkuśa by Bhava-Bhaṭṭa (1674-1701 A.D.)

26. According to Anūpa-Sangîta-ratnākara, by Bhava-bhatta (1674-1701 A.D.)

27. According to Sangita-narayana by Purushottama Misra, court poet of Narayana Deva of the Gajapati Dynasty (Circa 1730 A.D.)

28. According to Sangîta-Sārāmrtoddhāra by King Tulaji of Tanjore (1763-1787 A.D.)

29. According to Rāga-Kutūhala by Radha Krishna Kavi, composed in Samvat 1853-1781 A.D.

30. According to Sangīta-sara, compiled by Maharaja Sawai Pratap Sihma Deo of Jaipur (1779-1804 A.D.)

31. According to Bramhā.

32. According to the School of Bharata.

33. According to the School of Hanumāna.

34. According to the Hindi texts inscribed on the series of miniatures in the British Museum Ms. Add. Or. 2821.

35. According to a Hindusthānî (Urdu) Manuscript of Rāga-mālā by Saiyid "Abd-al-Wali" Uẓlat, (A.D. 1759).

36. According to Pandit V. N. Bhatkhande (Pundit Visnu Sarma), B.A., LL.B. of Bombay, as given in his Sanskrit treatise Abhinavaraga-manjari (Poona 1921).

APPENDIX 1.

Eleven Composite Játis (modes).

According to Dattila (Trivandram Edition, No. CII, 1930, p. 5, 49-54). The data of this text, if not the text itself, may be as early as second century A.D.

Names.	Component Jātis.
1. Sadja-Madhyamā	Sadjā, Madhamā.
2. Sadja-Kaiśikî	Sadjā, Gāndhārî.
3. Sadjodicyavatî	Sadjā, Gāndhārî, Dhaivatî.
4. Gāndharodîcyavā	Sadjā, Gāndhārî, Madhyamā, Dhaivati.
5. Madhyamodîcyavā	Gāndhārî, Madhyamā, Pancamî, Dhaivatî.
6. Rakta-Gāndhārî	Gāndhārî, Madhamā, Pancamî, Naiṣādî.
7. Āndhrî	Gāndhārî, Ārṣabhî.
8. Nandayantî	Gāndhārî, Ārṣabhî, Pancamî.
9. **Kārmāravî**	Gāndhārî, Niṣādî (*).
10. Gāndhāra-Pancamî	Gāndhārî, Pancamî.
11. **Kaiśikî**	Sadjā, Gandhārî, Madhyamā, Pancamî, Niṣādî.

* "Sa-niṣādastu gāndhāryah kuryu kārmāravîmimāh" 53.

The text differing from Bharata & Śārangadeva, appears to suggest that Kārmāravî is a composed of two modes:—Gāndhārî & Niṣādî.

APPENDIX 2.

The Eighteen Játis (modes).

According to Bharata's Nāṭya-Śāstra, C, 3rd Century A.D.

(Chapter 28, Verses 41-45.)

Sadja-grāma.	Madhyama-grāma.	
Sādjî (or Sādjā)	Gāndhārî (or Gāndhārā)	Madhyamodîcyavā.
Ārṣabhî	Madhyamā	Nandayantî.
Dhaivatî	Pancamî	Karmāravî.
Nîṣādinî (or Niṣādavatî)	Gāndhārodîcyavā	Āndhrî.
Sadjodîcyavatî or Odicyavā)	Gāndhāra-Pancamî	Kaiśikî.
Sadja-Kaiśikî	Rakta-Gāndhārî	
Sadjamadhyā (or madhyamā)		

Eleven Composite Játis.

(Chapter 28, Verses 48-54.)

	Names.	Component Jātis.
1.	Saḍja-Madhyamā	Sāḍjî, Madhyamā.
2.	Saḍja-Kaiśikî	Gāndhārî, Sādjî.
3.	Saḍjodîcyavā	Sāḍjî, Gāndhārî, Dhaivatî.
4.	Gāndhārodîcyavatî	Sāḍjî, Gāndhārî, Pancamî, (Madhyama, G), Dhaivatî.
5.	Madhyamodîcyavā	Gāndhārî, Pancamî, Madhyamā, Dhaivatî.
6.	Rakta-Gāndhārî	Gāndhārî, Pancamî, Niṣādî.
7.	Āndhrî	Gāndhārî, Ārṣabhî.
8.	Nandayantî	Ārṣabhî, Pancamî, Gāndhārî.
9.	Karmāravî	Niṣādî, Ārṣabhî, Pancamî.*
10.	Gāndhārapancamî	Gāndhārî, Pancamî.
11.	Kaiśikî	Sāḍjî, Gāndhārî, Madhyamā, Pancamí, Niṣādî.

* "Karmāravîm niṣādî sārṣabhî pancamï kuryuh" 53.

Classification or Jātis, according to the number of their notes (svaras).

(Chapter 28, Verses 57-64.)

	4 Sampūrṇa (Hepta-tonic)	4 Sāḍva (Hexa-tonic)	10 Auḍava (Penta-tonic)
Saḍja-grāma.	1 Saḍja-kaiśikî	1 Sāḍjî	5 { Ārṣabhî, Dhaivatî, Niṣāḍî, Saḍja-madhyamā, Saḍjodîcyavatî }
Madhyama-grāma	3 { Karmāravî, Gāndhāra-pancamî, Madhyamodîcyavā }	3 Gāndharodîcyavā, Āndhrî, Nandayantî	5 { Gāndhārî, Rakta-gāndharî, Madhyamā, Pancamî, Kaiśikî }

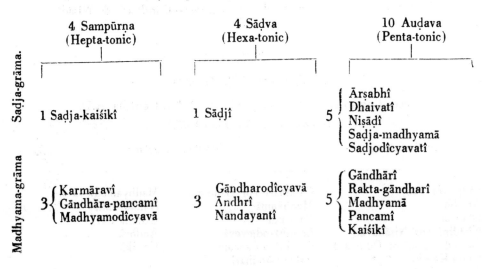

APPENDIX 3.

CLASSIFICATION OF RĀGAS.

Into Rāga-gîtis, Sādhārana-gîtis, Bhāṣā-gîtis, Bibhsá-gītis.

According to Brhaddeśî by Matanga (Circa 5th to 7th Century,) melodies, known under the generic name of *gîtis*, or folk-songs, or airs, were of seven varieties, one of which represented the *rága-gîtis* or melodies proper. The melodies had their derivatives known as *bhásās*, the latter being subdivided into Vibhāṣās. The *bháṣás* & *vibhásás*, correspond to rāgiṇîs of later times.

[Brhaddeśî (Trivandrum Edition) p. 82-133. The Author follows two earlier authorities Yāstika & Śārdûla.]

GÎTIS.

1. Śuddha-gîtis
2. Bhinnaka-gîtis
3. Gouḍîkā-gîtis
4. Sādharaṇî-gîtis
5. Rāga-gîtis
6. Bhāṣā-gîtis
1. Vibhāṣā-gîtis

SĀDHĀRANA-GÎTIS.

1. Śaka
2. Kakubha
3. Harmāṇa-Pancama
4. Rūpa-sādhārita
5. Gāndhāra-Pancama
6. Ṣadja-Kaiśika

These were later accepted in the classes of rāga proper, affiliated to the earliest rāga system.

RĀGA-GÎTIS.

1. Takka (-Tanka)
2. Souvîra
3. Mālava-Pancama
4. Khāḍava
5. Malava-kaiśika
6. Voṭṭa-Rāga
7. Hindo-loka
7. Takka-Kaiśika

BHĀSĀ-GÎTIS.

Ascribed to each of the rāgas.

1. TAKKA-RĀGA

1. Travaṇā
2. Travaṇodbhavā
3. Veranjikā
4. Chevātî
5. Mālavesarikā
6. Gūrjarî
7. Sourāṣtrî
8. Saindhabhî
9. Vesarikā
10. Pancamākyā
11. Ravi-Candrā
12. Aṃvā-herî
13. Lalitā
14. Kolāhalî
15. Madhyama-grāmikā
16. Gāndhāra-pancama

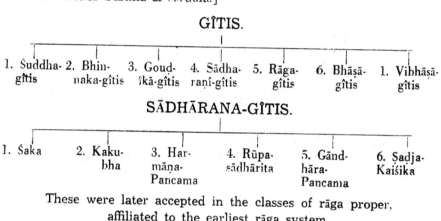

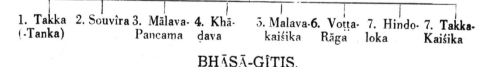

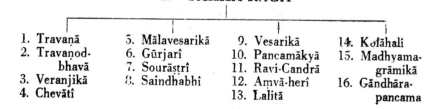

2. SOUVÎRAKA

1. Souvîrî
2. Vega-madhyamā
3. Sādhāritā
4. Gāndhārî

3. PANCAMA

1. Ābhîrî
2. Bhāvinî
3. Māngālî
4. Saindhavî
5. Gūrjarî
6. Dākṣiṇātyā
7. Āndhrî (?) (Āndhālî)
8. Tānodbhavā
9. Travanî
10. Kaiśikî

4. BHINNA-ṢAḌJA

1. Viśuddhā
2. Dākṣiṇātyā
3. Gāndhārî
4. Śrî-kanṭhî
5. Pourālî
6. Vangālî
7. Saindhavî
8. Kālindî
9. Pulindî

5. MĀLAVA-KAIŚIKA

1. Śuddhā
2. Ādya-vesarikā
3. Harṣa-pūrî
4. Māngālî
5. Saindhabhî
6. Ābhîrî
7. Khandanî
8. Gunjarî (?)

6. VOṬṬA-RĀGA

Mangalā.

7. HINDOLAKA

1. Vesarî
2. Prathama-Manjarî
3. Chevāṭî
4. Ṣaḍja-madhyamā
5. Madhurî (?) (Madhukarî)

8. TAKKA-KAIŚIKA

1. Drāviḍî
2. Mālavā
3. Bhinna-Lalikā

APPENDIX 4.

CLASSIFICATION OF RĀGAS.

According to *Sangīta Makaranda* by Nārada (circa 7th to 9th century A.D.)

Two systems are given one after another. According to the first scheme, the major melodies are eight in number, and the minor melodies twenty-four, aggregating thirty-two melodies. According to the second scheme, the major melodies are six in number, and the minor melodies, thirty-six, aggregating forty-two. Owing to a *lacuna* in the text, the second scheme is not available in its entirety.

The first scheme, with three rāginîs for each rāga, appears to be very old. But the text of *Sangīta-makaranda* is, probably, not as early as the 7th century.

[FIRST SCHEME.]

1. BHUPĀLA

| 1. Velāvalî | 2. Malaharî | 3. Vahulî |

2. BHAIRAVA

| 1. Devakriyā | 2. Pourālî | 3. Kāmbhārî |

3. ŚRÍ-RĀGA

| 1. Kāmbhojî | 2. Bhallātî | 3. Kuranjikā |

5. PAḌA-MANJARÎ

| 1. Deśî | 2. Manoharî | 3. Tuṇḍî |

5. NĀṬA

| 1. Sāranga | 2. Nāṭākhyā (?) | 3. Ahari |

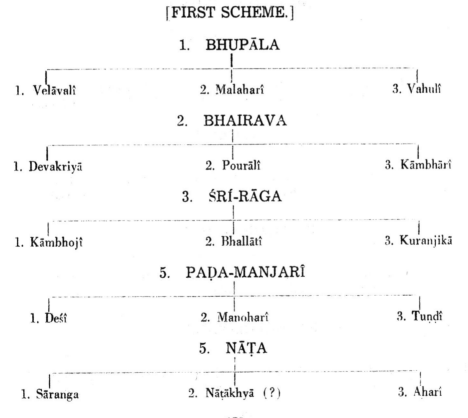

6. VANGĀLA

1. Nārāyaṇî
2. Gāndhārî
3. Ranjî

7. VASANTA

1. Parāṭî (? Varāṭî)
2. Drāvaḍî
3. Haṃsî

8. MĀLAVA

1. Guṇḍa-kriyā
2. Dhūrjarî (Gūrjarî)
3. Gouḍî

[SECOND SCHEME.]

1. ŚRÎ-RĀGA

1. Gouḍî
2. Kolāhalî
3. Drāvalî
4. Āndolikî
5. Mādhavî
6. Deva-Gāndharî

2. PANCAMA

1. Śuddha-Nāṭā
2. Sāverî
3. Saindhavî
4. Mālatî
5. Troṭi
6. Koumodakî

3. MEGHA-RĀGA

1. Sourāṣṭrî
2. Kāṃbhārî
3. Vangālî
4. Madhumādhavî
5. Devakrî
6. Bhūpālî

4. NĀTA-NĀRĀYANA

1. Vallabhā
2. Mādhavî
3. Vidaghdhā
4. Abhisārikā
5. Triveṇî
6. Megharanjî

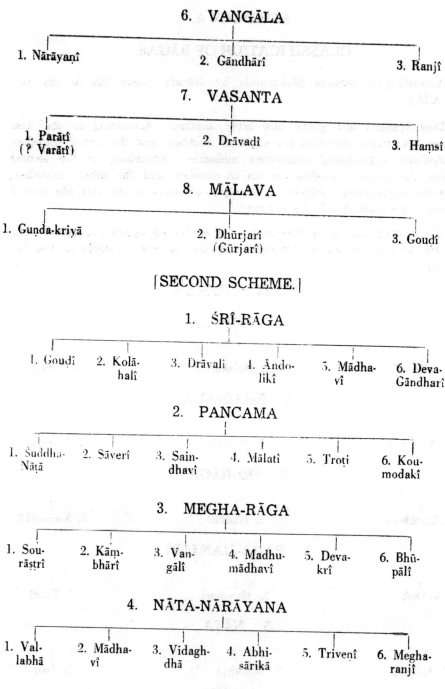

5. VASANTA

6. BHAIRAVA

(The rāgiṇîs of the melodies Vasanta and Bhairava do not appear in the text available.)

APPENDIX 5.

CLASSIFICATION OF RĀGAS

into six rāgas & thirty-six rāgiṇîs.

According to Mammaṭa (ācārya), author of *Sangîta-ratna-málá* as, cited in *Sangîta-nárâyaṇa*. Some scholars identify Mammaṭa, the author of this musical text, with Mammaṭ, the great authority on poetics, author of *Kávya-prakâśa*, who flourished about the eleventh century A.D.

1. KARNĀṬA

1. Vandhanî (?)	2. Mālavaśrî	3. Sindhu	4. Velāvalî	5. Prapātinî (?)	6. Vibhāṣā

2. NĀṬA

1. Kāṃbhojî	2. Nāṭabhāṣā	3. Tudikā	4. Gunamanjarî (?) (-Guṇakriyā (?))	5. Śekharî	6. Mukharî

3. (MEGHA)-MALLĀRA

1. Mallārî	2. Lalitā	3. Paṭamanjarî	4. Madhukirî	5. Bhāṣakārî	6. Deśî

4. DEŚĀKH

1. Gunjarî (-Gujjarî ?)	2. Rāmakirî	3. Guṇḍakirî	4. Sutodikā	5. Dhānasî	6. Varāṭî

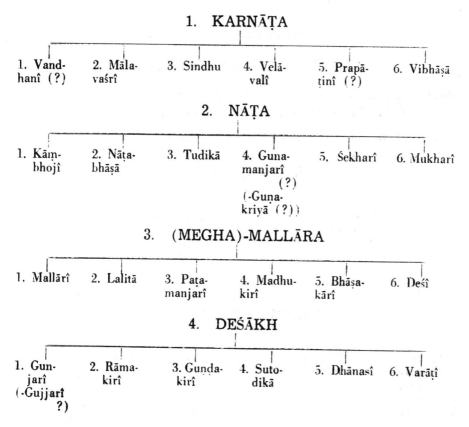

5. MĀLAVA

1. Śivi (?)
2. Kedāra
3. Meṣa-mā (?)
4. Jîvikā
5. Kandu-śritā (?)
6. Travaṇā

6. VASANTA

1. Bhai-ravî
2. Rega-hārî (?) (-Reva-guptā ?)
3. Megha-tālî
4. Supan-camî
5. Amvā-toji (?) (-Āmbho-jî ?)
6. Totka (?) (-Tan-ka)

(The absence of the Bhairava rāga, and the ascription of Bhairavî to the group of Vasanta lend an early date to this scheme.)

APPENDIX 6.

CLASSIFICATION OF RĀGAS

According to *Nāṭya-locana* (*circa* 850-1000 A.D.) into three groups of Śuddha, Sālaṃka & Sandhi (? Samkîrṇa) rāgas.

(Ms. No. 111, E. 158, in the Collection of the Asiatic Society of Bengal.)

ŚUDDH RĀGAS

1. Pancama-Mālava
2. Mādhavāri (?)
3. Hindola
4. Mālasikā
5. Velāvalî
6. Toḍî
7. Gāndhāra
8. Nāṭa

ŚĀLAṂKA-RĀGAS

1. Lalita
2. Nārada-Bhairavi
3. Bhāṣa
4. Vasanta
5. Gurjjarî
6. Koḍa-Deśāg
7. Deśa-Varāṭi
8. Vicitrā
9. Gouṇḍakirî
10. Varāḍî
11. Vangāla
12. Karṇāṭa
13. Rāmakirî
14. Sālaṃka
15. Deśāga
16. Mālava-rāga

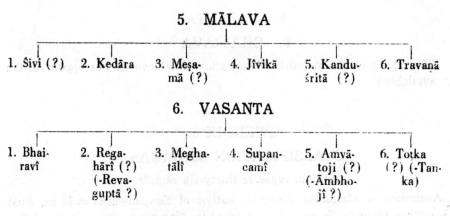

SANDHI-RĀGAS

1. Mallāra
2. Paṭhamanjarî
3. Dhanāsî
4. Kakubhā (?)
5. Himakirî
6. Savarî
7. Divāḍî
8. Khaṃvāvatî
9. Takka
10. Kāmoda
11. Devakîrî
12. Loungirātî (?)
13. Moṭakî
14. Bhallāta
15. Vāheḍî
16. Guṇakîrî
17. Kokîrikā
18. Madhukirî
19. Gouḍî
20. Anunî

APPENDIX 7.

CLASSIFICATION OF RĀGAS

According to King Nānyadeva's Sarasvatî—Hṛdayālaṃkāra (circa 1097 to 1154 A.D.) available in a single Ms. in the collection of the Bhandarkar Oriental Research Institute, Poona (No. 111 of 1869-70). The author mentions a class called Root-rāgas (mūla-rāga). Unfortunately, he does not specify them.

He gives full descriptions and notations of numerous rāgas, under three groups of 'Ṣaḍja-grāma, Madhya-grāma and Gāndhāra-grāma.

6 GITÎS

Śuddha | Bhinna | Gouḍa | Vesara | Sādhāraṇa

8 PRINCIPAL BHĀSĀS

Mālava- Vesarî | Desākhya | Mālava | Sourāṣṭrî | Saindhavî | Svarākya | Madhya-deha (?) — Pancama- lakṣita (?)

AN ALTERNATIVE LIST OF

10 BHĀṢĀS.

Bhammāni — Fourālî | Bhairavî | Hindolî | Sāverî — Pallavî | Vaṛāṭî | Āndhālî | Madhukarî — Ghanṭārava

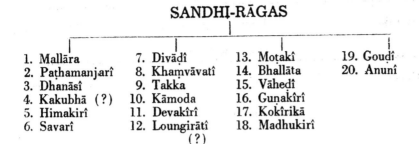

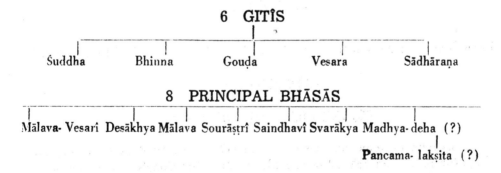

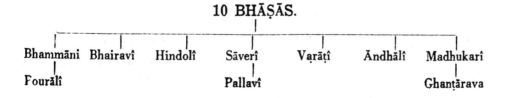

BHINNA-GÎTIS

- Bhinna-kaśika
- Bhinna- madhyama
- Bhima-sadja

Gounda-Gîtis

- Andhra-Gouda
- Gouḍa
- Kaiśika-Madhyama
- Gouḍa-Pancama

SĀDHĀRAṆA-GÎTIS

- Reva-Gupta
- Bhammāna-Pancama
- Rūpa-Sādhārita

ANTARA-BHĀṢĀ

- Protākhya
- Bhasalî
- Tānod-bhava
- Madhurî (?)
- Sālavāhinî

KRIYANGA (EARLIEST LIST).

- Kumuda-Krti
- Hanu- Krti
- Śiva- Krti
- Nāma- Krti
- Kumuda-Krti
- Rāma-Krti

KRIYĀNGA (LATER LIST).

- Deva- Kṛti
- Dāmva- Krti
- Tri-Netra- Kṛti
- Bhāva- Krti
- Dhānya- Krti

APPENDIX 8.

CLASSIFICATION OF RĀGAS

According to Someśvara Deva (Circa 1131 A.D.) cited in Rāga-darpaṇa (Raja Sir S. M. Tagore's Edition, 1881, P. 72). The Chapter in the author's Encyclopædia Mānsollāsa, does not give any classification of the Melodies. Probably this is given in his work Sangîta-ratnāvalî, the text of which is now lost.

1. ŚRÎ-RĀGA

1. Mālaśrî
2. Trivaṇî
3. Gourî
4. Kedārî
5. Madhu-Mādhavî
6. Pāhā-dikā

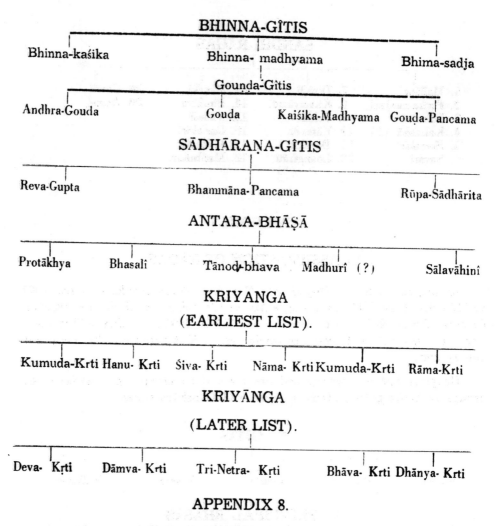

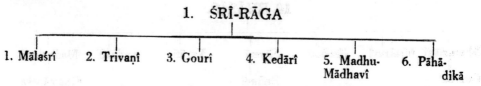

2. VASANTA

1. Désî
2. Devagiri
3. Varātî
4. Todikā
5. Hindolî
6. Lalitā

3. BHAIRAVA

1. Bhairavî
2. Gujjarî
3. Rāma-Kirî
4. Guna-Kirî
5. Vangālî
6. Saindhavî

4. PANCHAMA

1. Vibhāṣā
2. Bhūpālî
3. Karṇāṭî
4. Vadahaṃsikā
5. Mālavî
6. Paṭa manjarî

5. MEGHA-RĀGA

1. Mallārî
2. Sourāthi
3. Sāverî
4. Koușikî
5. Gāndhārî
6. Hara-Śṛngāra

6. NAṬṬA-NĀRĀYANA

1. Kāmodî
2. Kalyāṇî
3. Ābhîrî
4. Nātikā
5. Sārangî
6. Nāṭṭa-Hāṃvîra

APPENDIX 9.

CLASSIFICATION OF RĀGAS

According to Sangîta-Ratnākara by Śārangadeva (1210-1247 A.D.). He gives an historical survey of rāgas, according to Kaśyapa, Yāstika, and Matanga. He enumerates 30 grāma-rāgas, viz:—7 Śudda, 5 Bhinnakas, 3 Gouḍas, 8 Vesaras, and 7 Sādhāritas (Sādhāraṇa).

GRĀMA-RĀGAS

ŚUDDHA

- Ṣadja-Kaiśiki
- Ṣadja-Madhyama
- Śuddha-Sādhārita
- Ṣadja-grāma (? Ṣadjî)
- Pancama
- Ṣāḍva
- Śuddha-Kaiśika

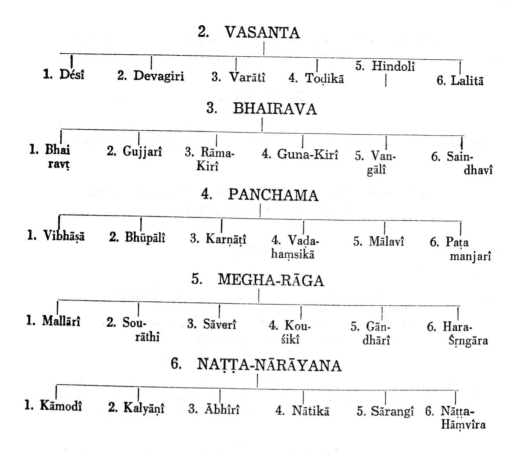

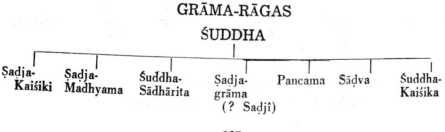

(Of these, the first four belong to the Ṣaḍja-grāma, and the last three to Madhyamā-grāma.)

BHINNAKA

- Kaiśika-Madhyama
- Bhinna-Ṣaḍja
- Tāna
- Kaiśika
- **Bhinna-Pancama**

(Of these, the first two belong to the Ṣaḍja-grāma, and the three to Madhyama-grāma.)

GOUḌA

- Gouḍa-Kaiśika-Madhyama
- Gouḍa-Pancama
- Gouḍa-Kaiśika

(Of these, the first two belong to Saḍjágrāma and the last two Madhyamā-grāma)

VESARA

- Ṭakka
- Vesara-Khaḍava
- Souvîra (?)
- Voṭṭa
- Mālava-Kaiśika
- Mālava-Pancama
- Ṭakka-Kaiśika
- **Hindola**

(Of these, the first two belong to Ṣadja-grāma, the next four to Madhyama-gràma and the last tu both grāmas.)

(These 8 Vesara melodies are designated as "Rāga-gîtis" by Matanga, Appedix 3.)

SĀDHĀRITA

- Rūpa-Sādhārita
- Śaka
- Bham-māṇā-Pancama
- Narta-Gāndhāra
- **Pancama**
- Saḍja-Kaiśika
- **Kakubha**

(Of these, the first three belong to Ṣaḍja-grāma, the second three to Madhyama, and the last to both gramas).

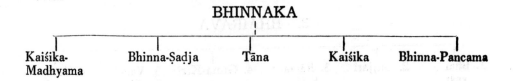

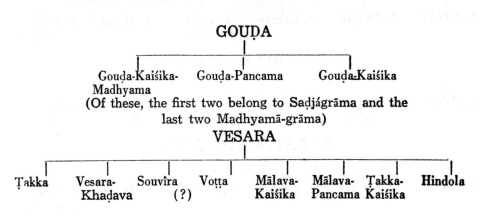

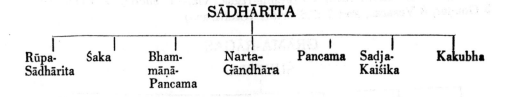

8 UPARĀGAS

Śakà-tilaka	**Takka-Saindhava**	Kokil	Reva-gupta	Pancama-Ṣaḍava	Bhāvanā-Pancama	Nāga-Gāndhāra	Nāga-Pancama

A group of 17 Rágas, wrongly stated to be 20 in number:

1. **Śrî-rāga**
2. **Naṭṭa**
3. **Vāngāla**
4. **Bhāṣā**
5. **Madhyama-ṣāḍava**
6. Rakta-hāṃsa
7. Kohla-hāsa
8. Prasava
9. Bhairava-dvani
10. Megha-rāga
11. Soma-rāga
12. Kāmoda
13. Abhra (Āmra)-Pancama
14. Kandarpa
15. Deśākhya
16. Kaiśika-kakubha
17. Naṭṭa-Nārāyaṇa

15 JANAKA or "PARENT" RĀGAS.

(on the authority of Yāstika).

1. **Souvîra**
2. **Kakubha**
3. **Takka**
4. **Pancama (Śuddha)**
5. Bhinna-Pancama
6. Takka-Kaiśika
7. Hindola
8. Bhoṭṭa
9. Mālava-Kaiśika
10. Gāndhāra-Pancama
11. Bhinna-Ṣadja
12. Vesara- Ṣāḍava
13. Mālava-Pancama
14. Tāna
15. Pancama-Ṣāḍabha

APPENDIX 10.

CLASSIFICATION OF RĀGAS

According to *Sangîta-samaya-sára by Párśvadeva* (circa 1250 A.D.).

(The author does not name the major melodies (janaka-rāga) **but only gives a classification of the** derivative rāgas, aggregating 101 rāgas. **Out of these he describes 44** rāgas).

20 RĀGĀNGAS

(Saṃpūrṇa)

- **Madhyamādi**
- **Śankarābharaṇa**
- **Toḍâî**
- **Deśî**
- **Hindola**
- **Śuddha-vangāla**

- Āmra-panca
- Ghaṇṭā-rava
- Gūrjari-somarāga
- Mālavaśrî
- Dîpa-rāga
- Varāṭi

(Ṣāḍava)

- Gouḍa
- Deśî
- Dhannāsi
- Deśākhyā

(Ouḍava)

- Bhairava
- Śrî-rāga
- Mārga-Hindola
- Guṇḍa-krî

47 BHĀṢĀNGAS

(Sampūrṇa)

- Kaiśiki
- Velā-uli
- Śuddha-varāṭi
- Ādi-kāmoda
- Nāṭṭā
- Ābhîri

- Vrhat-dākṣiṇātyā
- Laghvîdākṣiṇātyā
- Pourālî
- Bhinna-Pourālî
- Madhukari
- Ranganti
- Goranji
- Prathama-manjari
- Sāla-vāhini
- Naṭṭa-nārāyaṇa
- Utpalî
- Vegaranji
- Taranginṇi
- Dhvani
- Nādāntari

(Ṣāḍava)

- Karṇāṭa-vangāla
- Sāveri
- Andhāli
- Śrî-kaṇṭhi
- Utpali
- Goudî
- Śuddhā-sourāṣṭri
- Bhammāni
- Saindhî-rāga
- Chāyā-rāga

(Ouḍava)

- Nāgadvani
- Āhîri
- Kāmvoji
- Pulindi
- Kacchalli
- Cohāri-Goullî
- Gāndhāra-gati
- Lalitā
- Trāvaṇi
- Saindhava
- Domvaki
- Saindhavi
- Kālindi
- Khasikā

31 UPĀNGAS

(Sampūrṇa)

- Saidhava-varāṭi
- Antala-varāṭi
- Avasthāna-Varāṭi
- Drāviḍa-varāṭi
- Pratāp-Varāṭi
- Svara-varāṭi
- Turuṣka-Toḍḍi

- Sourāṣṭra-Gūrjarî
- Dakṣiṇa-Gūrjari
- Drāviḍa-Gūrjarî
- Karnāṭa-Gouḍa
- Drāviḍa-Gouḍa
- Chāyā-Gouḍa
- Lāulî-Gouḍa

- Bhairavi
- Samhala-Kamoda (Simhala)
- Devāla
- Mahuri
- Chāyā-nāṭṭā

(Ṣāḍava)

- Mahārāṣṭra-Gūrjari
- Khambhāti
- Gurunji
- Rāma-kri
- Hunji (kā)
- Bhallāti
- Mallāri

(Ouḍava)

- Chāyā-toḍḍi
- Deśāla-Gouḍa
- Turuṣka-Gouḍa
- Pratāpa-Velāuli
- Pūrnāṭa
- Mad-hāra

3 KRIYĀNGAS

(Sampūrṇa)

- Devaki (Devakri)
- (Trinetra-kri)
- Trinetraki

(Ṣāḍava)

- Svabhāvakri

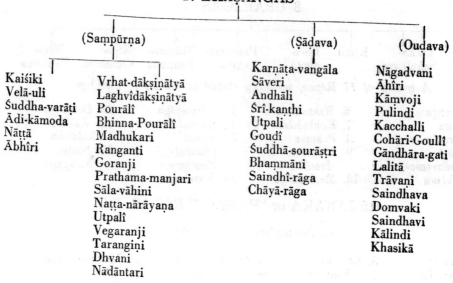

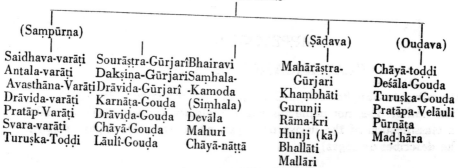

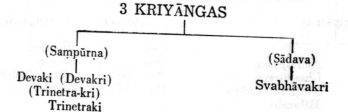

APPENDIX 11.

CLASSIFICATION OF RĀGAS.

According to Rāga-sāgara, attributed to the joint authors Nārada & Dattila (Ms. No. 1304, 13015 in the Govt. Or. Mss. Library, Madrass, Catalogue, Vol. XXII).

1. BHAIRAVA

1. Deva-kriyā
2. Megha-rañjanî
3. Kurañjî

2. BHUPALA

1. Vilaharî
2. Malaharî
3. Subhaṇḍî

3. ŚRÎ RĀGA

1. Mandālî
2. Sāhulî
3. Bhallātî

4. PAṬAMANJARÎ

1. Deśî
2. Mukhārî
3. Lalitā

5. VASANTA

1. Rāma-kriyā
2. Varālî
3. Goulî

6. MĀLAVA-RĀGA

1. Guṇḍakriyā
2. Ghurjarî(?)
3. Pālî

7. VANGĀLA-RĀGA

1. Kalyāṇî
2. Āhirî
3. Sāverî

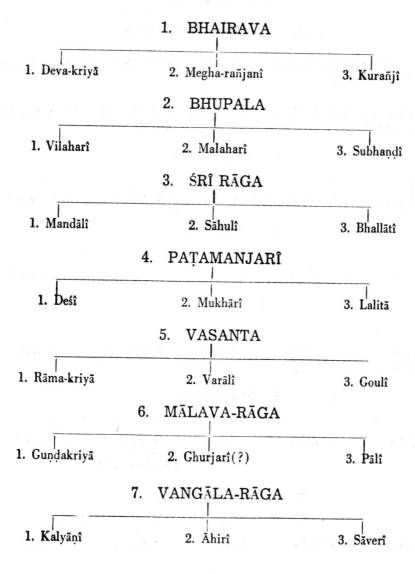

8. NAṬA-RĀGA

1. Ghanṭā-rava
2. Kāmbhojî
3. Śankarābharaṇa

APPENDIX 12.

CLASSIFICATION OF RĀGAS.

According to *Rágárṇava* as cited in the *Śárangadhara-Paddhati,* a work compiled in 1363 A.D.

The original text of *Rágárṇava* (datable about the 1300 A.D.) has not yet been traced.

1. BHAIRAVA

1. Vañgapāla
2. Guṇakari
3. Madhyamādi
4. Vasanta
5. Dhanaśrî

2. PANCAMA

1. Lalitā
2. Gurjjarî
3. Deśî
4. Varāṭî
5. Rāma-krit

3. NAṬA

1. Naṭa-Nārāyaṇa
2. Gāndhāra
3. Sālaga (Sālaṃka)
4. Kedāra
5. Karṇāṭa

4. MALLĀRA

1. Megha
2. Mallārikā
3. Mālava-Kouśika
4. Prati-manjarî(?) (-Paṭamanjarî)
5. Āsāvarî

5. GOUḌA-MĀLAVA

1. Hindola
2. Triguṇā
3. Dhānî (?)
4. Gouḍî
5. Kolāhala

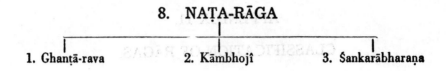

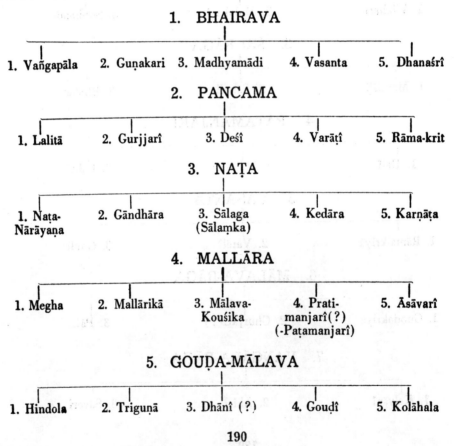

6. DEŚĀKH

1. Bhūpālî
2. Hari-pāla
3. Kāmodî
4. Dhoraṇî
5. Vilāvalî

APPENDIX 13.

CLASSIFICATION OF RĀGAS.

According to *Pancama Samhitá* by Nārada (Asiatic Society of Bengal Ms. No. 5040 with Colophon dated 1362 śaka-1440 A.D.).

1. MĀLAVA

1. Dhānasî
2. Mālasî
3. Rāmakirî
4. Sindhuḍā
5. Āsavārî
6. Bhairavî

2. MALLĀRA

1. Velāvalî
2. Pūravî
3. Kānaḍā
4. Māyurî
5. Koḍā
6. Kedārikā

3. ŚRÎ-RĀGA

1. Gāndhārî
2. Gourî
3. Subhagā
4. Kumārikā
5. Velawārî
6. Vairāgî

4. VASANTA

1. Tuḍî
2. Pancamî
3. Lalitā
4. Paṭamanjarî
5. Gujjarî
6. Vibhāṣa

5. HINDOLA

1. Mādhavî
2. Dîpikā
3. Deśakārî
4. Pāhiḍā
5. Varāḍî
6. Mārahāṭî

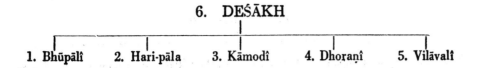

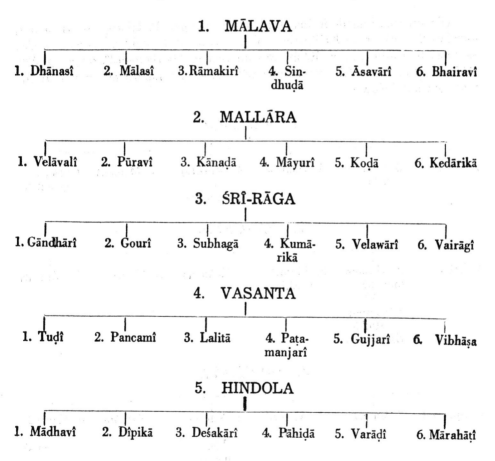

6. KARṆĀṬA

1. Nāṭikā
2. Bhūpālî
3. Gayḍā
4. Rāmakelî
5. Kāmodî
6. Kalyāṇî

APPENDIX 14.

CLASSIFICATION OF RĀGAS.

According to Kallinātha, (1460 A.D.) the famous commentator of *Sangîta-ratnākara.*

(Pandit Bhatkhande in his *Hindusthânî Samgîta Paddhati,* Vol. II, p. 201, ascribes ths system to Kallinātha. The system with slight variations is also ascribed to Kallinātha by Rādhā Mohan Sen in his *Sangîta-Taranga,* p. 222, 1225 sāl,-1818 A.D. The variations with alternate names are given in the table set out below.)

1. ŚRÎ-RĀGA

1. Gourî
2. Kolāhala
3. Dhavalā
4. Varorājî or Rada-rangî
5. Mālkouś
6. Deva-Gāndhāra

2. PANCAMA

1. Triveṇî
2. Hastaṃtaretahā (?) (-Staṃbha-tîrthikā-Khamā-icî)
3. Ābihirî or Āhirî
4. Kokabha
5. Verārî
6. Āsāvarî

3. BHAIRAVA

1. Bhairavî
2. Gujarî
3. Vilāvalî
4. Vihāga (or Vāda-haṃsî)
5. Karnāṭa
6. Kānaḍā (or Bhāṣā)

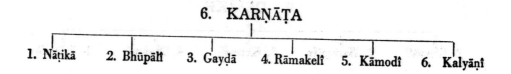

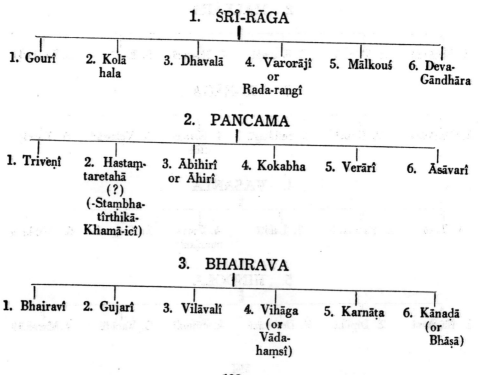

4. MEGHA

1. Vangālî
2. Madhurā (or Mudrā)
3. Kāmodî
4. Dhanāśrî (or Rahamā-śrî)
5. Deva-tîrthî
6. Devali (or Tîrthakî)

5. NAṬA-NĀRĀYAṆA

1. Tara-vaṇkî (or, Ḍevālî)
2. Tilaṃgî (or Tilakî)
3. Pūrvî
4. Gān-dhārî
5. Rāma (or Virāmā)
6. Sindha-mallārî (Siddā-mallārî-Śuddha-mallārî ?)

6. VASANTA

1. Āndhālî
2. Guṃa-kalî, (or Gamakî)
3. Paṭa-manjarî
4. Gouṇḍa-giri
5. Dhanki (? Tanki) (-Tanka) (or Dhāmakî)
6. Deva-sāga (Deva-śākha)

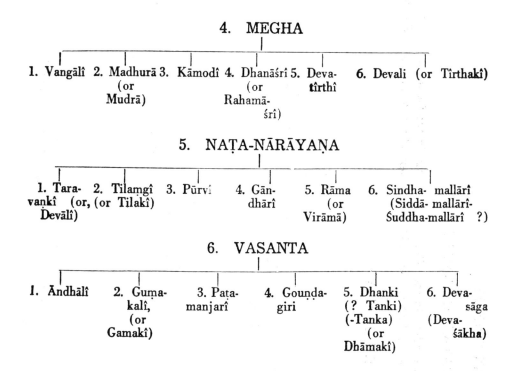

APPENDIX 15.

CLASSIFICATION OF RĀGAS.

According to *Rágamálá* by Meṣakarṇa, dated (according to the Colophon of a Ms. in the Collection of the Asiatic Society of Bengal No. 1195 (211)) in the Śaka year 1431 equivalent to 1509 A.D. The copy of the Ms. is dated Samvat 1833 equivalent to 1761 A.D.

1. BHAIRAVA

- 5 Wives
  - Vangālî
  - Bhairavî
  - Velāvalî
  - Punyakî
  - Snehakî
- 8 Sons
  - Vangāla
  - Pancama
  - Madhu
  - Harṣa
  - Deśākh
  - Lalit
  - Velāval
  - Mādhava

2. MĀLA-KOUŚIKA

- 5 Wives
  - Gunḍagrî (Gouḍakrî)
  - Gandhāriṇî
  - Mālaśrî
  - Śrîhaṭhî
  - Āndhreyakî or Dhanāśrî
- 8 Sons
  - Māru
  - Mevaḍa
  - Varvali
  - Miṣṭānga
  - Candra-kāya
  - Bhramara
  - Nandana
  - Kokkara-Khokhara

3. HINDOLA

- 5 Wives
  - Tilangî or Bhūpālî
  - Devagirî
  - Vāsantî
  - Sindhurî
  - Ābhirî
- 8 Sons
  - Mangala
  - Candra-vimva
  - Śubhrānga
  - Ānanda
  - Vibhāṣa
  - Vardhana
  - Vinoda
  - Vasanta

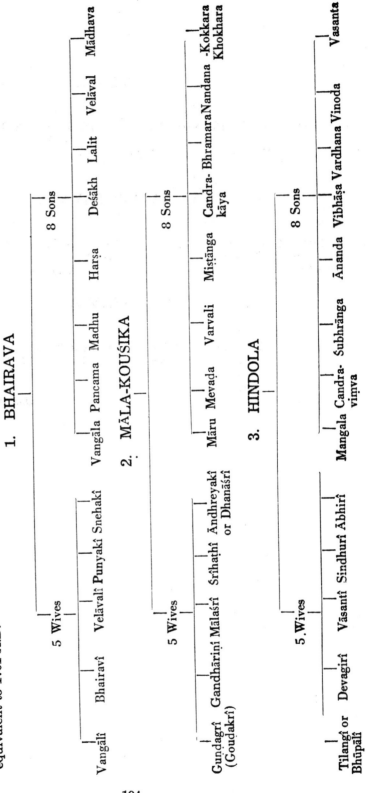

4. DÎPAKA

5 Wives

- Kāmodinî
- Paṭamanjarî
- Toḍî
- Gujjarî
- Kāhelî or Sārangî

8 Sons

- Kamala
- Kusuma
- Rāma
- Kuntala
- Kalinga
- Vahula
- Campaka
- Hemala

5. ŚRÎ-RĀGA

5 Wives

- Vairāṭî
- Karṇāṭikā
- Sāverî
- Gouḍî
- Rāmagirî

8 Sons

- Sindhavā
- Mālava
- Gouḍa
- Gambhîra
- Gunasāgara
- Vigaḍa
- Kalyāna
- Kurabha

6. MEGHA-RĀGA

5 Wives

- Mallārî
- Sorathî
- Suhāvî
- Āsāvarî
- Kokaṇî

8 Sons

- Naṭa
- Kanāra
- Sāranga
- Kedāra
- Guṇḍa Mallāra
- Guṇḍa
- Jalandhara
- Śankara

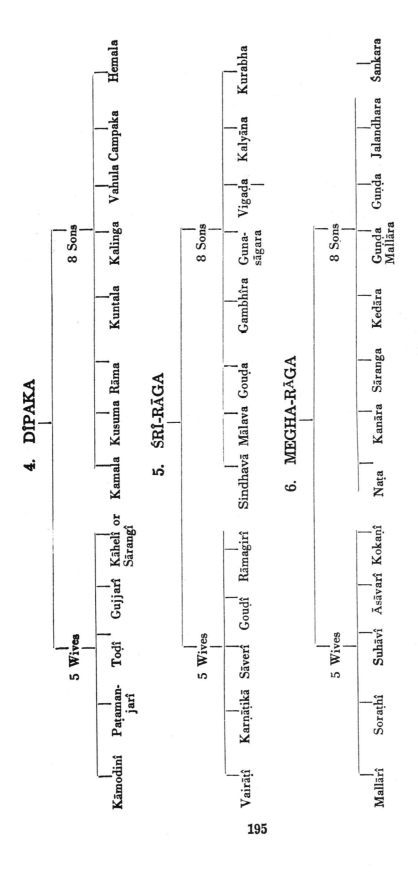

APPENDIX 16.

CLASSIFICATION OF RĀGAS.

According to Rāga-Tarangini by Locan-Kavi (Circa 1375 A.D.)

This scheme obviously belongs to the Southern or Carnatic School, according to which 12 root-rāgas or *melas* (major melodies) are chosen, and to each *mela* certain derivative rāgas (*janya-rāgas*) are ascribed. The melody Dîpaka-rāga, the last in the list, is not described and its derivative melodies are not indicated on the ground that at the time of the author, the Dîpaka had ceased to be current and had become unfamiliar to practising musicians.

Melas 12		Janya-Rāgas 77.
1. Bhairavî (?)	.. ..	(1) Bhairavî, Nilāmvarî.
2. Toḍî	.. .. ..	(1) Toḍî.
3. Gourî	.. .. ..	(1) Mālava, (2) Śrî-Gourî, (3) Caiti-Gourî, (4) Parāḍî (?) Gourî. (5) Deśî-Toḍî, (6) Deśa-Kāra, (7) Goura-(8) Trivaṇa, (9) Mūlatāni, (10) Dhanā-Śrî, (11) Vasanta, (12) Goura, (13) Bhairava, (14) Vibhāsa, (15) Rāma Kalî. (16) Gurjarî, (17) Vāhulî, (18) Revā, (19) Bhatiyāra, (20) Saḍ-rāga, (21) Mālava-Pancama, (22) Jayanta-Śrî, (23) Āsāvarî, (24) Deva-Gāndhāra, (25) Sindî-āsāvarî, (26) Gunakarî.
4. Karnāṭa	.. .. ..	(1) Kānara, (2) Vāgisvari, (3) Khamā-icî, (4) Soraṭha, (5) Paraja, (6) Māru, (7) Jay-Jayantî, (8) Kukubha, (9) Kāmodî, (10) Kedārî, (11) Chāyā-Goura, (12) Māla-Kauśika, (13) Hindola, (14) Sugharai, (15) Aḍānā, (16) Gāre-Kānarā, (17) Śrî-Rāga.
5. Kedāra	.. .. ..	(1) Kedāra-nāṭaka, (2) Abhîra-nāṭaka, (3) Khamvā-vati, (4) Śankarābharaṇa, (5) Vihāgarā, (6) Hamvîra, (7) Śyāma, (8) Chāyā-naṭa, (9) Bhupāli, (10) Bhîmpalaśrî, (11) Kauśika, (12) Māru-rāga.

6. Iman	(1) Śuddha-Kalyāna, (2) Puriyā-Kalyāṇa, (3) Jayat-Kalyāṇa.
7. Sāranga	(1) Paṭa-Manjarî, (2) Vṛndāvanî, (3) Sāmanta, (4) Vaḍa-haṃsaka.
8. Megha	(1) Megha-Mallāra, (2) Gouḍa-Sāranga, (3) Naṭa, (4) Velāvalî, (5) Ālahiyā, (6) Suddha-Suhāva, (7) Deśākha, (8) Śuddha-nāṭa.
9. Dhanā Śrî	(1) Dhanā Śrî, (2) Lalita.
10. Puravā	(1) Pūravā.
11. Mukhārî	(1) Mukhārî.
12. Dîpaka	

APPENDIX 17.

CLASSIFICATION OF RĀGAS

According to *Svara-mela-kalānidhi* by Rāmā-mātya (1550 A.D.)

The scheme belongs to the Southern or Carnatic School, according to which 20 root-rāgas, or *melas* (major melodies) are chosen, and to each *mela*, certain derivative rāgas (janya-rāgas) are ascribed. The lists of derivative rāgas given in this work are illustrative and not exhaustive. The table set out below is borrowed from Mr. M. S. Ramaswami Aiyar's edition of the work (Introduction, p. xliv, 1932).

I. Rāmāmātya's 'Genus-species' system.

Melas—(20)	Janya-Rāgas—(64)		
1. Mukhārî	Mukhārî and a few Grāma Rāgas.		
2. Mālavagoula	(1) Mālava-goula	(6) Mecaboulî	(11) Kuranjî
	(2) Lalitā	(7) Phala-manjarî	(12) Kannada-vangāla
	(3) Boulikā	(8) Gundakriyā	(13) Mangala-kouśika
	(4) Sourāṣṭra	(9) Sindhu-rāmakriyā	(14) Malharî, etc.
	(5) Gurjarî	(10) Chāyāgoula	
3. Śrîrāga	(1) Śrîrāga	(5) Śuddha-bhairavî	(9) Āndolî

	(2) Bhairavî	(6) Velāvalî	(10) Devagāndhārî
	(3) Goulî	(7) Mālavaśrî	(11) Madhyamādi, etc.
	(4) Dhanyāsî	(8) Śankarā bharaṇa	
4. Sāranganāṭa	(1) Sāranganāṭa	(4) Naṭṭanārāyaṇî	(7) Kuntalavarālî
	(2) Sāverî	(5) Śuddhavasanta	(8). Bhinnaṣadja
	(3) Sārangabhairavî	(6) Pūrvagoula	(9) Nārāyaṇî, etc.
5. Hindola	(1) Hindola	(2) Mārga Hindola	(3) Bhūpāla, etc.
6. Śuddha rāmakriyā	(1) Suddharāmakriyā	(3) Ārdradeśî	
	(2) Pāḍi	(4) Dîpaka	
7. Deśakṣî	Deśākṣî		
8. Kannaḍagoula	(1) Kannaḍagoula	(4) Chāyānāṭa	(6) Nāgadhani
	(2) Ghanṭārava	(5) Turuṣka-Toḍî	(7) Devakriyā, etc.
(3) Suddhavangāla			
9. Śuddhanāṭa	Śuddhanāṭa, etc.		
10. Āhirî	Āhirî, etc.		
11. Nādarāmakriyā	Nādarāmakriyā, etc.		
12. Suddhavarālî	Śuddhavaralî, etc.		
13. Rîtigoula	Rîtigoula, etc.		
14. Vasantabhairavî	(1) Vasantabhairavî	(2) Somarāga, etc.	
15. Kedāragoula	(1) Kedāragoula	(2) Nārāyaṇagoula, etc.	
16. Hejujjî	Hejujjî and	a few Grāma R	āgas.
17. Sāmavarālî	Sāmavarālî	do.	
18. Revagupti	Revagupti	do.	
19. Sāmanta	Sāmanta, etc.		
20. Kāṃbhoji	Kāṃbhoji, etc.		

APPENDIX 18.

CLASSIFICATION OF RĀGAS.

According to "Rāgamālā" by Pundarîk Viṭṭhala, (Ms. in the collection of the Bhandarkar Oriental Research Institute, Poona, with colophon dated śaka 1498-1576 A.D.)

1. ŚUDDHA-BHAIRAVA

Wives

Dhannāsî	Bhairavî	Saindhavi	Māravî	Āsāvarî

Sons

Bhairava	Śuddha-lalita	Pancama	Paraja	Vangāla

2. HINDOLA

Wives

Bhupālî	Varālî	Todikā	Prathama-mañjarî	Toḍî

Sons

Vasanta	Śuddha-vaṅgāla	Śyāma	Sāmanta	Kāmoda

3. DEŚIKĀR

Wives

Rāmakrî	Vahulî	Deśî	Jayata-Śrî	Gurjarî

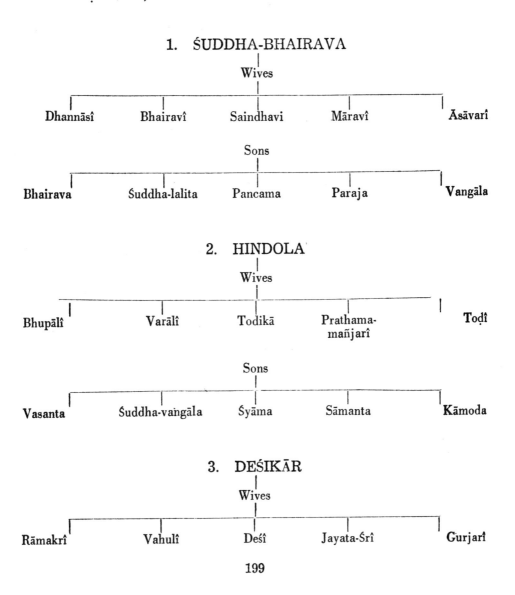

Sons

Lalita | Vibhāsa | Sāranga | Ravaṇa | Kalyāṇa

4. ŚRÎ-RĀG

Wives

Gouḍî | Pāḍî (? Pahadi) | Gunakarî | Nāda-rāmakri | Guṇḍkri

Sons

Takka | Deva-gāndhāra | Mālava | Śuddha-Gouḍa | Karṇāṭa-vangāla

5. ŚUDDHA-NĀTA

Wives

Mālaśrî | Deśāksî | Devakrî | Madhu-mādhavî | Ābhîrî

Sons

Jijāvanta | Sālanga-Nāṭa | Karñāṭa-rāga | Chāyā-nāṭa | Hamîra-nāta

6. NATTA-NĀRĀYANA

Wives

Velāvalî | Kāmvojî | Sāverî | Suhavî | Sourāṣṭrî

Sons

Malhāra | Gounḍa-rāga | Kedāra | Śankarābharaṇa | Vihāgaḍa

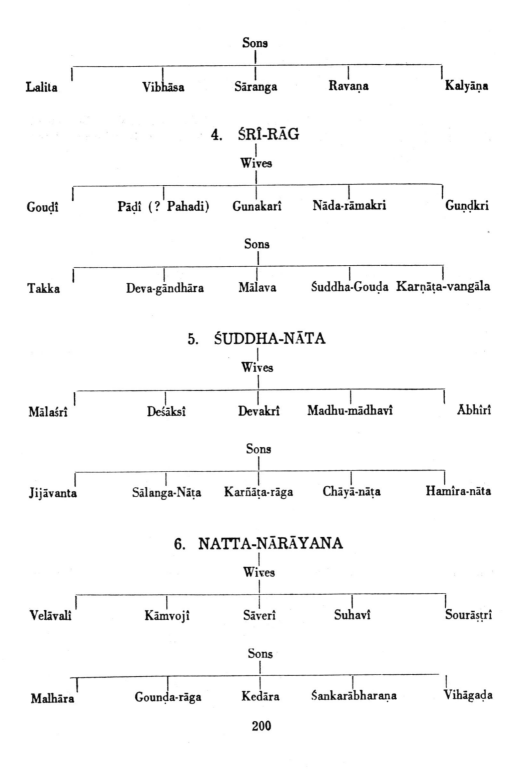

APPENDIX 19.

CLASSIFICATION OF RĀGAS.

According to *Catvārimśacchata-rāga-nirūpaṇam* by Nārada (circa 1525-1550 A.D.)

This treatise offers a scheme of 10 major male melodies, with five wives for each, four sons for each with four wives. It is quite possible that a scheme of 10 male rāgas is earlier than that of six male rāgas. More probably, this is an attempt to ammalgamate two alternative schemes.

10 Male rāgas. Śrî-rāga, Vasanta, Pancama, Bhairava, Kouśika, Megha-rāga, Natta-nārāyaṇa, Hindola, Dîpaka, and Haṃsaka.

1. ŚRÎ-RĀGA

Wives

Gouḍî — Kolāhalî — Āndhālî — Dravidi — Malu-kousiki

Sons

Śuddha-Gouḍa — Karṇāta — Mālava — Pūrvikā

Sons' Wives

Varāṭi — Voulikā — Madhyamādi — Ārabhî

2. VASANTA

Wives

Nîlāṃvarî — Dhanāśrî — Rāmakrî — Paṭa-manjarî — Gouḍa-krî

Sons

Śyāma — Soma — Rîti-Goula — Śankarābharaṇa

Sons' Wives

Kalyāṇî — Duhkha-vairāṭî — Sāverî — Taranginî

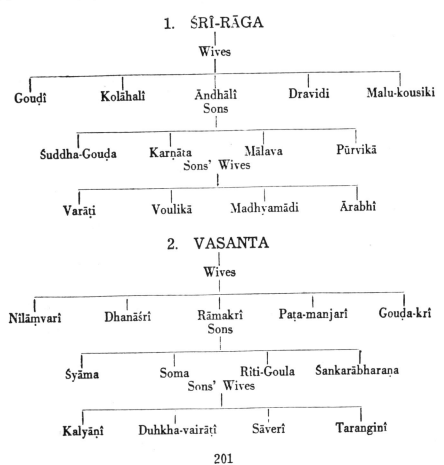

3. PANCAMA

Wives

Trivalî | Vallakî | Khaṃvāvatî | Kakubhā | Āharî

Sons

Valahaṃsa | Gāndhāra | Deva-Hindola | Pāvaka

Sons' Wives

Nārāyaṇî | Bhūpālî | Māru | Nava-rocikā

4. BHAIRAVA

Wives

Velāvalî | Bhairavî | Gurjarî | Lalita | Karṇāṭikā

Sons

Panca-vaktra | Kalhara | Lalita | Candra-śekhara

Sons' Wives

Kuranga-mālikā | Vîcî | Mangala-kouśikî | Māhulî

5. KOUŚIKA

Wives

Toḍî | Deva-gāndhārî | Desākhya | Guna-kriyā | Śuddha-sāverikā

Sons.

Vidun-māla | Modaka | Sāraga | Kāmoda

Sons' Wives

Naṭa-taranginî | Pūrṇa-candrikā | Pālikā | Jayanta-senî

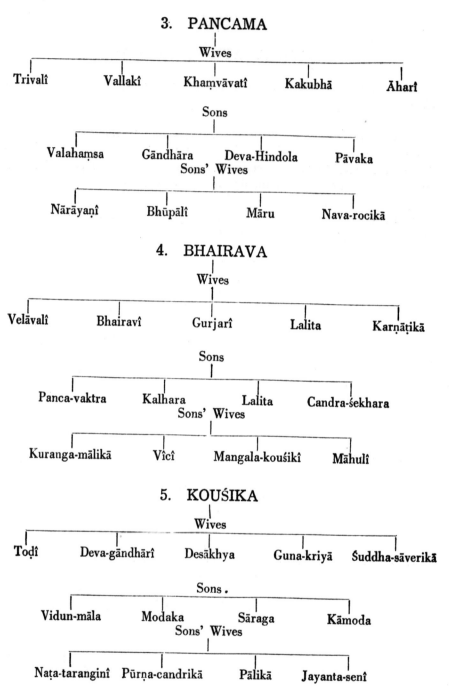

6. MEGHA-RĀGA

Wives

Troṭakî | Moṭakî | Aparā | Bṛhan-naṭā | Ahaṃ-naṭā

Sons

Ghauṭā-kaṇṭha | Kamala | Ghanṭārava | Rohaka

Sons' Wives

Sudhāmayî | Dombakrî | Mṛta-sanjîvanî | Megha-dhvani

7. NATA-NĀRĀYANA

Wives

Vaṇgālî | Śuddha-sālankā | Kāmbhojî | Madhu-mādhavî | Devakrî

Sons

Śuddha-vangāla | Naṭa | Garuḍa | Mohana

Sons' Wives

Trailingî | Lāngalî | Suratā | Hamvarî

8. HINDOLA

Wives

Deśî | Śiva-krî | Lalitā | Mallārî | Suhaṃsikā

Sons

Ramaṇîya | Mukhāri | Udaya-pancama | Śuddha-vasanta

Sons' Wives

Sindhu-rāmakriyā | Vega-vāhinî | Dhāranî | Chāyā-taranginî

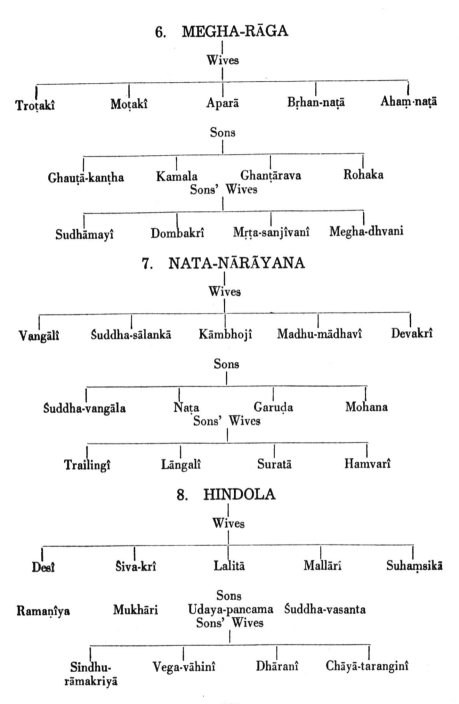

9. DÎPAK

Wives

Āsāverî | Nāṭikā | Dehalî | Karnāṭî | Kedārî

Sons

Kedāra-goulā | Vairanjî | Holî | Sourāṣṭra

Sons' Wives

Kuranja-manjarî | Nāga-varālî | Deva-ranjanî | Sura-sindhu

10. HAMSAKA-RĀGA

Wives

Śrî-ranjanî | Mālaśrî | Sarasvatî-manoharî | Gourî | Iśa-manoharî

Sons

Nāga-dvani | Sāmanta | Bhinna-pancama | Takka

Sons' Wives

Mālavî | Śyāma-kalyāṇî | Deśākṣî | Vilaharî

APPENDIX 20.

CLASSIFICATION OF RĀGAS.

According to "*Rága-vivodha*" by Soma-nātha (1609 A.D.)

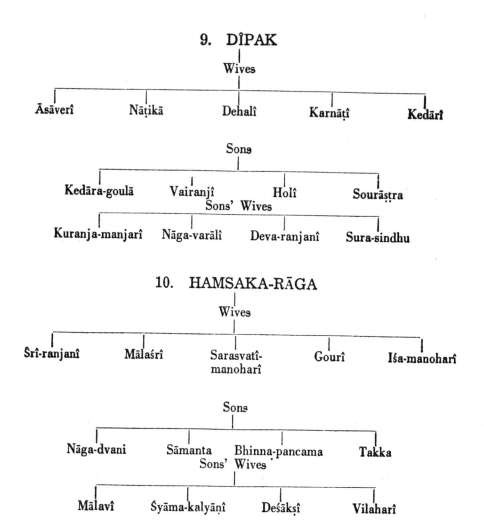

The scheme belongs to the Southern or the Carnatic system according to which the 23 root-rāgas or *mela-rágas* (major melodies) are chosen to which certain *janya-rāgas* (derivative melodies) are assigned on the basis of an analogy of note-structure. The number of derivative melodies cited are illustrative and not exhaustive.

Melas (23)	Janya-rāgas (76)
1. Mukhārî	(1) Mukhārî, (2) Turuṣka-Toḍî and others.
2. Revagupti	Revaguptî.
3. Sāma-varaṭî	(1) Sāma-varāṭî, (2) Vasanta-varāṭî and others.
4. Toḍî	Toḍî
5. Nāda-rāmakrî	Nāda-rāmakrî
6. Bhairava	(1) Bhairava, (2) Pouravikā
7. Vasanta	(1) Vasanta, (2) Takka, (3) Hijeja, (4) Hindola
8. Vasanta-Bhairavî	(1) Vasanta-Bhairavî, (2) Māravî
9. Mālava-gouḍa	(1) Mālava-gouḍa, (2) Gouḍî, (3) Pūrvî, (4) Pāhāḍî, (5) Deva-gāndhāra, (6) Gouḍa-kriyā, (7) Kuranjî, (8) Vāhulî, (9) Rāmakriyā, (10) Pāvaka, (11) Āsāvarî, (12) Pancama, (13) Vangāla, (14) Śuddha-lalita, (15) Gurjjarî, (16) Paraja, (17) Śuddha-gouḍa, (18) Caitî-Gouḍî and others.
10. Rîti-gouḍa	Rîti-gouḍa.
11. Ābhîra-naṭa	Abhîra-naṭa.
12. Hammira	(1) Hammira, (2) Vihangaḍā, (3) Ḳedāra
13. Śuddha-varāṭî	Śuddha-varāṭî
14. Śucî (Śuddha) Rāmakri	(1) Śuddha-rāmakrî, (2) Lalita, (3) Jaitaśrî, (4) Travaṇî, (5) Deśî and others
15. Śrî-rāga	(1) Śrî-rāga, (2) Mālava-śrî, (3) Dhanyāsî, (4) Bhairavî, (5) Dhavala, (6) Saindhavî and others
16. Kalyāna	Kalyāṇa
17. Kāmvodî	(1) Kāmvodî, (2) Devakrî
18. Mallārî	(1) Mallārî, (2) Naṭa-mallārî, (3) Pūrva-gouḍa, (4) Bhūpālî, (5) Gounḍa, (6) Śankarābharaṇa, (7) Naṭa-nārāyaṇa, (8) Nārāyaṇa-gouḍo, (9) Kedāra, (10) Sālanka-naṭa, (11) Velāvalî, (17) Madhyamādi, (13) Sāverî, (14) Sourāṣṭrî
19. Śamanta	Sāmanta
20. Karnāṭa-gouḍa	(1) Karnāṭa-gouḍa, (2) Addaṇā, (3) Nāga-dvani, (4) Śuddha-vangāla, (5) Varṇa-nāṭa, (6) Turuṣka-Toḍî-Irākha
21. Deśākṣî	Deśākṣî
22. Śuddha-nāṭa	Śuddha-nāṭa
23. Sāranga	Sāranga

APPENDIX 21.

CLASSIFICATION OF RĀGAS.

According to Rāga-Darpana by Dāmodara Miśra (circa 1625 A.D.)

The author first cites the scheme current in his time in the North, and then quotes the schemes according to the Schools of Someśvara, Hanuman, and "Rāgāraṇava." He also gives a list of twenty rāgas, which probably represented a traditional group, which may have been popular before the time of the author. Their names are:—Śrî-rāga, Naṭṭa, Vangāla, Bhāṣa, Madhyama, Ṣāḍava, Rakta-hamsa, Kohlāsa, Prabhava, Bhairava, Dhani, Megha-rāga, Soma-rāga, Kāmoda, Āmra-Pancama, Kandarpa, Deśākhya, Kukubha, Kaiśika, and Naṭṭa-Nārāyaṇa. Of these many must have ceased to be current in practice at the time of the author.

ŚRÎ-RĀGA

- Mālaśrî
- Trivanî
- Gourî
- Kedārî
- Madhu-mādhavî
- Pāhāḍi

VASANTA

- Deśî
- Devagirî
- Varātî
- Toḍi
- Lalitā
- Hindolî

BHAIRAVA

- Bhairavî
- Gurjjarî
- Rāmakirî
- Guṇakirî
- Vāngālî
- Saindhavî

PANCAMA

- Vibhāṣā
- Bhupālî
- Karnātî
- Vaḍahaṃsikā
- Mālavî
- Paṭa-manjarî

MEGH-RĀGA

- Mallārî
- Sourathî
- Sāverî
- Kouśikî
- Gāndhārî
- Hara-śṛngārā

VRHAN-NATA-NATTA-NĀRĀYANA

- Kāmodî
- Kalyāṇî
- Ābhirî
- Nāṭikā
- Sārangî
- Naṭṭa-Hamvîrā

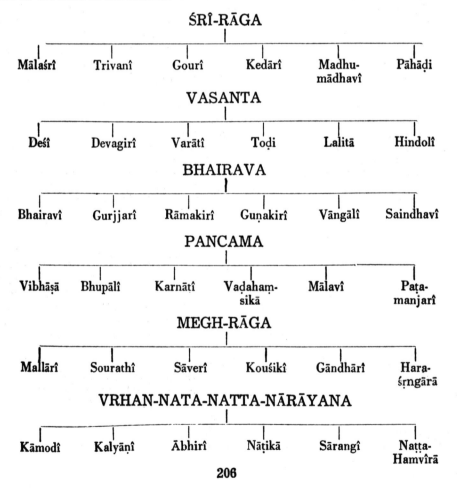

APPENDIX 22.

CLASSIFICATION OF RĀGAS.

According to "Hṛdaya-koutukaṃ" by Hṛdaya-Nārāyaṇa Deva (circa samvat 1724-1646 A.D.)

The author follows the Southern principle of classification of the 'genus and species system' on the basis of choosing certain major rāgas calling them *Samsthānam* (ṭhāṭa) in place of the name *Melaka* used by others.

He adopts 12 root-rāgas, from which he derives the minor melodies.

His 12 major rāgas include a new rāga said to have been created by his patron, the chief of Goḍā deśa (not identified) and called 'Hṛdaya-rāma.'

1.	Bhairavî	1. Bhairavî, 2. Nîlāmvarî
2.	Toḍî	Toḍî (mārga)
3.	Gourî	1. Mārga-Gourî, 2. Deśî-Gourî. 3. Mālava, 4. Śrî-Gourî, 5. Caitî-Gourī, 6. Pāhāri-Gaurī, 7. Deśî-Toḍî, 8. Deśa-Kāraka, 9. Gouḍa, 10. Trivaṇā, 11. Mulatānî-Dhānaśrî, 12. Vasantakā, 13. Goura, 14. Bhairava, 15. Vibhāṣa, 16. Rāmakarî, 17. Gurjari, 18. Vahulî, 19. Bhātiyāla, 20. Saṭa-rāga (khaṭ), 21. Mālaśrî, 22. Pancama, 23. Jayantaśrî, 24. Āśāvarî, 25. Deva-Gāndhāra, 26. Sindhî-Āśāvarî, 27. Gunakarî.
4.	Karṇāṭa	1. Karṇāṭa, 2. Kedārî, 3. Hindola, 4. Sugharāi, 5. Āḍanā, 6. Gāro-karṇāta, 7. Śrî-rāga.
5.	Kedāra	1. Kedāra, 2. Kedāra-nāṭa, 3. Jayant-kedāra, 4. Āhîra-naṭa, 5. Khamvāvatî, 6. Śankarā-bharaṇa, 7. Vihāgarā, 8. Hamvîra, 9. Śyāma-nāṭa, 10. Chāya-nāṭa, 11. Bhūpālî, 12. Bhîma-palāśikā, 13. Purîyā-kedāra, 14. Kouśika, 15. Māru.
6.	Imana	1. Imana, 2. Śuddha-kalyāṇa, 3. Purîyā, 4. Yayat-kalyāṇa
7.	Śāranga	1. Śāranga, 2. Paṭa-manjarî, 3. Vrindāvanî, 4. Sāmanta, 5. Vaḍa-haṃsa.
8.	Megha	1. Megha, 2. Mallāra, 3. Yoginî, 4. Madhya-mādi, 5. Gounḍa-Mallāra, 6. Devā-bharaṇa, 7. Goura-sāranga, 8. Naṭa, 9. Velāvalî, 10. Ālāhiyā, 11. Śuddha-suhāva, 12. Deśî-suhāva, 13. Deśākha, 14. Śuddha-nāṭa.

9.	Hṛdaya-rāma	Hṛdaya-rāma
10.	Dhanāśrî	1. Dhanāśrî, 2. Lalita.
11.	Pūrvā	Pūrvā
12.	Mukhārî	Mukhārî

An additional root-rāga called Dîpaka is intended to be included but it is not actually described ("Atha ṭhāṭa-prakaraṇa dîpak-saṃsthānaṃ lekhyaṃ").

APPENDIX 23

CLASSIFICATION OF RĀGAS.

According to *"Hṛdaya-prakāśa,"* by Hṛdayanāyaṇa Deva (Circa Samvat 1724-1646 A.D.)

In this treatise the author uses the term *mela* (genus) in place of *Saṃ*sthana (ṭhāṭa) used in his *Hṛdaya-Kautuka*. In the former work, he classifies the parent-scales into eleven *melas*, according to *Śuddha* or *Vikrita*-notes used in the structure of the melodies.

1.	Śuddha-mela	1. Saindhav, 2. Bhairvî, 3. Nilaṃvari.
2.	Mela with 1 vikṛta note ..	1. Karṇāṭa, 2. Kakubhā, 3. Jināvatî, 4. Sourāṣṭrî, 5. Sugharāyî, 6. Kāmoda, 7. Ādānā, 8. Vāgeśvarî.
3.	Ditto ..	Mukhārî
4.	Mela with 2 vikrta notes ..	Toḍî
5.	Ditto ..	1. Kedāra, 2. Śyāmā-naṭaka, 3. Khamvāvatî, 4. Hamvîra, 5. Śaṅkarābharaṇa, 6. Jayat-kedāra, 7. Pūriyā-kedāra, 8. Vihāgarā, 9. Āhîra-nāṭa, 10. Māru, 11. Bhîma-palāsikā, 12. Chāyā-nāṭa, 13. Khedāra-nāṭa, 14. Māla-kouśika, 15. Bhūpālî
6.	Mela with 3 vikrta notes ..	1. Îmana, 2. Pūriyā-Kalyāṇa, 3. Jayat-Kalyāṇa, 4. Śuddha-kalyāṇa.
7.	Ditto ..	1. Megha, 2. Śuddha-nāṭa, 3. Nāṭa, 4. Devagirî, 5. Goura-sāranga, 6. Ālāhiyā, 7. Devā-bharaṇa, 8. Deśākha, 9. Gound-Mallāra, 10. Suhāva, 11. Madhyamādi, 12. Mallāra
8.	Ditto ..	Hrdaya-ramā
9.	Mela with 4 vikrta notes ..	1. Gourî, 2. Mūlatānî-dhānasarî, 3. Śrî-rāga, 4. Saḍrāga, 5. Caitî-Gourî, 6. Vasanta, 7. Jayaśrî, 8. Rāmakali, 9. Paraja, 10. Pancama, 11. Gāndhāra, 12. Āsāvarî, 13. Deśî-Toḍî, 14. Bhairava, 15. Vahulî, 16. Gurjarî, 17. Gouḍa, 18. Guṇakarî, 19. Deśa-kāra, 20. Mālaśrî, 21. Vibhāsa, 22. Trivaṇa.
10.	Ditto ..	1. Sāranga, 2. Paṭamanjarî, 3. Sāmanta, 4. Vaḍahaṃsa.
11.	Ditto ..	Pūrva
12.	Mela with 5 vikrta notes ..	Dhanāśrî

APPENDIX 24.

CLASSIFICATION OF RĀGAS.

According to *Catur-dandi-Prakāśikā* by Vyānkatamakhî (otherwise called Vyāmkaṭeśvara Dikṣîta) (1660 A.D.)

The author belongs to the Southern, or Carnatic School. He severely criticises the author of *Svara-mela-kalā-nidhi,* who gives a list of 20 *melas,* whereas Vyankaṭamakî gives a list of 19 *melas.*

	(Janaka-melas)	(Janya-rāgas)
1.	Mukhārî	Mukhārî
2.	Sāma-varālî	Sāma-varālî
3.	Bhūpāla	1. Bhūpāla, 2. Bhinna-ṣadja
4.	Vasanta-Bhairavî	Vasanta-Bhairavî
5.	Goula	1. Goula, 2. Guṇḍakriyā, 3. Sālanga-nāṭa, 4. Nāḍa-rāma-kriyā, 5. Lalitā, 6. Pāḍî, 7. Gurjarî, 8. Vahulî, 9. Mallaharî, 10. Sāverî, 11. Chāyā-goula, 12. Pūrva-goula, 13. Karṇāṭaka, 14. Vangāla, 15. Sourāṣṭra.
6.	Āharî	1. Ābherî, 2. Hindola-vasanta
7.	Bhairavî	1. Bhairavî, Hindola, 3. Āhîrî, 4. Ghanṭā-rava. 5. Rîti-goula.
8.	Śrî-rāga	1. Śrî. 2. Sālaga-Bhairavî, 3. Dhanyāsî, 4. Mālava-śrî, 5. Deva-gāndhāra, 6. Āndhālî, 7. Velāvalî, 8. Kannāḍa-Goula.
9.	Hejujjî	1. Hejujjî. 2. Revaguptî.
10.	Kāmbhojî	1. Kāmbhojî, 2. Kedāra-goula, 3. Nārāyaṇa-goula.
11.	Śankarābharaṇa	1. Śankarā-bharṇa, 2. Ārabhî, 3. Nāgadvani, 4. Sāma, 5. Śuddha-vasanta, 6. Nārāyaṇa-Deśāksî, 7. Nārāyaṇî.
12.	Sāmanta	Sāmanta
13.	Deśākṣî	Deśākṣî
14.	Nāṭa	Nāṭa
15.	Śuddha-varālî	Śuddha-varālî
16.	Pantu-varālî	Pantu-varālî
17.	Śuddha-rāma-kriyā	Śuddha-rāma-kriyā
18.	Simha-rava	Simha-rava
19.	Kalyāṇî	Kalyāṇa

APPENDIX 25.

CLASSIFICATION OF RĀGAS.

According to *Anūpa-Sangîtānkuśa* by Bhāva-bhaṭṭa (1674-1701 A.D.)

The author belongs to the Northern School. He utilises both Southern and Northern texts both of which he quotes profusely. He accepts *Sangîta-Pārijāta* and *Sangîta-ratnākara* as leading authorities.

BHAIRAVA

- Madyamādî
- Bhairavî
- Vāngālî
- Varāti
- Saindhavî

MĀLAVA-KOUŚIKA

- Toḍî
- Khaṃvāvatî
- Gouḍî
- Guṇakirî
- Kakubhā

HINDOLA

- Velāvalî
- Rāmakirî
- Deśākṣî
- Paṭamanjarî
- Lalitā

DÎPAKA

- Kedārikā
- Deśî
- Kāmodî
- Nāṭikā
- Karṇāṭî

ŚRÎ-RĀGA

- Vasantî
- Mālavî
- Mālaśrî
- Sāverî
- Dhanāśrî

MEGHA

- Mallārî
- Deśakārî
- Bhūpālî
- Gurjarî
- Takka

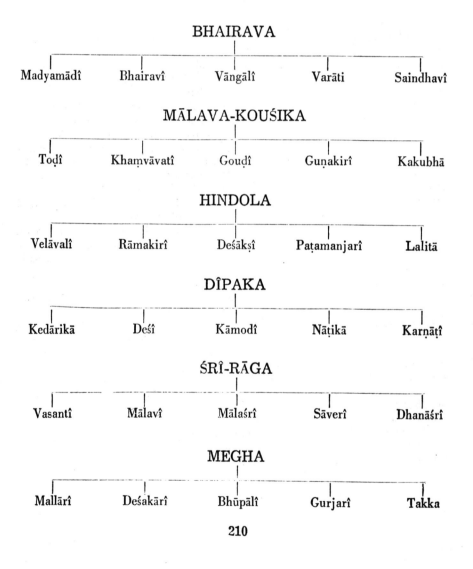

APPENDIX 26.

CLASSIFICATION OF RĀGAS.

According to *Anūpa-Sangīta-ratnākara,* by Bhāva-bhatta (1674-1701 A.D.)

The author belongs to the Northern School. But he treats the Northern and the Southern systems. In the *Anūpa-sangīta-ratnākara,* he cites 20 different *melas* (root-rāgas) with their derivatives. In another work he cites six rāgas and five rāgiṇīs (see Appendix 25).

1. Toḍī	Toḍī and others.
2. Gouḍī	1. Gouḍī, 2. Gurjarī, 3. Vahulā, 4. Rāmakali, 5. Āśāvarī, 6. Māru, 7. Guṇakri, 8. Paṭamanjarī, 9. Pancama, 10. Śuddha-lalita, 11. Takka, 12. Mālava-Gouḍa, 13. Pūrvī, 14. Vangāla, 15. Pāḍī.
3. Varāṭī	1. Varāṭī, 2. Śuddha-varāṭī, 3. Śyāma-varāṭī.
4. Kedāra	1. Kedāra, 2. Kedāra-Gouḍa, 3. Mallāra, 4. Naṭṭa-Nārāyaṇa, 5. Velāvalī, 6. Bhūpālī, 7. Kāmvojī, 8. Madhumādhavī, 9. Śankarā-bharaṇa, 10. Sāverī, 11. Suvāhī, 12. Nārāyanī, 13. Kedāranāṭa and others.
5. Śuddha-nāṭa	Śuddha-nāṭa and others.
6. Mālava-kaiśika	1. Mālava-śrī, 2. Dhannāsī, 3. Bhairavī, 4. Saindhavī, 5. Deva-Gandhāra and others.
7. Śrī-rāga	Śrī-rāga and others.
8. Hammira	Hammira and others.
9. Āherī	Āherī and others.
10. Kalyāna	Kalyāna and others.
11. Deśākṣī	Deśākṣī and others.
12. Deśīkāra	1. Deśīkāra, 2. Travaṇī, 3. Deśī, 4. Lalita, 5. Dīpaka, 6. Vibhāṣa.
13. Śāranga	Śāranga and others.
14. Karṇāṭa	1. Karṇāṭa, 2. Sāmanta, 3. Sourāṣṭrī, 4. Chāyā-nāṭaka.
15. Kāmoda	Kāmoda and others.
16. Hijeja	Hijeja, Bhairava and others.
17. Nāda-rāmakrī	Nādā-rāmakrī and others.
18. Hindola	1. Hindola, 2. Vasanta and others.
19. Mukhārī	Mukhārī and others.
20. Soma	Soma and others.

APPENDIX 27

CLASSIFICATION OF RĀGAS.

According to *Saṅgita-nārāyaṇa* by Puruṣottama Miśra, court poet of Nārāyaṇa Deva of the Gajapati Dynasty (Circa 1730 A.D.) The author quotes the differing views of the lists of rāgas as given by Nārada in the *Pancama-Sāra-samhitā* (Appendix 13), and Mammaṭa in *Saṅgita-ratna-mālī* (Appendix 5), and cites the system of rāgas as current in his time. The text available, that of the Ms. of the Asiatic Society of Bengal (No. 2513-69-E4) is very much corrupt, and undecipherable at various places.

BHAIRAVA

- Bhairavî
- Kaiśikî
- Bhāṣa
- Vẹlāvalî
- Vangālî

VASANTA

- Anonita (?)
- Deśākhya
- Nona (?)
- Prathama-manjarî
- Masravî (?) Mallārî (?)

MĀLAVA-KOUŚIKA

- Śaivî (?) Toḍî
- Guṇḍakirî
- Varāḍî
- Khamvāvatî
- Karṇāṭî

ŚRÎ-RĀGA

- Gāndhārî
- Deva-gāndhārî
- Mālava-śrî
- Sāverî
- Rāma-kirî

MEGHA-RĀGA

- Lalitā
- Mālasî
- Gourî
- Nāṭî
- Devakirî

NATA-NĀRĀYANA

- Saramani (?)
- Ābhāsa (?)
- Kāmodî
- Gunjarî
- Kakubhā

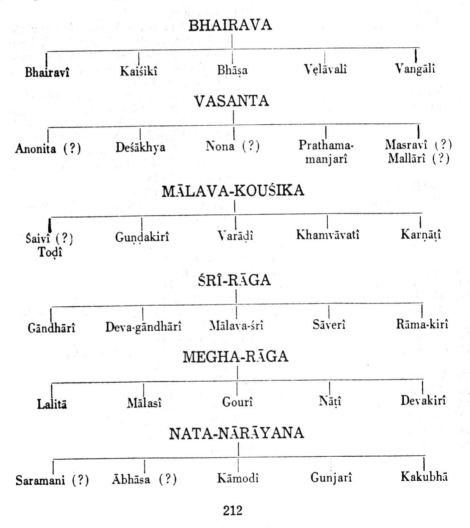

APPENDIX 28.

CLASSIFICATION OF RĀGAS.

According to Sangîta-Sārāmrtoddhāra

By King Tulāji of Tanjore (1763-1787 A.D.)

(Janaka-melas)	(Janya-rāgas)
1. Śrî-rāga	Kannaḍa-Gouḍa, Deva-gāndhāra, Sālaga-Bhairavî, Mādhava-manoharî, Suddha-deśî, Madhyama-grāma-rāga, Saindhavî, Kāphî, Husenî, Śrî-ranjanî, Malavaśrî, Deva-manoharî, Jayanta-sena, Maṇi-ranga, Madhyamādi, Dhanāśrî.
2. Suddha-nāṭa	Śuddha-nāṭî, Udaya-ravi-candrikā.
3. Mālava-gouḍa	Ādya-mālava-gouḍa, Sāranga-nāṭikā, Ārdra-deśî, Chāyā-gouḍa, Takka, Gurjjarî, Gunḍa-kriyā, Phala-manjarî, Nāda-rāma-kriyā, Sourāṣṭrî, Māgadhî, Gourî-manoharî, Māruva, Sāverî, Gouḍî-pantu, Pūrvî, Vibhāsa, Goula, Kannaḍa-vangāla, Vahulî, Pāḍi, Malla-hari, Lalitā, Pūrṇa-pancama, Śuddha-sāverî, Megha-ranjanî, Reva-Gupta, Mālavî.
4. Velāvalî	Velāvalî.
5. Varālî	Varālî.
6. Śuddha-rāma-kriyā ..	Śuddha-rāma-kriyā, Dîpaka.
7. Śankarā-bharaṇa	Śankarābharaṇa, Ārabhî, Śuddha-vasanta, Sarasvatî-manoharî, Pūrva-goula, Nārā-yaṇî-deśākṣî, Sāmanta, Kuranjî, Pūrṇa-candrikā, Sura-sindhu, Julāvu, Vilaharî, Gouḍa-mallāra, Kedāra.
8. Kāṃvojî	Kāṃvojî, Nārāyaṇa-gouḍa, Kedāra-gouḍa, Vaḍa-haṃsa, Nāga-dvani, Chāyā-taran-ginî, Jadu-kula-kāṃvojî, Naṭa-kurañjî, Kannaḍa, Naṭa-nārayaṇî, Āndhālî, Sāma-rāga, Manoha, Deva-kriyā, Mohana-kalyānî.
9. Bhairavî	Bhairavî, Āharî, Ghanṭā-rava, Indu-ghanṭā-rava, Ritî-goula, Hindola-vasanta, Ānan-da-Bhairavî, Ābherî, Nāga-gāndhārî, Dhanyāsî, Hindola.
10. Mukhārî	Mukhārî.
11. Vega-vāhinî	Vega-vāhinî.
12. Sindhu-rāma-kriyā	Sindhu-rāma-kriyā, Pantu-Varālî.
13. Hejujjî	Hejujjî.

14.	Sāma-varālî	Sāma-varālî, Gāndhāra-pancama, Bhinna-pancama.
15.	Vasanta-bhairava	Vasanta-bhairavî, Lalita-pancama.
16.	Bhinna-ṣaḍja	Bhinna-ṣaḍja, Bhūpāla.
17.	Deśākṣî	Deśākṣî.
18.	Chāyā-nāṭa	Chāyā-nāṭa.
19.	Sāranga	
20.	Toḍî	
21.	Kalyāṇî	

APPENDIX 29.

CLASSIFICATION OF RĀGAS.

According to a Hindî treatise Known as "Rāgā-Kutūhala" by Radha Krishna Kavi, composed in Saṃvat 1853-1781 A.D.

(Ms. in the possession of Kuñwar Brajendra Singh, Dholpur and described by him in the Hindî monthly *Saraswatî,* November 1933, p. 425).

BHAIRAVA

- Bhairavî
- Saindhavî
- Bairārî
- Madhumādhavî (? Madhya-mādî)
- Bangālî

MĀLKOUŚA

- Gourî
- Toḍî
- Guṇakalî
- Khamvāvatî
- Kukabhā

HINDOLA

- Vilāval
- Rāmakeli
- Lalit
- Deośākh
- Paṭamanjarî

DÎPAK

- Kanaḍā
- Deśî
- Kāmod
- Kedāra
- Naṭ

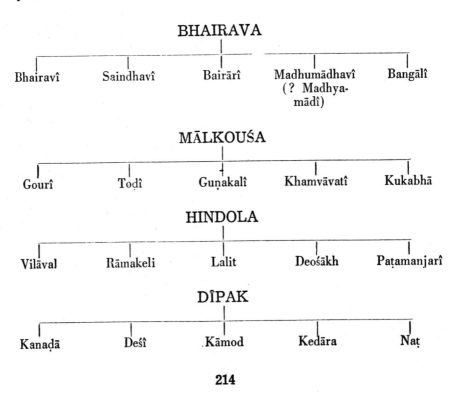

ŚRÎ-RĀGA

Vasanta | Mālaśrî | Āśāvarî | Mārvā | Dhanāśrî

MEGHA

Bhūpālî | Mallāra | Gujarî | Tanka | Deśakārî

APPENDIX 30.

CLASSIFICATION OF RĀGAS.

According to Sangîta-sāra, compiled by Mahāraja Sawai Pratap Simha Deo of Jaipur, (1779-1804 A.D.)

He purports to follow the School of Hanumāna, and after specifying the six rāgas and 30 rāginîs according to Hanumāna he adds the names and descriptions of the respective sons of the six rāgas, each having 8 sons according to the scheme set out below:—

BHAIRAVA

Vangāla | Pancama | Madhura | Haraṣa | Deśākh | Lalita | Vilāval | Mādhava

MĀLKOUŚA

Nandan | Khokar

HINDOLA

Vangāl | Candra-vimva | Śubhrānga | Ānanda | Vibhāṣa | Vardhana | Vanānta | Vinoda

DÎPAK

Kusuma | Kusum (?) | Rāma | Kuntala | Kalinga | Vahula | Campaka | Hema

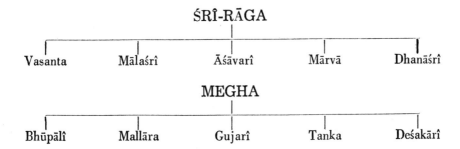

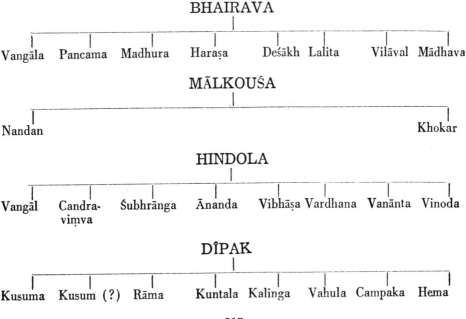

ŚRÎ-RĀG

SaindhavaMālava	Gouḍa	Gambhîra	Guna-sāgara	Vigaḍa	Kalyāna	Gaḍa	

MEGHA-RĀG

Nāga	Kanhāro	Sāranga	Kedāra	Goḍa	Mallāra	Jalandhara	Śankara

Note: Only two sons are assigned to Mālkos, viz. Nandan and Khokar.

APPENDIX 31.

CLASSIFICATION OF RĀGAS.

According to Bramhā. This name is more or less a mythical shadow, in Indian musical literature. According to old traditions, to Bramhā is ascribed the musical lore known under the title of *Gandharva Veda Sāram.* In the *Sangîta makaranda* of Nārada (G. O. S., Vol. XVI, p. 13, verse 18) Bramhā is mentioned as an ancient authority. But no authenticated work that could be ascribed to this author has yet been traced. The system of classification of melodies current under his name, is probably the opinion of some later authorities who ascribe it to Bramhā, in order to gain prestige and respectability. His system is followed by several authors.

BHAIRAVA

Bhairavî	Gujjarî	Rāmakelî	Guṇakelî	Saindhavî	Vangālî

ŚRÎ-RĀGA

Mālaśrî	Trivanî	Gourî	Kedārî	Madhu-mādhavî	Pahāḍî

MEGHARĀGA

Mallārî	Souraṭî	Sāverî	Kouśikî	Gāndhāri	Hara-śṛngārî

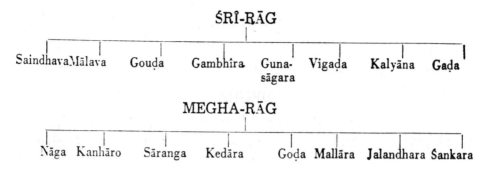

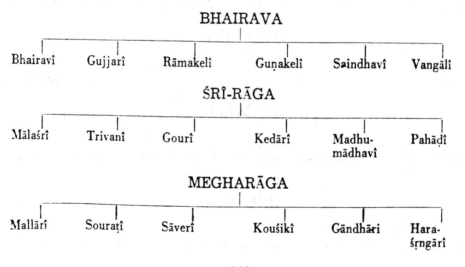

VASANTA

Deśî | Devagiri | Varāṭî | Toḍî | Lalitā | Hindolî

PANCAMA-RĀGA

Vibhāṣā | Bhūpālî | Karnāṭî | Vaḍha-haṃsikā | Mālavî | Paṭaman-jarî

NATA-RĀGA

Kāmodî | Kalyāṇî | Ābhirî | Nāṭikā | Sārangî | Hamvîra

APPENDIX 32.

CLASSIFICATION OF RĀGAS.

According to the School of Bharata.

Unless Bharata is taken to be some later musical authority other than the author of the *Nātya-sāstra,* the system of classification ascribed to him must be purely apocryphal. For, it is well-known, that at the time of Bharata, the rāgas, as understood in later times, had not evolved. The list ascribed to him by legend, must be a very late classification, attributed to him by way of courtesy, in order to acquire authority by association with a great name famous in musical history. The School of Bharata is referred to in Dāmodara's *Sangita-Darpaṇa* (Ch. I, verse 2). The system set out below is borrowed from Radha Mohan Sen's *Sangita-Taranga.* (Calcutta, 1818, Reprinted by Vangavāsî Press, 1203, at pp. 123-125.)

BHAIRAVA

Wives

Madhumādhavî | Bhairavî | Vangālî | Varārî | Saindhavî

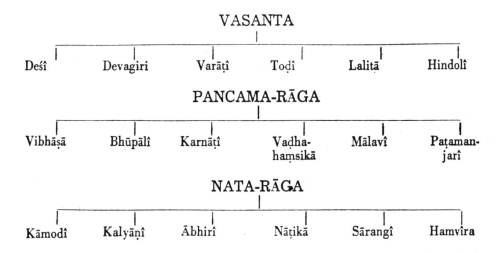

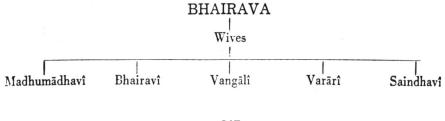

Sons

- Velāval
- Pancama
- Deśākh
- Deo-gāndhāra
- Vibhāṣa

Sons' Wives

- Rāmkalî
- Suho ? (Suhāi)
- Sugharāî
- Paṭamanjarî
- Toḍî

MĀLKOUŚA

Wives

- Gunakalî
- Khamvāvatî
- Gujarî
- Bhūpālî
- Gourî

Sons

- Soma
- Parasan
- Vaḍa-haṃsa
- Kakubha
- Vangāla

Sons' Wives

- Soraṭhî
- Triveṇî
- Karṇāṭî
- Āsāvarî
- Goḍa-girî

HINDOLA

Wives

- Velāvalî
- Deśākî
- Lalitā
- Bhîma-palāsî
- Mālavî

Sons

- Rekhav-haṃsa
- Vasanta
- Lokhāsa
- Gandharbha
- Lalita

Sons' Wives

- Kedāra
- Kāmodî
- Vehāgarā
- Kāphî
- Paraja

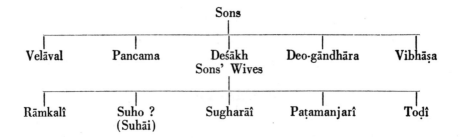

DĪPAKA

Wives

Naṭa, Mallārî, Kedārî, Kānarā, Bhārekā

Sons

Śuddha-kalyāṇa, Soraṭha, Deśakāra, Hāmîra, Māru

Sons' Wives

Vaḍa-haṃsî, Deś-varāṭî, Vairāṭî, Deogiri, Sindhavā

ŚRÎ-RĀGA

Wives

Vasantî, Mālavî, Mālaśrî, Sāhānā, Dhānaśrî

Sons

Naṭa, Chāyānaṭa, Kānaḍā, Iman, Śankarābharaṇa

Sons' Wives

Śyāma, Pūriyā, Gujarî, Hamirî, Āḍānā

MEGHA

Wives

Sāranga, Vankā, Gandharvvā, Mallārî, Mūlatānî

Sons

Bāhādurî, Naṭa-nārāyaṇa, Malavā, Jayatî, Kāmod

Sons' Wives

Pāhāḍî, Jayantî, Gāndhārî, Pūravî, Jaya-jayantî

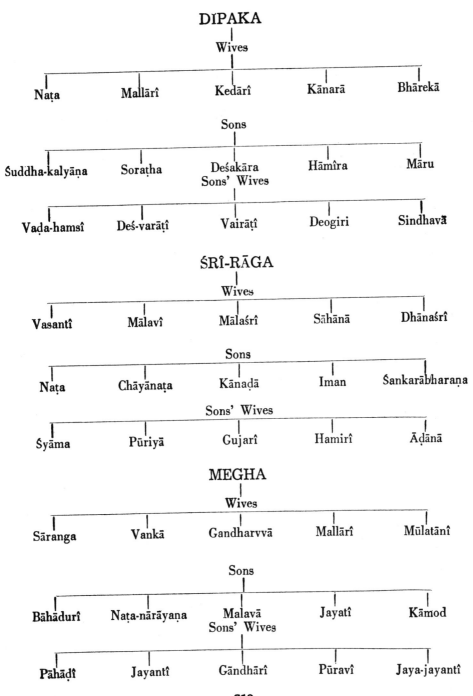

APPENDIX 33.

CLASSIFICATION OF RĀGAS.

According to the School of Hanumāna (Hanumat).

It is mentioned in the Persian Treatise known as *Tuphet-'ul-Hind* by Mahomed Rezza Khan (1813 A.D.) recently edited by the Viśva Bhārati, that at the time of this author, four classifications were current, one ascribed to Hanumāna, one ascribed to Bramhā, one ascribed to Bharata, and one ascribed to Kallinātha. The last named is set out in Appendix 14. Bharata has only mentioned certain grāma-rāgas (Appendix 2). and the classification ascribed to him must be by some later authors. As regards the School of Hanumāna, no text which could be ascribed to him appears to have survived. Ānjaneya (Hanumāna) as a musical authority is mentioned by Abhinava Gupta (C. 1930) and Śāranga-deva (C. 1247), and quoted by Sāradā-tanaya (C. 1250) and also by Kallinātha (C. 1460). In Govinda Dikṣîta's *Sangîta-sudhá,* Ānjaneyà is described as deriving the principles of Deśi-rāga, from Yāstika, an ancient authority earlier than Matanga. So that undoubtedly he is an ancient writer on music, although his actual work has not survived. The fact that his name is associated by Dāmodara in his *Sangîta Darpaṇa* (Calcutta edition p. 75-76) with the scheme of Rāga-raginîs shows that Hanumāna expounded the Northern, or the Hindusthānî system. He is also referred to by Ahovala, as a commentator on Bharata-nāṭya. The classification of Hanumāna is followed by Dāmodara, Harivallava, the anonymous author of Sangîta-mālā and various other authors, with minor variations and is supposed to be still current.

BHAIRAVA

Madhyamādî	Bhairavî	Vāngālî	Varāṭikā	Saindhavî

KOUŚIKA

Toḍî	Khaṃvāvatî	Gourî	Gunakrî	Kakubhā

HINDOLA

Velāvalî	Rāmakirî	Deśākhya	Paṭamanjarî	Lalita

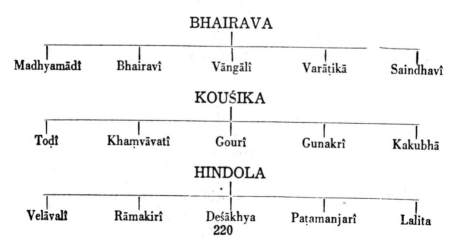

DÎPAKA

Kedārî | Kānadā | Deśî | Kāmodî | Nāṭikā

ŚRÎ-RĀGA

Vasantî | Mālavî | Mālaśrî | Dhanāsikā | Āśāvarî

MEGHA-RĀGA

Mallārî | Deśakārî | Bhūpālî | Gurjarî | Tanka

(According to the list cited in Rādhāmohan Sen's *Sangita-Taranga* (p. 123, Calcutta, 1818), Ramvā is substituted for Gaurî, and Mālinî for Mālavî).

APPENDIX 34.

CLASSIFICATION OF RĀGAS.

into six Rāgas and thirty Rāginis.

According to the Hindi texts inscribed on the series of miniatures in the British Museum Ms. Add. Or. 2821,—similar texts in the series in the Ghose Collection, Calcutta,—similar series in the Collection of Lala Shambhunath, Jaipur,—similar series in the Collection of Purātattva Samsodhaka Maṇḍalî, Poona.

BHAIRAVA

Bhairavî | Mālaśrî | Paṭamanjarî | Lalitā | Nāṭikā

MĀLKOUŚA

(?) Gourî | Gouḍa -Mālava-Gouḍ | Rāmakelî -Mānavatî | Khambāvatî | Gunakarî

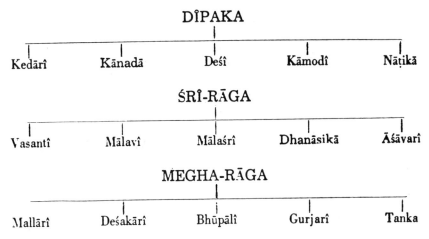

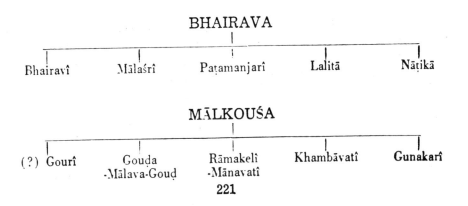

HINDOLA

Madhumādhavî | Gāndhārî | Toḍî | Deśākha | Vilāvala

DÎPAKA

Kanaḍā | Dhanāśrî | Varāḍî | Vasantî | Varāṭî

ŚRÎ-RĀGA

Pancama | Kāmoda | Setmalāra | Āsāvarî | Kedāra

MEGHA-RĀGA

Gourî | Kakubhā | Gujjarî | Vangālî | Vibhāṣā

APPENDIX 35.

CLASSIFICATION OF RĀGAS.

According to a Hindusthānî (Urdu) Manuscript of Rāga-mālā by Saiyid 'Abd-al-Wali' Uzlat, dated 25th Muharam, A.H. 1173, (A.D. 1759) in the India Office, London (No. 101 P-2380-C), described at p. 54, of Blumhardt's *Catalogue of the Hindustani Manuscripts* in the Library of the India Office, 1926.

According to this scheme of classification, the melodies are grouped under six rāgas, each having five rāgiṇîs, and each having a family of eight sons (*putras*) representing 84 different musical modes. As the list of the sons (*putras*) are not complete, they are not cited here.

BHAIRAVA

Bhairavî | Vilāvalî | Varārî | Kāmodî | Bangālî

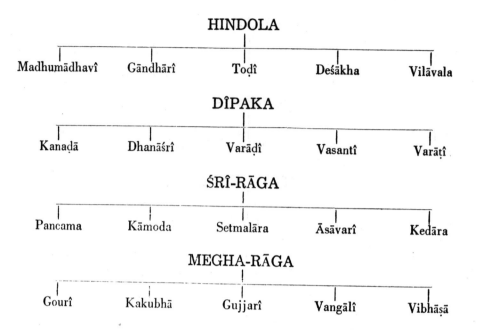

MĀLKOUŚA

- Gounḍakirî
- Gāndhāra
- Gāndhārî
- Sarasvatî
- Dhanāśrî

HINDOLA

- Tilangî
- Devakirî
- Vasantî
- Sindhurî
- Āhirî

ŚRÎ-RĀGA

- Karṇāṭî
- Kriyati (?)
- Gaurî
- Āśāvarî
- Sindhurā

DÎPAKA

- Surath
- Goṇḍ (?)
- Dhani
- Kankālî
- Suhā

APPENDIX 36.

CLASSIFICATION OF RĀGAS.

According to Pandit V. N. Bhatkhande (Pundit Visnu Sarma), B.A., LL.B. of Bombay, as given in his Sanskrit treatise *Abhinava-rága-manjarî* (Poona, 1921), in the *pariśiṣta* (appendix), pp. 1-12.

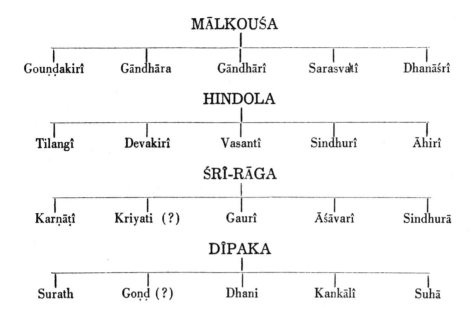

Mela-rāga:	Janya-rāga:
Kalyāṇî	1. Iman, 2. Bhūpālî, 3. Śuddha-Kalyāna, 4. Candra-Kānta, 5. Jayat-Kalyāna, 6. Mālaśrî, 7. Hindola, 8. Hammîr, 9. Kedāra, 10. Kāmoda, 11. Śyāma, 12. Chāyā-nāṭa, 13. Gouḍa-Sāranga.
Velāvalî	1. Śuddha-vilāvalî, 2. Ālhaiyā, 3. Śukhla-vilāvali, 4. Devagirî, 5. Yamanî, 6. Kakubhā, Second Kakubhā, 7. Naṭa-vilāvalî, 8. Laccha-sakhā, 9. Sarpardā, 10. Vihanga, 11. Desikār, 12. Hema-kalyāṇa, 13. Naṭa-rāga, 14. Pāhāḍî, 15. Mada-rāga, 16. Durgā, 17. Maluha, 18. Sankarā.

Khamāj	1. Jhinjhoṭî, 2. Khamāj, 3. Second Durgā, 4. Tailangî, 5 .Rāgeśvarî, 6. Khamvāvatî, 7. Garā, 8. Soraṭî, 9. Deśa-rāga, 10. Jayāvantî, 11. Tilok-kāmod.
Bhairava	1. Bhairava, 2. Rāmakrî, 3. Vangāla-Bhairava, 4. Sourāṣtra-tanka-rāga, 5. Prabhāta-rāga, 6. Śiva-Bhairava, 7. Ānanda-Bhairava, 8. Āhîra-Bhairava, 9. Guṇakrî, 10. Kalinga-rāga, 11. Jogiyā, 12. Vibhāṣa-rāga, 13. Megha-ranjanî.
Purvi	1. Pūrvî, 2. Puriyā-Dhānaśrî, 3. Jetaśri, 4. Praja, 5. Śrîrāga, 6. Gourî, 7. Mālavî, 8. Triveni, 9. Tankî, 10. Vasanta.
Māravā	1. Māravā, 2. Pūriyā, 3. Jeta-rāga, 4. Māligourā, 5. Sāj-girî, 6. Varāti, 7. Lalitā, 8. Sohanî, 9. Pancama, Second Pancama, 10. Bhattiyāra, 11. Vibhāśa-rāga, 12. Bhakkāra-rāga.
Kāphi	1. Kāphî, 2. Saindhavî, 3. Sindurā, 4. Dhānaśrî, 5. Bhimpalāsî, 6. Dhāni, 7. Paṭamanjarî, 8. Paṭa-Dîpakî, 9. Haṃsa-kankanî, 10. Pilu, 11. Vāgiśvari, 12. Sāhānā, 13. Suhā, 14. Sughāraikā, 15. Nāyakî-kānaḍā, 16. Devasāga-rāga, 17. Vāhāra-rāga, 18. Vrandāvanî-sāranga, 19. Madhyamādî-Sāranga, 20. Sāmanta-Sāranga, 21. Śuddha-Sāranga, 22. Miyā-Sārang, 23. Vaḍa-haṃsa-sāranga, 24. Śuddha-Mallār, 25. Megha-rāga, 26. Miyā (?) Mallāra, 27. Surat-Mallāra, 28. Gouḍ-mallāra.
Āśāvarî	1. Āśavarî, 2. Jaunpurî, 3. Deva-gāndhār, 4. Sindhu-Bhairavî, 5. Deśî, 6. Saḍrāga, 7. Kouśika-Kānḍā, 8. Darvārî-Kānaḍā, 9. Āddanā, 10. Dvitîya-nāyaki.
Bhairavî	1. Bhairavî, 2. Mālkośa, 3. Āśāvarî, 4. Dhanāśrî, 5. Vilāskhānî-toḍî.
Toḍî	1. Toḍî, 2. Gurjarî-Toḍî, 3. Mūla-tānī.